D1418429

Stemming Middle-Class Decline

The Challenges to Economic Development Planning

Stemming Middle-Class Decline

The Challenges to
Economic Development Planning

NANCEY GREEN LEIGH

Published by the Center for Urban Policy Research
New Brunswick, New Jersey 08903

Printed in the United States of America

Cover design: Helene Berinsky

Cover photograph:
Courtesy U.S. Department of Agriculture
Soil Conservation Service
Photographer: Gordon Smith

An earlier version of portions of chapter 6 that relate to California
appeared in the Winter 1989–1990 issue of *California History,*
a publication of the California Historical Society.

An earlier version of a portion of chapter 6 that relates to regional
economic shifts appeared in *Growth and Change* 24: 3–31 (1993).

Library of Congress Cataloging-in-Publication Data

Leigh, Nancey Green.
    Stemming middle-class decline : the challenges to economic
development planning / Nancey Green Leigh.
        p.   cm.
    Includes bibliographical references.
    ISBN 0-88285-149-7

    1. Income distribution — United States.   2. Middle class —
United States.   3. United States — Economic conditions — 1945 —
Regional disparities.   4. United States — Economic policy.   I. Title.
HC110.I5L43   1994
338.973 — dc20   94-18279
                                                            CIP

For my joyous academic distractions

Leigh and Kenan

Contents

Tables

Chapter 4

Chapter 5

Chapter 6

Figures

Acknowledgments

The work presented here is an outgrowth of research that was begun during my doctoral studies in the Department of City and Regional Planning at the University of California at Berkeley. This research was supported by a National Science Foundation Dissertation Improvement Grant and by the Woodrow Wilson Foundation through its Rural Development Policy Fellows Program. Additionally, I wish to acknowledge the administrative support of the Institute of Urban and Regional Development at the University of California at Berkeley that facilitated this initial research.

The original data analysis required significant refinement and interpretation to fulfill this book's aim of deciphering how the planning field has contributed to the plight of the middle economic class and how planning practice must change in order to improve the prospects of members and aspiring members of the middle economic class. This is a task I undertook as an Assistant Professor of Urban Planning at the University of Wisconsin–Milwaukee, and I am grateful for the institutional support that facilitated my work. [Nancey Green Leigh is currently Associate Professor in the City Planning Program at Georgia Institute of Technology, Atlanta. *Ed.*] I also wish to acknowledge the dedication and generosity of effort shown by my editor, Jeanne Thieme, in helping me to make this work more accessible to my audience. It was an important learning experience for us both.

Professors Michael B. Teitz and Edward J. Blakely at the University of California at Berkeley deserve special acknowledgment for their early guidance in this work and for their long-term interest and support. This work has also benefited from the ideas, criticisms, and suggestions of a number of other individuals, including Ed Bergman, Scott Campbell, Robert Cervero, Paul Chase, Carlos Davidson, Cliff Ellis, Amy Glasmeier, Lucy Gorham, Norton Grubb,

Bennett Harrison, John Landis, Jonathan Levine, Marc Levine, Robert Mier, Larry Mishel, Michael Reich, Sandra Rosenbloom, Charlie Shain, Philip Shapira, Michael Smith-Heimer, Lester Thurow, Lynn Thurston, Richard Walker, and Michael Wiseman.

A final special acknowledgment is due to Ken Preston for his enduring moral support and to Leigh and Kenan Preston for the generous and sweet spirit with which they accepted the seemingly endless hours I spent on this project.

1

Are Americans as Well-Off as We Used to Be?

Introduction

When the title question of this chapter is posed, we are asking: Do as many Americans today have a chance to attain the American dream as they did in the past? Attainment of the American dream is largely equated with achieving middle-class status. The 1980s saw the beginning of a debate over whether the American middle class was shrinking, with concern deriving from the importance attached to this segment for both the economy and society as a whole. The middle class is seen, in many ways, to represent the backbone of the U.S. economy and American society, with its values and life-style determining the outcome of our social and political systems. Much of the mass market is structured to satisfy the demands of the middle-class consumer, and the middle-class standard of living is a benchmark by which economic progress is measured. A position in the middle class is generally considered the goal of members of the lower class and of many who aspire to assist the lower class. Decline in the size of the middle class, therefore, has been equated with an erosion of the very foundations of America's society and economy.

Making sense of all the analyses that have been completed on changes in the size of the middle group of Americans is complicated by the fact that a consistent definition of what the middle of the income distribution is has not been used. The analyses have tended to make or infer a correlation between income or earnings

1

segments and social classes. Indeed, the motivation behind many
analyses of trends in the middle segment of the income or earnings
distribution derives from the desire to say something about what is
happening to a broadly construed middle class, but in reality, income class and social class are not that well correlated. Coleman
(1983), in his article synthesizing several decades of research into
social class, gives three reasons for this lack of correlation. First,
social class is derived more from occupational differentiation than
from income:

> Twentieth century America may illustrate this proposition to an ex-
> treme degree: blue-collar workers can outearn both white-collar
> workers and salaried professionals, yet they still do not rise above
> either in social status. To put this in the vernacular, the blue-collar
> workers "have more money than class," the white-collar workers
> "more class than money."

Second, income has historically varied systematically with
one's place in the age distribution and has largely been correlated
with work experience. The earnings of younger workers are usually
well below the average for the social class they are assigned to
based on their family and educational backgrounds as well as occupation.

The third reason that income and social class are not well correlated occurs because of family variations in the number as well
as gender of earners. Over the last twenty-five years, household
incomes well below and above the traditional range associated with
a particular class have had to be incorporated within the range.
This has been due, for instance, to such phenomena as middle-
class women becoming simultaneously divorced heads of households and low-income earners and middle-class women who are
married entering, in increasing numbers, into the labor force and
adding a second income to the household. These changes, combined with increases in the number of singles, retirees, and elderly
widowed, all contribute to the reduced correlation between income
and social class.

While there is no set definition of the middle class—although
it is a label that many members of upper- and lower-income groups
apply to themselves—the importance of the middle class in the

economic, social, and political spheres of American society is undisputed; any significant change in the size of the middle class is likely to alter the paths these spheres travel, often requiring more than minor adjustments along the way. Drawing broad conclusions about the fate of the middle class on the basis of changes in income distribution, however, must be regarded suspiciously for two reasons. First, as noted, the middle economic and social classes are not all that well correlated. Second, and critical to the intent of this book, even if we choose to focus on the more quantifiable aspect of the subject—that is, the middle economic class—we cannot assume that middle earning or income levels automatically correlate with middle standards of living. Indeed, **we will show in this book that there has been a widening gap between what middle-level earnings can purchase and what a middle standard of living costs.**

Because the motivation for this book was the desire to understand an important component of the changing prospects for economic development, our focus is on the middle *economic* class and not the *social* class. While broad conclusions about the middle social class will not be drawn, other important social issues will be addressed through an examination of change in the size and composition of the middle segment of the earnings distribution. For example, are there changing prospects for upward mobility for those in the lower segment? In what way is the changing labor force participation of women reflected in changes in the composition of the middle earner group?

This book's focus on the middle segment of the income distribution is a variation in the study of income inequality. A declining middle implies that one or both of the tails of the income distribution is growing, thus increasing inequality. Analyzing the impacts of changes in the middle segment of the income distribution is not meaningful without relating the changes to concurrent changes in the upper and lower segments of the distribution. In focusing on the middle of the income distribution, therefore, issues of overall income inequality continue to be addressed.

While the debate over the disappearing middle class is a variation on the age-old income inequality issue, it is a significant one. Although the body of research on the question of the disappearing middle class has expanded continuously, the debate has not been

resolved. Given the wide range of approaches taken by those analyzing the issue, this would seem inevitable, but a large part of the
reason for the lack of resolution must also be attributed to the po-
litically charged nature of any findings; the decline of the middle
class had been a major theme in the last two presidential cam-
paigns.

From the beginning of the debate, political analysts have discussed the potential impacts of a declining middle class on the nation. In one analysis, Thurow (1984) reminded us that Karl Marx
did not foresee the rise of the middle class and thus predicted that
capitalism would generate a bipolar income distribution. The lower
class was supposed to revolt against this distribution and establish
communism; however, the middle class that developed has an interest in preserving capitalism—its source of bread and butter. At
the same time, this middle class has "voted to alleviate the worst
excesses of capitalism with social welfare programs" (Thurow
1984). The implication is that without the middle class, and the
hope it offers to the poor, Marx's predictions of communism and
revolution could come to pass.

Ehrenreich (1986) referred to Marx's prediction as well, writ-
ing that although "it would be easy to conclude that the Marxist
vision at last fits America's future . . . America is unique in ways
that still make any prediction foolhardy." She claimed not only
that class consciousness was lacking in America but also that there
did not exist the political leadership necessary to articulate "both
the distress of the have-nots and the malaise in the middle." While
Ehrenreich's observations still seemed pertinent for former President George H. Bush's 1988 presidential campaign, by the 1992
campaign, Democrat Bill Clinton was successful enough in reach-
ing the lower and middle economic classes with his focus on industrial malaise, displaced workers, deteriorating educational systems, a stressed healthcare system, and an uncertain economic
future to defeat the Republican incumbent.

Returning to the debate over a shrinking middle *economic*
class, it should first be noted that which kind of income and what
income range should be used to define the middle class are critical
questions not easy to resolve. Using household or family income
enables one to look at the total income picture. If the main research concern is with impacts on the standard of living, then

household or family income—which includes earned and unearned income—may appear to be the most appropriate variable for analysis. However, it is important to understand how the pattern of earned income within households is changing in relationship to the household's ability to consume a middle standard of living. For example, does it now take two earners in a household to purchase the middle standard where previously it took only one?

If the primary concern is with the effect of the declining middle class on employment and earning opportunities, then individual earnings is the appropriate variable to analyze. Understanding the underlying causes of changes in household income distributions requires an equal understanding of what is happening to the individual earnings distribution. While it would be ideal to examine both, such a task is formidable. The two distributions continue to be strongly related but in a more differentiated manner than in the past. At one time, the individual male's earnings were predominantly synonymous with household income. Today, the two-earner household increasingly makes up the family income unit while, at the same time, there are growing numbers of single-earner, single-occupant households.

There has been less agreement over whether the middle of the family or household income distribution has been declining since the late 1960s as compared to the individual earnings distribution. Still, even if the middle segment of the household income distribution was shown not to be declining, it would be important to understand the ways in which the profile of middle-income households may be changing as a result of overall economic transformation. For instance, does it take more than one earner in a household to achieve a middle-class income and life-style? If so, is this because the middle of the earnings distribution is dropping or because real earnings and income overall have declined or because of both? Can we say we have made economic progress or even maintained the same standard of living overall if it takes two earners to maintain a middle-income household where one could do so previously? What about the additional resources that must be consumed by the second worker in order to work? Does it not imply a less efficient use of resources if more must be consumed in order to generate the same level of income?

With the increase in female labor force participation of the last twenty-five years, the earning of wages has become an activity engaging a greater proportion of the adult population than at any other time in the United States' economic history. For those engaged in full-time work, earnings constitute all but 2% to 3% of their total income. Thus, earnings are nearly synonymous with total income for the active participants in the economy.

This book will describe the changing middle economic class from the perspective of individual earnings, showing how the middle segment of the earnings distribution decreased over a twenty-year period between 1967 and 1987. We will show that the shifting middle ground has created problems in geographical regions associated with economic growth as well as in those associated with economic decline. We will discuss which earners—in terms of part- and full-time employment status, race, gender, education level, industry of employment, and regional location—have been affected by the economic restructuring that occurred between 1967 and 1987. The period of this book's analysis—beginning in the latter part of the postwar boom, passing through the 1973 turning point in the economy, and continuing to 1987—has predictive value. The economy underwent profound structural change during this period, setting in motion earnings and cost-of-living trends whose paths are unlikely to alter significantly in the near future without substantial new policy direction and planning activity.

This book seeks to make a contribution to our understanding of the changed economic development context of the United States and to help identify what areas of policy require the greatest attention. Its focus is on individual earnings, the ability of middle earnings to purchase a middle standard of living, and what this means for economic development planning. While a changing market basket over the last twenty-five years makes it difficult to measure the middle-class standard of living, one feature of the basket can be selected as a constant index of middle-class economic status: home ownership. We will describe the declining ability of the aspiring middle class to purchase a home with middle-level earnings; in addition, this book considers fringe benefit recipiency because access to healthcare and provision for retirement are two additional and measurable marks of middle-class economic status.

The nation is not, to use the classic regional science terminology, a homogeneous plain. To offer insight for regional economic development planning, this book explores regional variations in the pattern of the declining middle economic class by the categories of urban and rural; by the four major U.S. Census Bureau regions— Midwest, North, South, and West—and by the largest state in each of the four census regions—Illinois, New York, Texas, and California, respectively.

The decline in the middle segment of the earnings distribution has not been experienced equally by all workers and we will discuss which subgroups of the labor force are most at risk of losing or never attaining middle-class economic status. A significant point to be raised is that the historical notion of a broad middle class supported by a family wage may never have reflected reality. At the beginning of our period of analysis—1967—more than half of all full-time middle earners did not earn enough to provide a family with a middle standard of living. The subsequent increase in female-headed households, dual-earner families, and single-person households means that the "Ozzie and Harriet" model, which reflected an ideal and media image rather than the majority's reality in 1967, needs to be retired while topics such as support for working families with dependents and affordable single-earner housing must be given more attention by planners and policymakers.

The decline of the middle class, which occurred during a period of industrial restructuring, appears to be a long-term trend. This problem is more than just a temporary phenomenon associated with a disproportionate share of the labor force being baby boomers in the early phase of their earning life cycle; thus, that group's aging cannot be expected to result in significant changes in the earnings distribution and in the ability of earnings to purchase the middle standard of living. Further, the problem cannot be solved with comparable worth policies because it results from more than just an increasing percentage of white women in the labor force.

The best explanation for the industrial restructuring that characterized the 1967 to 1987 period and beyond points to increased international manufacturing competition, which resulted in an industry profit squeeze that ultimately forced upon workers wage and benefit cuts, changes in hiring practices, and weakened unions. Restoring well-paying, or union, jobs with more comprehensive fringe benefits is an obvious remedy from the point of view of current and aspiring members of the middle class. However, such a "solution" does not take into account the reasons for industrial restructuring that began when U.S. manufacturers lost ground to international competitors. By the same token, the most commonly proposed national "economic development" solutions—taxation and transfer policies—simply are not adequate to solve the problem, as will become clear when we examine the more complex causes of the restructuring.

What is needed is more public-sector planning. The problems presented by strong international competition and subsequent industrial restructuring in the United States have been treated primarily as private-sector issues, on an ad hoc basis, and with a short-term perspective. Public planning activities throughout the postwar period have tended to be local rather than national and have primarily influenced the middle standard of living rather than the middle earnings position. There has been little systematic focus on the plight of the middle class or on related issues, such as jobs/housing imbalances, the need for worker training, or policies to support working families. In contrast, America's chief international competitors have developed national industrial policies through the cooperation of industry and government or of labor, industry, and government. By refusing to do likewise, the United States puts its industry at a competitive disadvantage and its citizens at risk of a declining standard of living.

Furthermore, a broader historical perspective shows that local-level public planning and what limited national-level planning there was helped create the situation that led to pricing the middle standard of living out of the reach of middle earners. The failure of planners to acknowledge how the national highway system made possible suburban development and how the long-run consequences of local zoning ordinances led to suburban development standards that increasingly only upper-income households can afford means that planners also failed to do their part to help bridge the gap between middle earnings and a middle standard of living. This local planning in a vacuum has had significant negative effects on the ability of the nation's citizens to attain and maintain a middle standard of living.

The Organization of This Book

The remaining six chapters of this book are organized as follows. Chapter 2 examines what happened to middle-level earners at the national level between 1967 and 1987. It provides an overview of the changing earnings distribution for the beginning and ending points of the twenty-year research period and profiles earners by part- and full-time employment status, gender, race, educational attainment, and levels of fringe benefit recipiency.

Chapter 3 examines the middle standard of living, discusses problems of measuring changes in the standard of living over time, and explores two approaches to measuring such changes.

Chapter 4 investigates why industrial restructuring is more compelling than demographic restructuring as an explanation for changes in middle-level earnings and in making a prognosis for the employed's ability to purchase a middle standard of living. An overview of the industrial structure that employs earners is presented, and the twenty-year period of analysis is divided into three periods, 1967 to 1973, 1973 to 1979, and 1979 to 1987. Particular attention is paid to pre-1973 and post-1973 trends because it has been since 1973 that declines in real incomes have been observed. The earnings distributions of a broad nine-sector industrial classification system are examined for the three intervening time periods. In addition, the earnings distributions of two separate, but not mutually exclusive, industrial classifications—high technology and defense and trade-impacted industries—are examined.

Chapter 5 and 6 are regional analyses of the changing earnings distribution. At the regional level, change in the earnings distribution and levels of fringe benefit recipiency are studied in relationship to changes in the industrial structure that employs the region's earners and to the characteristics of the earners themselves. In addition, and where the data permit, the attainability of the middle standard of living, as it is reflected in the cost of home ownership, is examined for the regional categories. The aggregate metropolitan and nonmetropolitan regions of the United States are examined in chapter 5. The four major census regions are studied in chapter 6, along with the largest state in each region.

Finally, chapter 7 explores how the practice of implicit national planning and explicit local planning contributed to the growth of the middle economic class after World War II and to the divergence between middle-level earnings and a middle standard of living after 1967. To the question of what should be done to counteract the diverging trend between middle earnings and the middle standard of living, chapter 7 concludes with a set of planning and policy prescriptions ranging from the national to the local level.

2

What Is Happening to Middle-Level Earners?

This chapter focuses on whether the end of the postwar growth boom has resulted in a smaller middle economic class and a decline in the American standard of living. It does so by examining changes in the distribution of earnings. The earnings distribution is comprised of income gained through employment while the household income distribution is comprised of all sources of income to the household, such as employment earnings of all household members, investment income, Social Security income, alimony, and pension and/or disability income.

Earnings are an especially pertinent gauge of the status of the middle economic class for two reasons. First, earnings are the primary source of income and the primary source with which to purchase a middle standard of living. For full-time workers, earnings have been in excess of 95% of their income for the last twenty years.[1] If planning and policy actions are to be prescribed to promote economic development and counter the declining middle trend, then it is necessary to focus on the primary source of income—earnings—and on the changes that are affecting opportunities for participating in that primary income-generating activity.

Second, during the postwar boom era, it was widely perceived that the *earnings* of one full-time worker could purchase a middle standard of living for a household, which was typically characterized as the "Ozzie and Harriet" family, with one adult male breadwinner, one adult female who did not work outside the home, and two children.[2] If that was the case then but is no longer the case today, we have evidence of a decline in the middle economic class: Some Americans are not as well-off as they used to be.

The focus here is on *individual* earnings as opposed to the combined earnings of a household—when there is more than one earner—because of the historical notion of a family wage; that is, the earnings of one full-time worker could provide the income to support a household.[3] It may be argued that the concept of a "family wage" is a historical one that is no longer relevant for economic development, in part because so many households have more than one earner due to the influx of women into the labor market. It could further be argued that the family wage is a mythical concept as the proportion of households who were traditional and actual recipients of family wages was far smaller than commonly perceived. It certainly was not a concept that characterized most black households twenty years ago. There have always been single-parent households, single-adult households, and adult-couple-only households. Our best estimate of the proportion of Ozzie and Harriet households in the late 1960s is less than 10%.[4]

It is argued here, however, that the family wage is still a useful concept not to be discarded lightly. In the first place, can we say we have made economic progress if there has been an increase in the extent to which a household requires more than one earner in order to generate enough income to purchase a middle standard of living? The additional resources the second earner must consume in order to work indicate a less efficient use of resources to generate the same standard of living.

Second, a household's economic status can be viewed as *less secure* if two individuals must be employed in order to generate the earnings necessary to maintain its standard of living. When only one household member works for wages, there exists the possibility that another could work to replace lost wages if the first became unemployed.

Finally, it can be argued that, from an economic development policy perspective, a variant of the family wage standard should be considered an ideal. At one time or another, and often at more than one phase in an individual's life, everyone is dependent on someone else for financial support. Consequently, it is a reasonable goal that an individual's full-time earnings should be able to support that individual and at least one dependent, be it a child, a mate, or a dependent adult.

For these reasons, this book examines how the ability of individual earnings to purchase the middle standard of living changed over a two-decade period, from 1967 to 1987. Our analysis uses data from the March sample of the U.S. Census Bureau's Current Population Survey (CPS), the largest annual survey taken in the United States, providing data on income, earnings, race, gender, age, occupation, industry, and education for a nationally representative sample, ranging from around 48,000 households in 1967 to around 56,500 in 1987.

The two decades of analysis correspond to the period when America's economy began to experience slow growth and more rapid economic transformation due to industrial restructuring and the changing composition of the labor force. The question "Are we as well-off as we used to be?" refers to the way things were when Americans were experiencing the postwar boom that lasted until the late 1960s.

The beginning and ending points of the two decades were chosen for the middle range they represent in the business cycle. In a point-to-point analysis such as this one, this procedure helps to minimize possible distortions in the structural changes that appear to have taken place. The business cycle encompassing 1987, the end year of the analysis, peaked in July 1990. The recessionary economic conditions of the early 1990s suggest that an appropriate new ending year for extending this analysis would not occur before 1993.

Since this analysis is concerned with the ability of earnings to purchase a middle standard of living, it will examine both changes in the middle segment of the earnings distribution over the twenty-year period as well as their relationship to the middle standard of living.

Defining the Middle-Earnings Segment

The definition of the middle employed here is 50% to 200% of the median earnings figure for all earners (part- and full-time) nationwide (Appendix 2.A). Defining the middle of the earnings distribu-

tion as a range around the median point is the predominant
method used by researchers and is one with broad intuitive appeal.
Nevertheless, it is important to note the fundamental flaw in this
approach. First, middle-level earnings do not necessarily correspond to a middle standard of living. Second, even if they were
found to correspond at one point in time, they do not necessarily
do so at all other points. Draper has written: "The postulate that
adequacy at prevailing levels of living is always at median consumption, and that other standards remain in fixed percentage relationship to the median, is inherently unsupportable" (Watts
1980).[5] Extending her point, in an economy with falling real incomes, equating median earnings with median consumption will
track a falling middle standard of living. This can be a rather de-
ceptive way of answering the question of "Are we as well-off as we
used to be?" The ideal approach to this question would entail an
analysis of changes in the ability of the middle economic class to
purchase a middle standard of living embodied in a specific consumption basket. However, there is no officially defined consumption basket representing the middle standard of living. Chapter 3
will explore the concept of a middle standard of living, and it will
identify a proxy for that standard. That proxy measure is then used
to analyze whether changes in the earnings distribution in combination with changes in the middle standard suggest that we are—
or are not—as well-off as we used to be.

Dividing the Labor Force into Part- and Full-Time Earners

While the earnings of a part-time worker should not be expected to
be sufficient to purchase a middle standard of living, it is impossi-
ble to fully understand the changing earnings distribution and how
it is affected by structural economic change without also considering the trends for part-time workers. If full-time workers appear
to be making gains, that is, experiencing upward earnings shifts,
while part-time workers are experiencing a decline, and/or the percentage of involuntary part-time workers is growing, then it would
be a mistake to conclude that the ability to achieve a middle-class
standard of living has improved across the board. Rather, there are
diminished opportunities for upward mobility and a falling stan-

dard of living for individuals who must work part-time because they cannot find full-time jobs or because the hours at their full-time jobs have been cut back due to slack demand or materials shortages. Indeed, data from the U.S. Bureau of Labor Statistics indicate that the percentage of part-time workers who would rather be working full-time rose from 9% to 19% between 1968 and 1987.[6] This will be an important point to keep in mind as we discuss the changing earnings distribution for full-time workers.

A further reason for analyzing part-time workers separately from full-time workers is that structural labor market change may take the form of eroding labor's position at the expense of part-time workers. Part-time jobs do not offer the same level of benefits in the form of paid vacation and sick leave, as well as health and insurance benefits, as do full-time jobs. Dividing a full-time job into two part-time positions may enable an employer to reduce the level of overall compensation paid and may also reduce both legal requirements on termination procedures and unemployment compensation. Change in the institutional arrangements and rules between workers and employers that have evolved over the postwar period—including, but not limited to, unionization and internal labor markets—and that played a fundamental role in creating a widespread American middle class may be seen first in structural shifts between full- and part-time work.

The definition of middle earnings used here is based on the median point of the all-earners' distribution, thereby acting as a constant reference point for the full- and part-time workers' earnings distributions, facilitating comparisons between the two distributions. As a result, the middle and upper segments of the part-time earners' distribution are expected to be small and the lower segment to be large, in comparison with those for the all-earner distribution (Figure 2.1). Of primary interest will be the degree of change in each of the segments over the period of analysis. The full-time earners' distribution is expected to have larger middle and upper segments relative to that of the all-earner distribution. The degree of change in all three segments of the full-time earners' distribution is the primary focus in this analysis.

As previously indicated, our focus in examining the lower, middle, and upper segments of the part- and full-time earnings distributions is not so much on their absolute size but on the degree

FIGURE 2.1

Distribution of Earnings by Low, Middle,
and Upper Segments, 1967 (Percent)

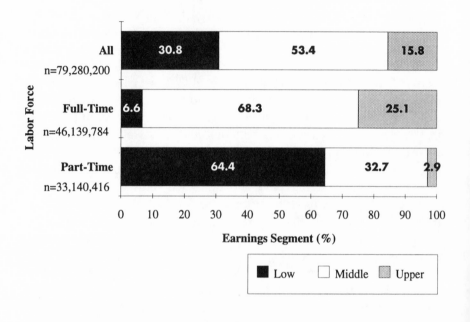

Source: Calculated from Current Population Survey (CPS) microdata files.

of change or movement among the segments. If the middle segment decreases while the lower segment increases, this is a sign of a negative economic development trend. In a democratic, egalitarian society, many would argue this to be the case even if the upper segment were increasing in conjunction with the lower segment. Not only equality but political stability, as well, is greatest when most of the population is in the middle. Concern over bipolarization of the income distribution has been at the heart of the worry over a shrinking middle class.

Even when the lower earnings segment is shrinking and an upward shift appears to be occurring, we cannot assume that Americans are better off than they used to be. Before making this conclusion, it must be established that the cost of the middle standard of living has not also increased. Further, consideration must be given to workers' overall compensation packages and not just to their earnings; the extent to which each worker's employment provides health coverage and financial security in his or her old age can be quite significant in attaining and retaining the middle standard of living. If earnings levels appear to remain the same, or even if earnings increase but benefit recipiency decreases by more than an offsetting amount, the attainability of a middle standard of living is eroded.

Worker Characteristics

For the purpose of economic development planning and policy-making, it is not enough to know that the earnings distribution is changing or even how the distribution has changed for full- and part-time workers. It is also necessary to know the characteristics of the workers who are experiencing the changing earnings distribution along with the characteristics of their earnings sources, that is, the industrial structure.

Workers can be analyzed according to many variables, but in general the primary ones for analysis are gender, race, and education.[7] Between 1967 and 1987, the proportion of women and minorities in the work force increased significantly. Education levels for all groups increased as well. For targeting limited planning and policy resources, it is essential to determine if there are distinctions in the earnings distributions of workers by their gender, race, or education levels. It is also necessary to understand the distinctions in earnings distributions among different industrial sectors. Finally, since earners and industries are located in space, and economic development planning is generally targeted at workers and industries in specific places and regions, understanding how change in the earnings distribution has been distributed geographically is fundamental. While this chapter examines only the aggregate national-level picture, subsequent chapters examine the industrial and spatial distribution of earners.

The Nation's Changing Earnings Distribution, 1967 to 1987

The number of earners (full-time and part-time) increased by nearly 37.5 million from 1967 to 1987. The composition of the all-earner distribution changed significantly by gender, primarily because the white male share declined and the white female share increased. Together, they made up 89% of all earners in 1967 and 86% in 1987. The white male share declined from 53% in 1967 to 46% in 1987 while white females increased their share from 36% in 1967 to 40% in 1987 (Figure 2.2). Blacks—both male and female—remained at 11% of all earners throughout the period of analysis.

The relative size of part- and full-time earner groups has re-

FIGURE 2.2

Distribution of All Earners by Gender and Race, 1967 and 1987

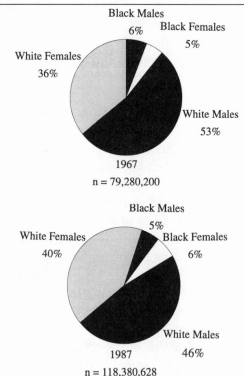

Note: Percents may not total 100% because "other" races are omitted.

Source: Calculated from CPS microdata files.

mained essentially the same over the entire analysis period.[8] Part-time workers made up 42% of all earners in 1967 and 41% in 1987. Full-time workers were 58% and 59% of all earners at the beginning and end of the period, respectively.

As would be expected, the full-time earnings distribution has larger middle and upper segments. We would not necessarily expect, however, to find that the full-time earner distribution made a more pronounced upward shift than that of all earners. The upper segment has increased more than 6% and comprises nearly one-quarter of the distribution. The middle-earner segment has declined almost 4% but still makes up nearly 65% of the distribution. Low full-time earners have declined from 7% to 4% of the total. During the same period, the proportions of upper, middle, and low workers in the part-time earnings distribution have remained the same.

In essence, over a period of two decades, the earnings of full-time workers have shifted upward while part-time workers have experienced no improvement. The result is an increasing earnings gap, which is apparent when the median earnings of both groups are compared with the all-earner median (Appendix 2.B). The ratio of median earnings for full-time earners to all earners has increased; thus, the gap between the median earnings of full- and part-time workers has widened.

Comparing the Part- and Full-Time Earnings Distributions by Gender and Race Groups

Some rather dramatic changes occurred in the position along the earnings distribution of the four gender/race subgroups. Among white male full-time workers, there were almost no low earners (less than 3%) at both the beginning and end of the analysis period (Table 2.1). In contrast, upper earners grew from roughly one-third to nearly one-half of the full-time distribution. Among black male full-time workers, the middle-earner group declined. Nevertheless, the earnings distribution of black males shifted upward dramatically. The percentage of black upper earners nearly tripled, growing from 7.6% to 20.6% in two decades. Likewise, the percentage of low earners was reduced, shrinking from 11.6% to 7.3%.

TABLE 2.1

Full-Time Workers' Distribution of Earnings and Net Additions to Earnings Groups, 1967 and 1987

| Earner Group | Year | Earnings Group | | | Total |
		Low	Middle	Upper	
All Earners	1967	3,050,186	31,497,833	11,591,765	46,139,784
	%	6.6	68.3	25.1	100.0
	1987	3,337,389	46,362,481	21,436,042	71,135,912
	%	4.7	65.2	30.1	100.0
	Change	287,203	14,864,648	9,844,277	24,996,128
	%	9.4	47.2	84.9	54.2
White Males	1967	839,386	17,422,262	10,630,764	28,892,412
	%	2.9	60.3	36.8	100.0
	1987	1,093,701	20,123,591	16,309,462	37,526,754
	%	2.9	53.6	43.5	100.0
	Change	254,315	2,701,329	5,678,698	8,634,342
	%	30.3	15.5	53.4	29.9
White Females	1967	1,362,751	10,427,086	546,312	12,336,149
	%	11.0	84.5	4.4	100.0
	1987	1,546,485	19,193,714	3,275,536	24,015,735
	%	6.4	79.9	13.6	100.0
	Change	183,734	8,766,628	2,729,224	11,679,586
	%	13.5	84.1	499.6	94.7
Black Males	1967	325,724	2,258,361	213,439	2,797,524
	%	11.6	80.7	7.6	100.0
	1987	281,147	2,794,651	800,394	3,876,192
	%	7.3	72.1	20.6	100.0
	Change	−44,577	536,290	586,955	1,078,668
	%	−13.7	23.7	275.0	38.6
Black Females	1967	502,607	1,123,293	39,561	1,665,461
	%	30.2	67.4	2.4	100.0
	1987	345,070	2,955,255	326,792	3,627,117
	%	9.5	81.5	9.0	100.0
	Change	−157,537	1,831,962	287,231	1,961,656
	%	−31.3	163.1	726.0	117.8

Note: The sum of the black and white groups may not equal the total because "other" races are not being reported. "Other" represents around 1% of the sample in 1967 and 3% in 1987.

Source: Calculated from *Current Population Survey* (CPS) microdata files.

Some 79.9% of white female full-time workers have consistently been in the middle-earner range; however, this group experienced an upward shift out of the lower and middle segments into the upper segment. In contrast, black female full-time workers show dramatic change. They are the only group to show an increase in the middle-earner segment, and it was a substantial increase—from 67.4% to 81.5%. The upper-earner group for black females was the smallest among the four groups, but it increased from 2.4% to 9%. Black female low earners declined from 30.2% to 9.5% of the distribution.

Although shares of the part-time earnings distribution held by low, middle, and upper earners have basically remained unchanged, there were significant changes within the four gender/race groups (Table 2.2). Overall, the position of males deteriorated between 1967 and 1987 while that of females improved. White and black males' part-time earnings shifted downward from the middle segment to the lower segment. Three percent of white females and 5% of black females shifted out of the low-earner group into the middle or upper groups.

The downward slide of white and black males in the part-time earnings distribution together with upward movement for white and black females is leading to an equalization of economic status by gender within the part-time labor force. If it is a leveling, however, it also is a lowering of economic position. Males make up more than 40% of the part-time labor force, and while the picture for females improved over the two decades, nearly 70% were still low earners in 1987. This suggests that for those who cannot or who choose not to work full-time, an earnings penalty is being incurred. This penalty is further exacerbated by the pattern of fringe benefit recipiency, as will be discussed below.

We conclude our comparison of the four gender/race groups' earnings positions by looking again at median earnings (see Appendix 2.B). Among full-time earners, white males continued throughout the period to have the highest ratio of median earnings to the median for all earners. However, the gap between this group and the black male, white female, and black female groups narrowed, with the ratio of black female earnings to all earnings showing the greatest improvement.

When median earnings are examined for part-time earners, we

TABLE 2.2

Part-Time/Year Workers' Distribution of Earnings and Net Additions to Earnings Groups, 1967 and 1987

Earner Group	Year	Earnings Group			Total
		Low	Middle	Upper	
All Part-Time/Year Earners	1967	21,346,029	10,849,574	944,813	33,140,416
	%	64.4	32.7	2.9	100.0
	1987	31,128,165	14,530,103	1,586,449	47,244,717
	%	65.9	30.8	3.4	100.0
	Change	9,782,136	3,680,529	641,636	14,104,301
	%	69.4	26.1	4.5	42.6
White Males	1967	6,687,951	5,343,679	811,888	12,843,518
	%	52.1	41.6	6.3	100.0
	1987	10,051,224	5,899,691	1,052,773	17,003,688
	%	59.1	34.7	6.2	100.0
	Change	3,363,273	556,012	240,885	4,160,170
	%	80.8	13.4	5.8	32.4
Black Males	1967	1,091,283	679,711	33,901	1,804,895
	%	60.5	37.7	1.9	100.0
	1987	1,653,852	643,665	53,115	2,350,632
	%	70.4	27.4	2.3	100.0
	Change	562,569	−36,046	19,214	545,737
	%	103.1	−6.6	3.5	30.2
White Females	1967	11,518,980	4,259,824	89,685	15,868,489
	%	72.6	26.8	0.6	100.0
	1987	16,276,035	6,855,300	377,474	23,508,809
	%	69.2	29.2	1.6	100.0
	Change	4,757,055	2,595,476	287,789	7,640,320
	%	62.3	34.0	3.8	48.1
Black Females	1967	1,831,446	442,122	4,828	2,278,396
	%	80.4	19.4	0.2	100.0
	1987	2,185,469	661,089	47,085	2,893,643
	%	75.5	22.8	1.6	100.0
	Change	354,023	218,967	42,257	615,247
	%	57.5	35.6	6.9	27.0

Note: The sum of the black and white groups may not equal the total because "other" races are not being reported. "Other" represents around 1% of the sample in 1967 and 3% in 1987.

Source: Calculated from CPS microdata files.

see further evidence over the two decades of a deteriorating position for males, especially white males. Earnings for white male part-time workers fell 7% relative to the all-earner median. The ratio for black males fell 3%. White and black females' ratios improved slightly.

This is further confirmation that part-time male workers, and white males in particular, lost ground over the two decades of analysis. They shifted out of the middle-earner segment into the lower segment, and the gap between the lower segment's earnings and those of earners overall has widened.

Comparison of Employee Benefits for Full- and Part-Time Earners in 1986

The financial security that employee benefits provide is very often critical for an individual's or a household's ability to attain—and retain—a middle standard of living. That real average hourly earnings have not grown since the mid-1970s while real average hourly compensation, that is, wages and benefits, has grown consistently suggests that the presence of a benefit package is becoming increasingly important for maintaining a middle-class standard of living. As a percentage of total compensation, benefits increased 6% between 1970 and 1986 (Employee Benefit Research Institute 1988a,b).

The CPS did not collect information on benefits received by wage and salary workers at the beginning of the research period, 1967, but data are available from 1979 onward. The actual dollar amount of benefits received was not collected; however, data do reveal whether an earner is included in an employer's pension plan and/or group health plan. In the latter case, the data also show whether the employer paid for all or part of the group health insurance.

According to the Employee Benefit Research Institute (1988a,b), the two benefit categories of group health insurance and pension and profit sharing were 4.1% of total compensation in 1970 and 6.6% of total compensation by 1986. If the 1970 percentage is applied to the median wage and salary for all earners in 1967 ($4,092), an estimated median total compensation for 1967 is

$4,280.[9] Applying the 1986 compensation percentage to the 1986 all-earner median ($13,840) results in an estimated median total compensation of $14,813.

Analysis of CPS data on pension and health benefits suggests these benefits have the effect of further skewing the earnings (or perhaps we should say compensation) distribution. The higher one's earnings group, the greater one's chances of being included in an employer's pension plan and/or group health plan (Table 2.3). Furthermore, higher earnings increase the likelihood that an em-

TABLE 2.3

Pension and Health Benefits of Earners by Distribution of
Earnings, 1986

			Full-Time Earners		
Earnings Group	*% of All Full-Time Earners*	*% of Group Included in Employer Pension Plan*	*% of Group Included in Employer Group Health Plan*	*% of Group for Which Employer Paid for ALL Group Health*	*% of Group for Which Employer Paid for PART Group Health*
Lower	3.7	16.8	35.7	13.5	18.7
Middle	64.6	53.0	77.0	30.5	43.1
Upper	31.7	76.2	91.7	39.9	49.1

Note: n = 68,690,029.

			Part-Time Earners		
Earnings Group	*% of All Part-Time Earners*	*% of Group Included in Employer Pension Plan*	*% of Group Included in Employer Group Health Plan*	*% of Group for Which Employer Paid for ALL Group Health*	*% of Group for Which Employer Paid for PART Group Health*
Lower	63.9	7.3	14.8	5.6	7.9
Middle	32.7	36.7	58.7	24.2	31.0
Upper	3.4	67.9	82.2	40.4	38.6

Note: n = 48,007,740.
Source: Calculated from 1987 CPS microdata files.

ployer paid all or part of the costs of a group health plan. These trends were present for full-time as well as part-time earners; the rate of benefit recipiency, though, was much lower among part-time earners. The lower rate among part-time workers is to be expected. When combined with earlier observations of the downward leveling of the part-time earnings distribution, it suggests that there is a widening gulf between full- and part-time workers in the returns to labor force participation.

Educational Attainment among Full-Time Earners

"Education," it has been observed, "translates an individual's theoretical right to political and economic freedom into practical powers" (U.S. Congress, Office of Technology Assessment 1988). The tradition of providing quality public education is at the heart of giving future workers an equal opportunity in the labor force. The deindustrialization that occurred over the 1967 to 1987 period led to widespread elimination of a segment of manufacturing jobs that required relatively low educational attainment, that is, high school or less. These were often unionized jobs that paid good middle-level or higher wages. In this section, we examine, for full-time workers, how changes in the earnings distribution have corresponded with changes in levels of educational attainment. Have the returns to education increased over time in the analysis period? Or are higher levels of education expected in 1987 than in 1967 for the same level of earnings?

As with the earnings distribution, the distribution of educational attainment shifted upward. The percentage of full-time workers who had less than a high school education fell more than 22% in the last two decades. The group of full-time workers with some college (but not a college degree) grew the most (9.1 percentage points), followed by the groups with college degrees or postgraduate training; see the totals in Table 2.4.

Although the distributions of both earnings and educational attainment have shifted upward, the shift in educational attainment has been more rapid and pronounced. We have calculated from CPS data that 83.3% of full-time workers who were low earners in 1967 had a high school education or less. Two decades later,

TABLE 2.4

Full-Time Workers' Level of Educational Attainment by Level of Earnings, 1967 and 1987 (Percent)

Earnings Group	Year	Total	Educational Attainment					
			Less Than High School	High School Grad	Some College	College Grad	Post-Graduate	Total
Lower	1967	3,050,186	56.7	26.6	10.9	3.8	2.0	100.0
	1987	3,337,389	28.6	41.9	20.3	5.0	4.0	100.0
Middle	1967	31,497,833	39.4	38.9	13.1	5.3	3.3	100.0
	1987	46,362,481	15.8	42.4	24.1	11.1	6.6	100.0
Upper	1967	11,591,765	18.8	31.4	18.4	16.6	14.8	100.0
	1987	21,436,042	5.5	25.8	22.4	22.6	23.6	100.0
Total	1967	46,139,784	35.4	36.2	14.3	8.1	6.1	100.0
	1987	71,135,912	13.0	37.1	23.4	14.5	11.9	100.0

Source: Calculated from CPS microdata files.

those with only a high school education or less were 70% of low earners. Less than 22% of middle earners in 1967 had more than a high school education; two decades later, this figure had risen to 42%. In two decades, the percentage of upper earners who had postsecondary education increased from half to almost 70%. Additionally, upper earners with postgraduate education increased from 15% to 24%. Thus, the higher one's educational level, the more likely is it that one will be in a higher income group.

At the same time, these data indicate that while educational attainment has become increasingly important in determining the level of one's earnings, returns to education are decreasing. Earners with at least a high school education, who were likely to have been upper earners in the late 1960s, were more likely to be only middle earners in the late 1980s, and this trend was even more pronounced for earners with postsecondary education. For example, more than 60% of middle- and upper-level earners had less than a high school education in 1967, but two decades later only 20% of these earners were without high school degrees. At the other extreme, while less than 20% of middle and upper earners had postgraduate training in 1967, 30% had such training two decades later. These data lend support to the U.S. Congress, Office of Technology Assessment's (1988) findings that the value of education has been "particularly pronounced for younger workers entering an increasingly competitive labor market. The real mean hourly earnings (1985 dollars) for civilian males aged 20–24 fell 26 percent between 1973 and 1986, but the earnings of high school dropouts fell 42% while earnings for college graduates fell only 6 percent."

These trends take on additional meaning when differences in educational attainment by gender/race group are considered (Table 2.5). If educational attainment will have increasing bearing on earnings levels, the outlook for black males is problematic. They had the largest percentage of full-time earners with less than a high school education in 1987 (21.6%).

Opportunities to secure middle or upper earnings increasingly appear to require postsecondary education. Nonetheless, approximately 40% of black females, black males, and white females had only high school diplomas by 1986, although this did represent an increase in educational attainment. For blacks, this percentage was

TABLE 2.5

Full-Time Earners' Level of Educational Attainment by Gender/Race Group, 1967 and 1987 (Percent)

| Gender/Race Group | Year | Educational Attainment | | | | | |
		Less Than High School	High School Grad	Some College	College Grad	Post-Graduate	Total
Black Females	1967	48.0	32.5	9.1	6.4	4.1	100.0
	1987	15.1	42.3	23.3	12.3	7.0	100.0
	Change	−32.9	9.8	14.2	5.9	2.9	
Black Males	1967	62.0	24.9	8.7	2.9	1.5	100.0
	1987	21.6	41.7	22.0	8.5	6.3	100.0
	Change	−40.4	16.8	13.3	5.6	4.8	
White Females	1967	27.3	45.7	14.4	7.6	5.0	100.0
	1987	9.4	40.9	25.8	18.9	10.1	100.0
	Change	−17.9	−4.8	11.4	11.3	5.1	
White Males	1967	35.6	33.6	15.0	8.9	7.0	100.0
	1987	14.0	35.2	22.0	15.3	13.5	100.0
	Change	−21.6	1.6	7.0	6.4	6.5	
Total	1967	35.4	36.2	14.3	8.1	6.1	100.0
	1987	12.8	37.5	23.3	14.6	11.8	100.0
	Change	−22.6	1.3	9.0	6.5	5.7	

Source: Calculated from CPS microdata files; includes additional 3% males and females of "other" races.

an upward shift in attainment from the "less than high school" group from 1967. For white females, the change was due to an upward shift into the "some college" group. More than 20% of each gender/race group had some college education but no degree. This category was largest for the black and white female groups. The highest percentages of college degrees and postgraduate training were found among whites, both males and females, while black males had the lowest postsecondary educational level.

The need to strengthen the educational attainment of black earners and white female earners is suggested by these data. This in turn suggests an expansion of policies to make postsecondary education more accessible and affordable.

Conclusion

This chapter has analyzed change in the U.S. earnings distribution from 1967 to 1987, focusing in particular on the middle segment of earners. The intent of the analysis has been to determine how the earnings distribution changed and to offer one approach to answering the question "Are we as well-off as we used to be?" The 1967 starting point for the analysis marks the end of the postwar boom era and is considered a widely prosperous period.

Observed in *current* dollars, the results of this analysis of shifts in the earnings distribution may seem more favorable than not. The analysis has been conducted in current dollars because, in chapter 3, we will examine current housing prices as our gauge of changing costs in the middle standard of living. Evidence from other sources indicates that real income and earnings peaked around 1973 and have since been stagnant (Levy and Michel 1991; Mishel and Simon 1988).

If we were to conduct our analysis of the earnings distribution in real dollars, we would still find an upward-shifting distribution but not as great a movement into the upper segment. However, since real earnings peaked around 1973, a pertinent question for us to consider is how much better off we would be today if economic growth had continued at its pre-1970s rate.

Analyses conducted for this chapter indicate that the relative position of full-time workers improved over the two-decade period.

The position of the full-time worker shifted upward without exception among gender/race groups. While the white male full-time earner group still had the highest median earnings, the gap between it and all other gender/race groups narrowed significantly. The gap between the median earnings of part- and full-time earners, though, widened over the period of analysis. White females constitute more than one-half of the part-time labor force. The shares of the part-time distribution held by low, middle, and upper earners remained the same over the two decades, although male earners shifted downward along the distribution.

The above evidence, together with the fact that the percentage of part-time workers who would rather be working full-time doubled between 1967 and 1987, indicates that the initial responses to deindustrialization in combination with shifts of employment to service-related functions created a growing disparity between part- and full-time earners. Clearly, part-time workers would have been better off if economic growth had continued at its pre-1970s rate. That full-time workers would also have been better off is demonstrated in chapter 3.

APPENDIX 2.A

Three-Part Definition of the Earnings Distribution:
Middle Segment Is 50% to 200% of the Median Earnings for All
Workers Nationwide

Earnings Group	1967	1973	1979	1987
Low Earners				
Less Than	$2,046	$3,291	$5,033	$7,278
Middle Earners	$2,046	$3,291	$5,033	$7,278
	to	to	to	to
	$8,184	$13,164	$20,132	$29,110
Upper Earners				
Greater Than	$8,184	$13,164	$20,132	$29,110

Source: Calculated from CPS microdata files.

APPENDIX 2.B

Median Earnings and Ratio of Full- and Part-Time Earners' Medians to All-Earner Median, 1967 and 1986

Earnings Group	Smoothed Median		All-Earner Ratio	
	1967	1986	1967	1986
All Earners	$4,092	$13,727	1.00	1.00
All Full-Time Earners	5,938	20,527	1.45	1.50
White Males	7,194	25,720	1.76	1.87
Black Males	4,486	18,122	1.10	1.32
White Females	4,121	16,375	1.01	1.19
Black Females	2,985	14,369	0.73	1.05
All Part-Time Earners	1,296	4,512	0.32	0.33
White Males	1,907	5,490	0.47	0.40
Black Males	1,376	4,204	0.34	0.31
White Females	1,095	4,042	0.27	0.29
Black Females	867	3,489	0.21	0.25

Note: Reported medians are "smoothed" medians.

Source: Calculated from CPS microdata files.

3

The Middle Standard of Living

What is a middle standard of living? There is no precise answer, but Levy and Michel (1986, pp. 33–39) attempted to capture its essence when they wrote:

> A central theme of modern American life is the chance to enjoy a "middle-class standard of living." This standard is not officially defined anywhere, but it exists in many subtle forms throughout our society, from television advertisements to casual conversations. The middle class American dream has come to include such material goods as a single-family home, one or two cars (including a new one), a washing machine and dryer, a dishwasher, a color TV, raising and educating children, providing for a lengthy period of retirement, and so on.

While the middle-class standard of living is not officially defined, it subtly permeates our society even as it is in constant change. What represented the middle standard in the 1960s would not constitute the middle standard in the 1990s. Items such as microwave ovens, camcorders, and VCRs, which did not exist in the 1960s, have become staples in middle-class homes of today. The home within the middle-class consumption basket has changed as well; two bathrooms and a two-car garage are becoming the norm.

In the general focus on the plight of the middle class, the implicit assumption has been that the middle class consumes a middle standard of living. Instead of analyzing changes in the ability of the middle class to purchase the middle standard of living embodied in a specific consumption basket, however, the research approach has consistently been one that identifies a range of middle-level income or earnings that households and/or individuals receive. While this approach does not attack the research question directly, it is not to be faulted. Avoidance of the direct approach is based on a recognition of the inherent difficulty and subjectivity involved in any attempt to define a consumption basket that represents a middle standard of living.

Ideally, there would be an official, government-defined middle standard of living akin to the official standard of poverty that currently exists.[1] At the beginning point of this book's analysis, 1967, there was a government-produced household budget series that defined three standards of living—low, moderate, and high (U.S. Department of Labor, Bureau of Labor Statistics 1967). In an effort to explore what a consumer-basket definition of the middle standard of living might have looked like, an exercise was undertaken using this household budget series. The moderate budget of this series is the closest representation available of a middle standard of living in the late 1960s. It is used in this exercise as the basis for determining the amount of earnings necessary to purchase a middle standard of living consumption basket.

The prevailing view from the 1950s through the late 1960s was that the earnings of one full-time worker could purchase a middle standard of living for a household; the consumer-basket definition of the middle standard of living that is created here incorporates this perception. The household budgets for lower, moderate, and higher standards of living published by the U.S. Bureau of Labor Statistics (BLS) in 1967 were for a "typical family" of four: a thirty-eight-year-old, full-time employed husband who had fifteen years or more of work experience; a wife who was a full-time home-maker; and two children, a thirteen-year-old boy and an eight-year-old girl. These budgets included family consumption items, such as food, housing, transportation, clothing and personal care, and medical care; costs of gifts and contributions; personal life insurance; occupational expenses; and taxes, including Social Security and disability and personal income. In the moderate and high budgets, the household occupants were homeowners while in the low budget they were renters. For the spring of 1967, the budget costs for a BLS-designated lower standard of living were $5,915; for a moderate standard of living, $9,076; and for a higher standard of living, $13,050.

From the BLS household budget series, a consumption-based definition of the earnings distribution is delineated with five earnings segments, three of which make up the middle earners' group because many individuals with widely ranging incomes consider themselves to be middle class—and the middle class is widely believed to make up the broadest segment of our American society and economy.

Having determined for full-time workers in the U.S. Census Bureau's Current Population Survey that earnings as a percent of total income varied between 97% and 98% over the two-decade period, the lower, middle, and upper ranges that divide up the earnings distribution were based on the ability to purchase 97% of the BLS's lower, moderate, and higher budgets. The middle range was further subdivided into a low-middle segment, a mid-middle segment, and an upper-middle segment, using the midpoint first between the moderate and lower budgets and next between the moderate and higher budgets as the midpoints of the low-middle and upper-middle ranges, respectively (Appendix 3.A). The five-part definition of the earnings distribution for 1967 that this procedure created generated a three-part middle earnings range of $6,380 to $11,571 (Table 3.1). In summary, the consumer basket–based definition of the middle of the earnings distribution starts with the amount of earnings necessary to purchase 97% of the middle stan-

TABLE 3.1

Consumer-Basket–Defined Five-Part Delineation of the Earnings
Distribution in 1967

Earnings Segment	Earnings Range
Lower	Less than $6,380
Low-Middle	$6,380 to $7,663
Mid-Middle	$7,663 to $9,393
Upper-Middle	$9,393 to $11,571
Upper	More than $11,571

Source: Calculated by the author.

dard of living, as defined in the BLS's moderate household budget, and determines how many workers have earnings adequate to meet the figure.

The BLS discontinued production of the family budget series in 1981, so a late 1980s version of the 1967 low, moderate, and higher standard of living budgets is not available. Simply inflating the cost of the 1960s basket by some form of consumer price index to late 1980s figures would not provide a satisfactory basis of comparison of changes in the ability of consumers to purchase a middle standard of living over the two-decade period. If a late 1980s basket is not defined, then the issues of changing household composition, of changing relative prices of consumer items, and of changing the concepts of goods and services associated with a middle-class standard of living are not addressed. This is problematic because not only has the middle-class consumption basket changed over the 1967 to 1987 period, as we have discussed, but the middle-class household consuming the basket has changed as well. For example, the average family size decreased from 3.58 persons in 1970 to 3.19 persons in 1987 (U.S. Department of Commerce, Bureau of the Census 1988). Further, the percentage of total households that were husband-wife families decreased, and in such families the percentage of wives who worked in the paid labor force increased. It is precisely these changes in the content of the middle-class consumption basket, as well as the household consuming the basket, that make it so difficult to define an encompassing definition of the middle standard of living.

The primary problem with an attempt to pursue construction of the consumer-basket definition, however, arises out of the issue of the changing contents of the basket rather than the issue of who is purchasing it, for even though the Ozzie and Harriet–type family may be an anachronism, at one time this family type was widely perceived to purchase a middle standard of living out of the earnings of one full-time worker. Thus, if we have made progress or at least held our own, the same or a larger percent of full-time earners should be able to purchase the middle consumption basket whether or not they are the primary earner in an Ozzie and Harriet household.

Since it is not possible to track changes between 1967 and 1987 in the attainability of the middle standard of living consumption basket, the issue will instead be addressed by examining changes in the affordability of the most important consumption item in the middle-class basket, that is, home ownership, which has long been significant for middle-class status. The building of equity through home ownership accounts for more than half of the net wealth of many families, and the long-term appreciation of home values contributes to a family's financial security (Levy and Michel 1991).

Before examining home ownership affordability, an examination of the 1967 consumer basket–based definition is useful for dispelling two aspects of middle-class mythology in the United States. First, the middle-class standard of living was not nearly as pervasive as was commonly thought: 54% of full-time earners could not purchase the middle standard in 1967[2] (Figure 3.1). Second, the Ozzie and Harriet–type family was not nearly as pervasive in the late 1960s as was commonly thought. While the percentage of households represented by this group cannot be determined for 1967, the 1970 census showed that four-person, husband-wife families were 17.1% of all families; those with only one member in the labor force were 8.4%.

The BLS consumption package taken to represent the middle-class standard of living for this analysis included home ownership. Further, it specified that the earnings of only one full-time worker were enough to enable the consumer to purchase the home. Under the consumer basket definition, the median point of the earnings segment was $8,304 in 1967. Inflating this to 1987 dollars, we get $28,243. A rule of thumb by which to determine the price of a house one can afford is two and a half times one's annual earnings. In 1967, this meant a house priced at just under $21,000 could be purchased with the middle earnings figure while in 1987 the house would be priced at around $70,600. In 1968 (a comparable 1967 figure was unavailable), the median sales price of existing single-family houses sold was $20,100 (Arnold and Kusnet 1985), clearly affordable with the middle earnings figure. In 1987, though, the median sales price of existing single-family homes was $85,600, with the median sales price of new one-family houses sold at $104,500 (U.S. Department of Commerce, Bureau of the Census 1991). These median prices are significantly above the affordable figure for 1987, meaning home ownership has clearly become

FIGURE 3.1

Distribution of Full-Time Earnings by Consumer-Basket
Definition of the Middle, 1967

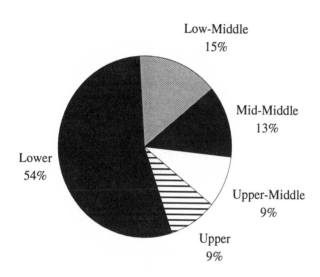

Source: Calculated from Current Population Survey (CPS) microdata files.

less attainable. For those who can afford to buy a home, the burden of doing so has increased substantially. The after-tax cost of home ownership—the cash burden—consumed 22.2% of first-time buyers' income in 1967 and 33.9% in 1986 (Joint Center for Housing Studies of Harvard 1988). The first-time buyers' income referred to here is the median family income of a married couple who rent and who are ages twenty-five to twenty-nine. We would expect the cash burden for individual full-time workers to be much higher and, in many cases, simply unbearable. As a result, more and more households require two earners to be able to buy a home.

Even though the earnings distribution shifted upward between 1967 and 1987 and 6% more full-time workers became upper earners while another 65% maintained their position in the middle-

earner group, the possibility of purchasing a home with the earnings of one full-time worker significantly declined. Thus, the decreasing opportunities for home ownership—the single most important characteristic of middle-class status—suggest that
Americans were really not as well-off in the late 1980s as they were
in the late 1960s.

APPENDIX 3.A

Calculating the Consumer-Basket
Delineation of the Earnings Distribution in 1967

CHART 1

*Ninety-Seven Percent of 1967 BLS Lower, Moderate, and
Higher Standards of Living:*

Lower	Moderate	Higher
$5,738	$8,304	$12,659

CHART 2

*Midpoints Between Lower, Moderate, and Upper Budgets, Which Become the Midpoints of
the Low-Middle and Upper-Middle Ranges:*

Low-Middle Midpoint	High-Middle Midpoint
$7,021	$10,482

CHART 3

*The Middle Earnings Ranges Based on 97% of the BLS-Defined Lower, Moderate, and
Higher Standard of Living Budgets for 1967:*

Lower	Low-Middle	Mid-Middle	Upper-Middle	Upper
$0	$6,380	$7,663	$9,393	$11,571

Source: Calculated from CPS microdata files.

4

Industrial Restructuring's Influence on the Distribution of Earnings

Industrial transformation—that is, change in what is produced and how it is produced—is manifested in a changing income distribution: who gets what and how. As economies shift from agricultural to industrial modes of production, they first experience an increasing inequality; subsequent movement toward greater equality, which is reflected in a growing middle-income sector, occurs as industrialization advances (Williamson and Lindert 1980).

The most recent, continuing transformation of the American economy has been given the label of *post*-industrialism. Postindustrial is widely used to describe service economies, implying that the manufacture of goods is no longer the basic economic activity. In the United States, manufacturing clearly is no longer the primary source of employment: eight of every ten jobs are in the obscurely labeled service sector, but as Cohen and Zysman (1987), among others, have argued, manufacturing is still an economic foundation upon which major portions of service jobs are dependent.

In the early 1980s, it was claimed that America's postindustrial phase was really deindustrialization and that deindustrialization was causing the permanent loss of good manufacturing jobs, that is, those paying middle-level wages (Bluestone and Harrison 1982; Magaziner and Reich 1982). Since there was growth in nonindustrial or postindustrial sectors, however, this suggested to others that even if deindustrialization was occurring, it was not a cause for concern (Lawrence 1984b). Toward the end of the 1980s, the term reindustrialization came into use to describe the economic recovery of areas that had been part of the industrial core that had suffered from severe manufacturing losses. But even though the United States appears to be moving beyond deindustrialization, basic questions are yet to be satisfactorily answered, including: What has happened to middle-level jobs? and What will be the sources of new middle-level jobs?

This chapter explores why the issue of structural change has come to be the fundamental concern in the debate over the disappearing middle class and examines the evidence of its impact on the earnings distribution at the national level.

The Debate over Structural Change

That the middle economic group is being squeezed is now widely accepted, but this was not the case in the early 1980s. The beleaguered middle class as a national economic problem of political consequence did not become a theme until former President George H. Bush's 1988 presidential campaign. It emerged again as one of the primary issues in President Bill Clinton's successful 1992 campaign.

The initial phase of the debate over the disappearing middle class was characterized by several interrelated themes. Was the disappearing middle class a real trend? If so, what was its cause and when would it end? The debate first centered on whether the declining middle class was due to a changing demographic or a changing industrial structure. From there, the question became whether the disappearing middle class was a temporary or a relatively permanent phenomenon. If it was temporary, it was due to either demographic origins that would disappear as the labor force changed or to macroeconomic causes that were cyclical and relatively easy to correct through monetary and fiscal policies. If the declining middle class was a more permanent trend, it was a result of fundamental changes in industrial structure, the counteraction of which required strategic industrial policy implementation on the part of the national government.

The Demographic Explanation

In the early phases of the debate over the declining middle class, the demographic explanation—that is, the changing age distribution of the labor force—gained the most acceptance. The argument was that entrance into the labor force of the baby boom generation could explain the decline in the middle-earnings sector and, concurrently, the growth in the low-earnings sector.

The baby boom explanation of the changing earnings distribution hinged upon two concepts in labor economics: crowding and the life cycle of earnings. Crowding referred to the fact that the baby boom cohort—individuals born between 1946 and 1964—constituted an unusually large number of new workers entering the labor force at one point in time, which was supposed to result in a relative lowering of their wages.

Lawrence (1984b) wrote that the baby boomers' entrance into the labor force between 1969 and 1983 was accompanied by declines in earnings relative to those of the total work force. In particular, the ratio of the median earnings of males under age twenty-five to those over age twenty-five dropped from 74% to 55%. Lawrence further observed that the decline in the middle-earnings sector was accompanied by an expansion in the lower-earnings sector for younger workers, whereas for all workers age thirty-five and older, it resulted in an expansion of the upper-earner group. Among females, the middle-earnings sector declined only for the group age twenty-five or younger, leading to an expansion of the low-earner group. Citing Russell's (1982) conclusion that "the reductions in earnings due to a large cohort appear to be greatest in the early stages of careers and to diminish thereafter," Lawrence suggested that the declining middle-class phenomenon would be temporary and that as the large baby boomer cohort aged, the middle of the earnings distribution would increase. The demographic explanation for the declining middle class has largely been dispelled through subsequent analyses and accumulating evidence that the economy was in fundamental distress.

The Life-Cycle Explanation

That a worker's aging is correlated with higher earnings is a principle of the life-cycle earnings model. Earnings are expected to grow over the course of an individual's work force participation, peaking in the middle years, after significant skills and experience have been acquired. According to the life-cycle model, if the declining middle class were due to the baby boomer cohort entering the labor force, the trend was a temporary one that would disappear as the baby boomers aged (Linden 1984). However, taking into account the effects of crowding, this conclusion is overly simplistic.

Blackburn and Bloom (1985) found the median age of middle-income groups had been increasing since 1969, implying that it took longer for a younger earner to enter the middle sector. It is not clear, though, when and if the effects of crowding will wear off.

Thurow (1984) criticized an implied assumption in the life-cycle explanation that supply creates its own demand:

> A larger supply of middle-aged workers does not lead to more middle-income jobs. A larger supply of middle-aged workers leads partly to lower wages for those, since they are competing with one another for the existing supply of jobs. These workers are also filtering down into what are less desirable jobs once held by the young or old, disrupting conventional job distribution.

Thus, even if the economy were not experiencing significant structural change, the baby boomer cohort might always be subject to the effects of crowding. If fundamental structural changes are occurring within the economy that reduce the number of jobs offering middle-level earnings at the same time the baby boomer cohort is moving through the labor force, though, the baby boomers' prospects for attaining middle standards of living are further reduced; so are those for the cohort following the boomers and for any workers preceding the boomers who were unfortunate enough to be displaced from their middle-earning jobs. The question, therefore, is whether structural changes present a temporary or a more permanent problem.

The End of Growth

In the early 1970s, the postwar engine of growth in the United States began to experience mechanical difficulties that directly and negatively impacted the standard of living of American workers.

The frequently cited symptoms of the economy's troubled state were declining productivity, stagnant real income and wages, ballooning federal deficits, erosion in international market position, and increasing reliance on imports that displaced American manufacturing activity.

Essentially, the postwar economic era has been divided into two phases. Prior to 1973, American workers and their families experienced a steadily rising standard of living over a period of unprecedented economic growth and expansion. Inflation-adjusted wages grew 2% to 3% annually (Levy 1987). Real median family income grew more than 3% annually (Congressional Budget Office 1988). However, since 1973, real wages have been declining at the rate of more than 1% per annum and real family income has been stagnant (Mishel and Simon 1988).

The post-1973 productivity slowdown and stagnant income growth are *partially* explained by the large increases in energy prices, rapid labor force growth, a decade of self-sustained inflation, and an inadequate response to slow-growing markets. Levy (1987) noted that some of these problems resolved themselves only to have been replaced by problems of extraordinary financial debt and import consumption, as well as dependency on foreign capital. He distinguished between the two sets of problems, noting that the former were beyond our control whereas the latter are not. Thus, with substantial government intervention, the post-1973 period of stagnation might become known as a bad episode instead of a structural crisis. The government intervention that Levy specified would induce "short-run sacrifice" on the part of American workers and families because of deficit-reducing measures involving higher taxes and reduced federal expenditures.

A prescription such as Levy's implies that other factors that generate middle-level jobs would remain constant. Large corporations would continue to maintain their layered personnel structures, with large proportions of middle-management jobs; the service sector would continue to perform strongly, providing multiple opportunities for professional employment; and the strength and compensation levels of unionized blue-collar labor would remain intact. This was not to be the case, though. The early years of the 1990s have brought a continual erosion of the unionized sector, service sector retrenchment, and wide-scale elimination of middle-management jobs as corporations have sought to adopt leaner and more flexible organizational patterns.

Consequently, others have not been as sanguine as Levy over the causes and cures of the post-1973 malaise. In particular, Harrison and Bluestone (1988) argue that its cause was a "profit squeeze" or structural crisis in American capitalism that began in the mid-1960s and led to the reversal in income growth after 1973. This profit squeeze was an outgrowth of heightened international competition to which U.S. corporations were initially blind. In this heightened international competition, all the major industrialized, as well as newly industrializing, countries ended up producing similar products, leading to global excess capacity.

The delayed response by America's businesses took the form of corporate restructuring that resulted in "qualitative changes amounting almost to a 180-degree U-Turn in the prevailing relationship between business and its workforce," the restructuring of financial relationships within and between firms, and a significant change in government posture toward supporting business interests over worker interests (Harrison and Bluestone 1988).

Although in agreement with Levy that significant government intervention is required to reverse the post-1973 malaise, Harrison and Bluestone called for far more extensive and specific actions, which can be grouped into seven areas: industrial and corollary educational policies; workplace democracy; renewed public support for unionization; management of international trade; rebuilding of the national physical infrastructure; reregulation of specific, and especially financial, private market activities; and the provision of universal healthcare, child care, and elder care.

The government intervention prescribed by Harrison and Bluestone, if successfully implemented, would have generated substantial gains in the standards of living and in the overall quality of life of American workers and their families. In contrast, Levy's prescription was guaranteed to produce short-run further declines in the standard of living and did nothing to reverse declines in or replace such factors as unionization and fringe benefit growth, which had helped to raise the American standard of living and lessen overall inequality in the postwar period. It would, however, be naive not to include a reduction in the federal deficit as a criterion of successful government intervention. Levy's measures would specifically reduce the deficit; Harrison and Bluestone's, while not directly focused on the deficit, would—if they reignited the economy's growth machine—also help to reduce it.

By the early 1990s, we still have not been able to conclude that the post-1973 malaise was only a temporary phase. The depth and scope of industrial restructuring continue, hastened in the manufacturing sector by global corporations reorganizing their production strategies in response to continued international competition and now to free trade movements.

Recognizing the significance of the industrial restructuring that has occurred since 1973, we now need to examine how this structural change has affected the earnings distribution—especially the middle of the distribution—to more fully understand the prospects for attaining and retaining a middle standard of living. The pattern of change in the earnings distribution that we identify in what follows, particularly after 1973, may very well be our best indicator of the pattern characterizing the remainder of this century unless some significant new government intervention, such as the development of a strategic industrial policy, is forthcoming.

An Industrial Classification System

To understand the pattern of change in the earnings distribution requires analysis of the production sectors that employ the labor force along with a determination of who middle earners are in terms of gender and race and what proportions they make up of the various production sectors. Additionally, to understand the influence of the growing internationalization of the economy on the distribution requires analysis of whether the U.S. industries employing middle-level earners are gaining or losing their trade advantage.

In this research, earners are placed, according to their primary industrial affiliation recorded in the Current Population Survey (CPS), into sectors defined by an industrial classification system adapted from the U.S. Congress, Office of Technology Assessment (OTA; 1988). OTA aggregated all industries into production sectors "likely to be affected in similar ways by changes in technology, trade patterns, and regulation."[1] A description of the nine production sectors constituting this classification system can be found in Appendix 4.A. The relatively unknown OTA classification is superior to recent approaches that employ only broad industry groups, such as durable and nondurable manufacturing, mining and construction, agriculture, and services (Levy and Michel 1991).

The nine production sectors in which earners have been grouped are: natural resources; construction; traditional/low-wage manufacturing; high-tech/medium-wage manufacturing; smokestack/high-wage manufacturing; transportation and trade; transactional activities, such as financial and business services; personal services; and social infrastructure, such as government, healthcare, and education.[2]

At first, it may seem odd to analyze earners by their earnings segment within industry groups that have been labeled low-, medium-, and high-wage. What it is important to make clear is that OTA has grouped the manufacturing industries based on the average level of annual compensation per a full-time equivalent employee in 1984. This is distinctly different from creating low-, middle-, and upper-earnings segments based on the median point, as is done in this analysis, because within those industries with either low, medium, or high average wages there is still a segmented distribution of earners. Shifts across the low, middle, and upper segments of the three manufacturing groups will inform our analysis of the changing earnings distribution.

The nine OTA sectors have been aggregated into three major groups to facilitate comprehension of the analysis results: "high growth" is made up of transportation and trade, transactional activities, and social infrastructure; "manufacturing" is made up of traditional/low-wage manufacturing, high-tech/medium-wage manufacturing, and smokestack/high-wage manufacturing; and "other" is made up of natural resources, construction, and personal services. The "high growth" group was so labeled because these sectors were observed to experience the greatest additions in employment over the two decades of analysis. Use of this modified OTA classification more directly illuminates factors that have been identified as negatively affecting the middle economic class.

From Appendix 4.A, we see that the grouping of manufacturing industries by wage levels produces sectors that are commensurate with well-recognized qualitative criteria. Traditional/low-wage manufacturing represents traditional apparel, footwear, and furniture making. High-tech/medium-wage manufacturing includes the manufacture of electrical and electronic equipment, communications equipment, and scientific instruments. The smokestack/high-wage sector is dominated by motor vehicles, iron and steel, construction machinery, and glass manufacture.

Defense and High-Technology Sectors

In addition to examining changes in the earnings distribution by the nine-sector production classification, two sectoral analyses that focused on only certain segments of the production system were conducted. These subanalyses studied defense and high technology as well as trade impacts, areas of industrial restructuring that have received wide attention and speculation as to their impact on economic development and income change.

The first of these subanalyses focused on defense and high-technology activity, a subset of the high-tech/medium-wage and smokestack/high-wage groups in the nine-sector classification. High technology is an important analytical category because the creation of industry and jobs in this sector has been the primary focus of economic development policy and practice for more than a decade. The sector is considered an important new source of middle- and upper-earnings jobs. Seeking to emulate the perceived successes of Silicon Valley in California and Route 128 in Massachusetts, state and local development agencies tried to jump on the high-tech bandwagon by building high-tech research parks, by targeting high-tech industries in their industrial recruiting efforts, and by creating special university-level programs to grow their own high-tech industries throughout the 1980s.

Although there is considerable overlap between the defense and high-technology sectors, the defense sector has unique characteristics that warrant its analysis as a separate entity. It does not operate in a competitive market, where it would be subject to pressures to hold down production costs, including labor costs. Instead, it produces a public good for a monopsonistic buyer, that is, the federal government, which determines what the products of the defense sector are to be, who the suppliers of the products will be, and the location of their production facilities on the grounds that defense is a public good. It is important to recognize, however, that this government defense policy constitutes a de facto or implicit industrial and economic development policy. Markusen (1985a) has called this the "quiet industrial policy." While the size of the defense sector may be relatively small, if it is geographically concentrated, it could create pockets of population enjoying high standards of living.

The overall period of this analysis of the changing earnings distribution, 1967 to 1987, is one in which growing controversy developed over U.S. defense activity. Further, the latter part of the period saw increasingly organized attention given to issues of economic conversion of the defense industry. The defense buildup under former President Ronald Reagan fueled much of the recent debate over the defense sector's role in the American economy. Therefore, a number of adverse consequences have been attributed to defense spending: it creates inflationary pressures; it has unequal distributional consequences for different socioeconomic groups; and it undermines industry competitiveness and technological leadership (Browne 1988; Markusen 1985a).

No clear support has emerged for arguments that defense-related expenditures are responsible for the economy's deteriorating performance and that they hinder high-tech competitiveness (Browne 1988; Leitenberg and Ball 1983), nor has it emerged for the closely related issue of whether defense spending has put the U.S. economy at a considerable " 'growth disadvantage' compared with countries where military spending is lower" (for example, Japan and West Germany; Leitenberg and Ball 1983).

Although we lack a consensus on what effect defense and high-technology sectors have on the growth of our economy, it is important, given the attention that these two sectors receive, to understand what the earnings distribution looks like for these two categories and what percentage of employment is found within them. Additionally, the end of the cold war is expected to lead, in particular, to a downsizing of the defense sector, which further warrants its examination. The size of these sectors may not appear significant on the national level yet they are significant to regional economies within the United States.

The Role of Comparative Advantage

Because of the growing interdependency of the international economic system, a changing international trade position affects the domestic earnings distribution and standard of living. Therefore, we also should consider trends in the earnings distributions of industries that are gaining or losing trade advantage.

The benefit of increased trade between countries, as suggested by international trade theory, is that a nation can maximize its comparative advantage by concentrating on the selling of those goods and services it produces most efficiently. Throughout much of the postwar period, the United States' comparative advantage across industries was so broad that the nation dominated the postwar international economy. Factors contributing to this comparative advantage included high levels of education, easy access to capital, and the possession of technologically advanced production processes. However, the United States no longer holds a monopoly on these factors and, in fact, has experienced a significant erosion in their presence.

The convergence of living standards of the United States and foreign countries should, in itself, be viewed positively because it has been a result of the accelerated growth of less-developed economies. Still, the continued presence of the factors that contributed to this convergence creates the threat of further convergence, resulting in the American standard of living falling in real terms.

The factors that contributed to this convergence and to the erosion of the U.S. economy's comparative advantage can be summarized as follows (U.S. Congress, Office of Technology Assessment 1988):

1. Other nations have benefited from being in a position of playing catch-up with the United States as a technological leader rather than having to be the ones to first succeed in new and untested areas.
2. The United States as, historically, the world's technical leader could not recover the real value of its exported technology or training.
3. U.S. industries have suffered from complacency and mismanagement.

4. The major international competitors of the United States
   have benefited from postwar recovery incentives and access to this country's markets.
5. There has been a weakening of the product cycle, which,
   until recently, seemed to guarantee the self-perpetuation of
   America's industrial leadership.

The OTA analyzed changes in the U.S. trade advantage by individual industries over a twelve-year period, from 1972 to 1984.
Advantage in trade was measured by a change in the ratio of the
value-added gained due to exports to the value-added lost due to
imports. A declining comparative advantage was found for nearly
all manufacturing industries, with particularly strong losses observed in production areas in which the United States had traditionally been a leader, including electronic components and acces-
sories, office computing and accounting machines, aircraft and
parts, and engines and turbines. Additionally, major losses were
observed for automobile manufacturing and apparel industries.

OTA found that 75% of the high-technology industries had lost
their comparative advantage. It further found that the United
States was gaining comparative advantage where it would expect to
be losing ground to developing nations, that is, in labor-intensive
and raw material–dependent industries.

To determine what influence the United States' changing international trade position has had on the distribution of earnings
in our analysis, OTA's trade categories have been adapted to create
an industry classification composed of three broad groupings—
Gainers, Losers, and Holders—of apparent trade advantage. This
was done for full-time earners by cross-referencing the CPS industry codes with OTA's trade categories.

We turn now to look at what changes occurred in the relationship between industrial restructuring, labor force composition, and
the distribution of earnings in the pre-1973 and post-1973 periods.
Unless there is substantial redirection of the current political cli-
mate, our observations of post-1973 trends may provide a good indication of what the last decade of this century may look like for
the American economy and its workers. Consequently, if the future
outlook appears negative, our observations can help focus attention on the necessary policy and planning actions needed to alter
that outlook.

Change in the Distribution of Earnings from 1967 to 1973, 1973 to 1979, and 1979 to 1987

Over the period as a whole, earnings for full- and part-time workers shifted from the middle segment. Full-time earners shifted upward from the middle while part-time earners shifted downward. As a result, inequality among the work force increased between 1967 and 1987; however, it did not increase steadily, as we will see in a later section.

Further, while full-time earners shifted upward along the distribution, their progress was counteracted by decreases in benefit recipiency. The trend in benefit recipiency combined with large increases in the cost of home ownership suggests an erosion in the attainability of the middle standard of living. In turn, this erosion differentially affects the work force depending on the gender, race, and educational attainment of the earner.

Our twenty-year examination of shifts in the earnings distribution is divided into three segments that correspond to commonly analyzed periods of the business cycle: 1967 to 1973, 1973 to 1979, and 1979 to 1987. Among full-time workers, low earners as a group shrank over the 1967 to 1987 period, with the greatest shrinkage occurring between the peak business cycle years of 1973 and 1979 (Table 4.1). The pattern of the middle- and upper-earner segments has not been as consistent. A downward shift in the earnings distribution of full-time workers from the upper to the middle segments occurred between 1967 and 1973, which reversed itself slightly in the next period. This shift from the middle to upper segments became more pronounced between 1979 and 1987, with the upper segment increasing by nearly 7%.

The position of full-time workers does not appear to be such an improvement if their benefit recipiency is taken into account. Between 1979 (the earliest year for which benefit data are available) and 1987, the percent of full-time earners who were included in an employer's pension plan declined almost 7% (Table 4.2). Decreases in those included in an employer's group health plan and in the percentage of full-time earners whose employers helped to pay for their group health insurance also occurred. These 1980s trends intensified in the 1990s. The lack of affordable health insurance has become a crisis for much of the nation's low earners and

TABLE 4.1

Change in the Distribution of Earnings, 1967–1973–1979–1987

| Labor Force | Year | Earnings Segment (%) | | | Total | |
		Low	Middle	Upper		
Full-Time Earners	1967	6.6	68.3	25.1	46,139,784	100.0
	1973	5.8	72.0	22.2	51,258,377	100.0
	1979	4.9	71.7	23.4	58,784,561	100.0
	1987	4.7	65.2	30.1	71,135,912	100.0
Part-Time Earners	1967	64.4	32.7	2.9	33,140,416	100.0
	1973	63.3	34.3	2.4	29,227,861	100.0
	1979	61.8	35.4	2.8	36,081,526	100.0
	1987	65.9	30.8	3.4	47,244,716	100.0

Source: Calculated from Current Population Survey (CPS) microdata files.

TABLE 4.2

Percent of Full-Time Earners by Gender with Benefit Recipiency, 1979 and 1987

Benefit	Year	Males	Females	Total
Included in Pension Plan	1979	65.3	58.3	62.8
	1987	58.0	53.6	56.2
	Change	−7.3	−4.7	−6.6
Included in Group Health	1979	84.7	75.8	81.5
	1987	79.2	71.5	76.1
	Change	−5.5	−4.3	−5.4
Employer Helped Pay for Group Health	1979	80.1	71.1	76.9
	1987	75.9	68.5	72.9
	Change	−4.2	−2.6	−4.0

Note: n = 58,784,561 in 1979; n = 71,135,912 in 1987.

Source: Calculated from CPS microdata files.

unemployed. It is also approaching crisis levels among the middle-earner group, particularly for the rising number of self-employed middle earners who do not benefit from premium costs savings that are given to group policyholders.

Shifting the focus to part-time workers, there was, overall, a downward shift in their earnings distribution between 1967 and 1987, primarily as a result of changes between 1979 and 1987 (see Table 4.1). Low earners who were more than 64% in 1967 decreased to about 62% in 1979 and then grew to almost 66% by 1987. The middle-earner segment shrank almost 5% between 1979 and 1987 while upper earners increased slightly.

The question has been raised as to whether or not the improvement in earnings, that is, upward shifts for full-time workers, is a result of an increased work effort (Mishel 1988). The indicator of work effort—"average weekly hours worked"—does not support this claim.[3] Full-time workers in 1968 (comparable 1967 figures were not available) worked an average of 43.4 hours per week.[4] In 1987, they worked slightly less—43.1 hours per week. Thus, the *overall* upward shift of the full-time earnings distribution does not seem to be explained by this indicator of hours worked yet it could explain some of the shift between 1979 and 1987, as the average hours worked in 1979 was 42.7 per week. More significantly, the hours-per-week indicator does not support explanations of *decreased* work effort having lead to the downward shift in the part-time earners' distribution: their average hours worked per week increased.

Earnings Inequality among Full-Time Workers

An examination of the middle segment of the earnings distribution is really a subset of research into inequality. Displacement of middle-level earners, whether to the upper or lower segments or to both, implies that inequality within the distribution is growing. Growing inequality is a critical public policy issue as it can lead to growth in the rate of poverty and its accompanying underclass, to greater needs for transfer programs, and to a middle-class decline, with possibilities for associated political instability.

Inequality is measured here for full-time earners only; that is, those who work more than thirty-five hours a week, fifty weeks a year. Because the range of weeks and hours per week worked has wide variation among part-time earners, measures of inequality among this group would be difficult to interpret.

There are a number of measures of inequality to choose from, but as Allison (1978) noted, the choice of a measure is, in fact, a choice among alternative definitions of inequality rather than simply a choice among alternative ways to measure a single theoretical construct. The inequality index employed here is the Theil,[5] an index based on information theory. It is a measure of dispersion divided by the mean, which makes it sensitive to transfers and therefore particularly suited to the measurement of income inequality (Allison 1978). The Theil index satisfies the principle of transfers, which specifies that the measure of inequality should increase whenever income is transferred from a poorer to a richer person. Further, under the assumption that income has diminishing marginal utility, the Theil index reflects that when a transfer of income among low earners occurs, it is more consequential than a transfer of an equal amount among upper earners.

Computations using the Theil index revealed *decreasing* inequality for full-time earners as a group between 1967 and 1979, followed by a sharp rise in inequality between 1979 and 1987.[6] However, as might be expected, the trend toward growing inequality appears sooner within the middle-earnings segment, beginning in 1973 (Table 4.3).

TABLE 4.3

Theil Index of Inequality for Full-Time Earners, 1967–1973–1979–1987

Year	All Full-Time Earners Theil	Middle Earners Theil
1987	0.178	0.055
1979	0.154	0.056
1973	0.163	0.054
1967	0.168	0.049

Source: Calculated from CPS microdata files.

Declining inequality for full-time earners throughout the decade of the 1970s at first glance appears highly unlikely. It is also contrary to the results of a number of analyses, the two most recent being the one by Grubb and Wilson (1987) and the other by Harrison and Bluestone (1988). Both sets of authors, though, analyze all earners combined. Reiff (1986), who analyzed full-time workers, as was done here, also found decreasing inequality between 1968 and 1983. Since the increase in inequality shows up for all workers but not for full-time workers until later, its earlier onset must be explained by changes in the position and earnings of the part-time segment of the labor force. This is the conclusion reached by Grubb and Wilson, Harrison and Bluestone, and Reiff, and it correlates well with findings presented earlier indicating that the part-time labor force is becoming increasingly marginalized.

What explains the observed decreasing inequality for full-time earners during the 1970s and the sharp increase during the 1980s? Grubb and Wilson, Harrison and Bluestone, and Reiff reached similar conclusions that changes in the gender and racial composition of the labor force, regional shifts, and sectoral shifts—such as from manufacturing to services—are inadequate to explain increasing inequality. The data on the distribution of earnings by gender presented in Appendix 4.B also support their findings. The shift of women out of the low-earner segment has been dramatic in all industry sectors. Eighty percent of women who worked full-time were in the middle-earner segment in 1987, compared to 55% of men. Thus, increased labor force participation of women has had the effect of decreasing earnings inequality.

Harrison and Bluestone (1988) concluded that the greater openness of the U.S. economy to international trade and investment was insufficient to explain the increasing inequality. Instead, they found that the best explanation of increasing inequality was captured in a phrase adapted from Richard Freeman: "rule changes." These rule changes occurred in the relationship between employers and employees and especially affected full-time earners, resulting in an uneven incidence across industries of wage freezes, concessions, and establishment of two-tiered wage systems.

The increasing openness of the U.S. economy and its accompanying declining international trade position, however, is precisely what has been the primary motivating factor for the rule changes. Some American employers were experiencing an uncomfortable "profit squeeze" while others were threatened with business failure. They focused on reducing labor costs in their efforts to recover. In doing so, they directly attacked organized labor, which played a major role in generating high and stable wages for the unionized and nonunionized employment sectors throughout the postwar period. Organized labor itself made a series of strategic errors that led to its diminished presence in the manufacturing sectors without an accompanying growth in presence in the non-manufacturing sectors of the economy.

The declining influence of unions on the earnings structure of the U.S. economy may go a long way toward explaining the increasing inequality among full-time workers. Edsall (1984) wrote that organized labor had a "deceptively cooperative alliance with big business" during the postwar growth period and was unprepared for big business's attack, which began in the mid-1970s. That the attack did not show up in rising inequality for full-time earners until the end of the 1970s may be explained by the unionized sector's automatic cost-of-living salary increases, which were pegged to increases in the Consumer Price Index (CPI). Because the CPI was heavily weighted toward oil and mortgage interest rates, economic trends in the 1970s resulted in wage rises of 6% to 8% above the actual increase in the cost of living. As Edsall (1984) observed:

> The result was, just at a time of increased overseas competition, an inadvertant CPI-pegged wage hike that functioned to push United States wage rates up, in international terms, to noncompetitive levels, levels that were, in the view of at least management, economically not sustainable. . . . [I]n the late 1970s and early 1980s . . . management drives have gone past efforts to reduce the union/non-union wage differential and have become successful efforts to break unions altogether.

At the end of our period of analysis, 1987, the unionized labor force was around 17%, down from a high of 29%, in 1975, in the postwar period. As is well acknowledged, unions have been a fundamental source of good-paying—that is, middle-earnings—jobs and have contributed to the growth of nonunionized good-paying jobs in that nonunionized employers have tried to match unionized wages in an effort to remove organizing incentives for their employees.

Rule changes and declining unionization are the most logical factors to explain the growing inequality for full-time earners and even the increasing marginalization of part-time workers. These trends lend themselves well to analyses of changes in the labor market and the earnings structure based on dual labor market theory. The primary labor market and its accompanying internal labor market structure within large firms are being eroded through employers' efforts to cut labor costs and to achieve flexibility in production.

Employment Shifts across Production Sectors

Industrial restructuring has led to changed employment and sources of middle-level earnings in the economy's production sectors.

Concerns over the offshoring of production to economies that pay their manufacturing workers a fraction of U.S. wages were voiced with increasing frequency over the 1967 to 1987 period. Thus, it may come as a surprise that while the traditional low-wage manufacturing sector had the smallest share of employment among part- and full-time earners it actually grew in absolute terms in both groups. In fact, every production sector of the full-time earner distribution has gained employment. In contrast, part-time earners decreased in the high-tech/medium-wage and smokestack/high-wage manufacturing sectors, as well as in the personal services sector.

Full-time employment grew most in the transportation and trade, transactional activities, and social infrastructure sectors. Significant shifts in the shares of employment in each of the production sectors have occurred between 1967 and 1987 (Figure 4.1). Employment in high-tech/medium-wage manufacturing declined the most while social infrastructure gained the largest share, becoming the largest sector, and transactional activities experienced the second largest share increase. While transportation and trade increased its share by less than 1%, it held its position as the second largest sector.

FIGURE 4.1

Distribution of Full-Time Earners by Production Sector, 1967 and 1987

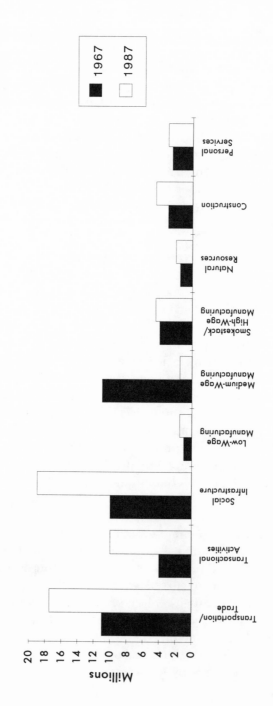

Note: n: 1967 = 46,139,784; 1987 = 71,135,912.

Source: Calculated from CPS microdata files.

Therefore, between 1967 and 1987, the production of social infrastructure, such as government, education, and private and public healthcare, replaced manufacturing as the dominant employer of full-time workers. Transportation and trade became the second largest employer of full-time workers so that the distribution of goods overtook the actual manufacturing of goods as the activity engaging full-time workers.

For part-time workers, the two largest employing production sectors increased their dominance, and these two sectors were the same as those for full-time workers. Transportation and trade and social infrastructure combined employed 47% of the part-time workers in 1967 and 56% in 1987. Nearly one-third of all part-time workers were employed in the transportation and trade sectors (Figure 4.2).

Gender and Race Distribution by Production Sector

Employment shifts across production sectors over the twenty-year period were accompanied by shifts in gender and race of employees within the sectors. White males were the largest employed group in every sector in 1967. However, after two decades, white females had become the largest group in the fast-growing transactional activities and social infrastructure sectors. Further, white females overtook black males as the second largest employed group in natural resources and construction. The most significant changes in the distribution of employees by gender/race groups occurred in personal services, transactional activities, and social infrastructure (Table 4.4).

Personal services employed less than 5% of full-time workers throughout the twenty-year period, but black females were 21% of the sector's workers in 1967. By the end of the period, they were only 5%. More than a quarter of personal service workers were low earners in 1967. Twenty years later, this group shrank by more than one-half while the middle-earner group grew by 10%.

Within the personal services sector, more than 17% of all black women were employed as private household workers in 1967, comprising nearly 59% of all private household workers (see Table 4.4). By 1987, this industry employed just 1.5% of all full-time black

TABLE 4.4

Percent Distribution of Each Gender/Race Group by Selected Sectors

Major Industry Sector and CPS 2-Digit Industry	Year	Black Females	Black Males	White Females	White Males	Percent of Full-Time Employment
Personal Services Sector						
Private Household	1967	58.5	2.1	32.9	4.8	1.1
	1986	19.6	1.9	62.6	10.0	0.4
Repair Services	1967	0.0	10.4	6.0	83.0	0.9
	1986	0.0	5.1	11.5	82.6	1.4
Personal Services Excluding Private Household	1967	13.7	7.0	37.2	39.8	2.0
	1986	7.0	6.6	45.2	35.7	1.8
Entertainment and Recreation Services	1967	4.8	10.1	17.0	67.5	0.6
	1986	2.6	6.7	32.3	56.2	0.8
Transactional Activities						
Communications	1967	3.1	1.4	41.7	53.0	1.9
	1986	6.3	3.8	35.2	52.8	1.9
Banking and Other Finance	1967	3.0	1.2	49.9	45.3	2.5
	1986	7.3	1.7	53.9	32.9	3.6
Insurance and Real Estate	1967	1.6	3.8	34.1	59.6	2.9
	1986	5.0	3.9	49.4	39.1	3.9

Business Services	1967	1.0	6.9	29.0	62.1	1.4
	1986	5.6	6.5	35.0	50.6	3.6
Social Infrastructure						
Hospitals	1967	14.7	7.6	53.5	22.7	3.5
	1986	13.5	4.5	56.5	20.2	4.6
Health, Except Hospitals	1967	7.3	2.0	68.1	21.4	1.4
	1986	10.1	3.2	63.5	19.1	3.4
Education	1967	6.7	4.0	47.3	41.0	7.3
	1986	7.3	4.2	50.9	35.5	7.7
Social Services	1967	4.2	5.6	31.7	57.4	1.0
	1986	17.4	4.6	54.6	21.0	1.3
Public Administration	1967	3.8	7.6	25.4	62.0	3.0
	1986	6.4	6.8	29.1	55.1	6.6
Other Professional Services	1967	1.7	1.8	33.8	60.5	1.4
	1986	3.2	2.8	38.7	52.7	3.6
Total Employment	1967	3.6	6.1	26.7	62.7	100.0
	1986	5.0	5.4	33.3	53.3	100.0

Notes: 1967 total full-time employment = 46,139,784; 1986 total full-time employment = 68,690,029.

Source: Calculated from CPS microdata files.

FIGURE 4.2

Distribution of Part-Time Earners by Production Sector, 1967 and 1987

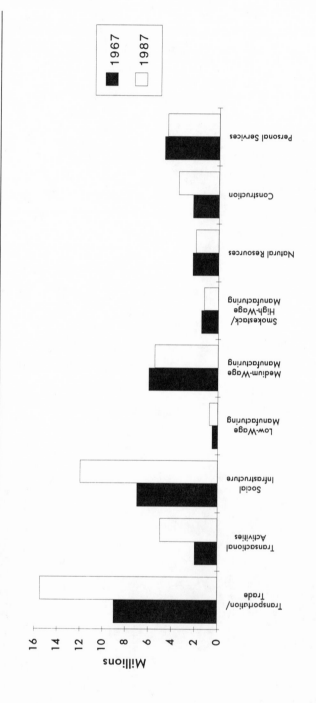

Note: n: 1967 = 33,140,416; 1987 = 47,244,716.

Source: Calculated from CPS microdata files.

women workers. Black males were 10.4% of the employees in 1967 in repair services, another industry in the personal services sector, and only 5.1% by 1987 (see Table 4.4). In contrast, white females grew from 6.0% to 11.5% in repair services employment.

In the remaining two industries in the personal services sector, white females gained significant shares of employment while the three other gender/race groups all lost shares. The white females' share of the personal (excluding household) services industry employment increased from 37.2% to 45.2% while their share in the entertainment and recreation industry increased from 17.0% to 32.3%.

The transactional activities sector is the second of the three sectors to experience significant shifts in the gender and race distribution of its workers. This sector's share of full-time employment increased from around 9% to 13% between 1967 and 1987. The sector had a slightly smaller share of low earners and a greater share of upper earners than full-time earners overall in 1967, as well as in 1987. In the twenty-year period, there was a shift in the distribution from middle to upper earners.

Within transactional activities, white males' employment fell 11%, black males' share increased slightly to 4%, white females' share increased to 46%, and black females' share increased to 6%. Of the four industries making up the transactional activities sector—communications, banking and other finance, insurance and real estate, and business services—only communications' share of full-time employment did not increase (see Table 4.4). Within this industry, blacks' share of employment doubled but white males were still more than half of the industry's employees. The banking and other finance industry was largely female in 1967 and has become even more so, as the white males' share fell more than 12%. The white females' share increased to one-half of the insurance and real estate industry. Finally, business services' share of total employment more than doubled over the last two decades. While it is still a predominantly white male industry, it has become significantly less so. White females' share has increased to 35.0% and black females' to 5.6%. Within the transactional activities sector, this industry employs the largest percentage of black males, 6.5%.

The third sector experiencing dramatic shifts is social infrastructure. With close to nineteen million employees, this sector

had the largest share of full-time earners in 1987 at 27.2%. Social
infrastructure's earnings distribution closely mirrored that of the
distribution of all earners combined. The middle segment gradually
increased until 1979. Between 1979 and 1987, it decreased sharply
as a result of a shift to the upper segment. Over the last two decades, 2% of the decline in the white males' share of this sector's
employment went to black females while 6% went to white females.

Six industries make up the social infrastructure sector: hospitals, health (except hospitals), education, social infrastructure,
public administration, and other professional services (see Table
4.4). In the education industry, white males, who were once 41%
of the employees, shrank to 35.5%. However, the most dramatic
change in white males' share of employment occurred in the social
services industry. They were more than 57% of the industry in
1967 and dropped to 21% two decades later. The white and black
females' shares increased substantially to 4.6% and 17.4%, respectively.

White males have the largest shares of employment in the public administration and other professional services industries,
where they are more than 50%. Still, their shares have experienced
declines from 1967, when they were more than 60%. With almost
a 30% share of public administration employment in 1987, white
females were slightly underrepresented compared to their 33%
share of all full-time employment while black females and males
were slightly overrepresented. The reverse situation occurred in
the other professional services industry.

Intertemporal Change in the Earnings Distribution by Production Sector

The direction of movement in the earnings distribution has not
been uniform over the 1967 to 1987 period, which will become
evident as we look at intertemporal changes divided into three periods: 1967 to 1973, 1973 to 1979, and 1979 to 1987. The first
period, 1967 to 1973, represents the tail end of the postwar growth
period. During this time, the middle segment of the full-time earnings distribution grew at the expense of the upper segment. During
the 1970s' decade of stagflation (stagnant economic growth accom-

panied by inflation), little change in the distribution of earnings among the low, middle, and upper groups occurred for all full-time earners combined and for those employed in the three high-growth sectors. The biggest changes have come since 1979, and these have been in the form of upward shifts (Table 4.5).

Full-time workers in only one of the three high-growth sectors, transactional activities, had a higher percentage of upper earners than that of all sectors combined. Another high-growth sector, transportation and trade, has had a stable and relatively large low-earner segment, around 7%, and a smaller upper-earner segment. The earnings distribution of the remaining high-growth sector, social infrastructure, is the one that most closely parallels that for all sectors combined. These three sectors are major sources of future employment.

High-tech/medium-wage manufacturing, the third largest employing sector, shows a less than 0.5% increase in its low-earner segment since 1979 and a more than 5% increase in its upper-earner segment.

The most dramatic shift in a sector's earnings distribution occurred in smokestack/high-wage manufacturing. While its low-earner segment hovered between 1% and 2%, much larger vacillations occurred in its middle and upper segments. Between 1967 and 1973, a downward shift of nearly 7% from the upper to the middle segment occurred. This shift completely reversed itself between 1973 and 1979 and intensified after 1979, when the middle segment was around 60%, to 1987, when the upper segment was more than 53%.

One explanation for the downward shift in the 1970s is that it was a result of declining unionized employment in the smokestack industry, which in subsequent restructuring led to the use of more capital-intensive production processes with higher skilled and paid labor. The full-time labor force grew 21% between 1979 and 1987 while the smokestack/high-wage sector grew less than 5%. The high-tech/medium-wage sector declined 0.5%. The traditional/low-wage manufacturing production sector grew almost 18% during the same period, although it has less than one million workers compared to nearly twelve million in the high-tech sector and more than four million in the smokestack sector.

The other sector particularly worth noting because of its re-

TABLE 4.5

Intertemporal Change in Full-Time Workers' Distribution of Earnings, 1967–1973–1979–1987
(Percent)

Production Sector	Earnings Group	1967	1973	1979	1987	1967–87 % Change
High-Growth Sectors						
Transportation and Trade	Low	6.8	6.4	6.0	6.9	
	Middle	69.9	72.0	71.8	66.2	
	Upper	23.3	21.6	22.3	26.9	
	Total	11,024,493	11,451,719	13,139,833	17,147,419	55.5
Transactional Activities	Low	4.7	3.9	3.6	2.9	
	Middle	67.0	70.4	72.2	63.4	
	Upper	28.3	25.7	24.2	33.7	
	Total	4,028,558	4,934,177	6,264,591	9,626,381	139.0
Social Infrastructure	Low	6.5	4.6	4.0	3.7	
	Middle	69.4	74.1	76.1	66.7	
	Upper	24.2	21.3	20.0	29.6	
	Total	9,652,717	12,984,142	15,979,013	19,128,291	98.2
Manufacturing Sectors						
Traditional/Low-Wage	Low	8.1	9.1	5.0	4.5	
	Middle	78.4	78.6	81.4	82.0	
	Upper	13.5	12.3	13.6	13.5	
	Total	727,449	782,548	816,226	961,604	32.2
High-Tech/Medium-Wage	Low	4.1	3.4	2.7	3.1	
	Middle	70.8	75.4	72.1	66.6	

Upper	25.1	21.2	25.2	30.3	
Total	11,232,121	11,174,718	11,877,498	11,818,790	5.2
Smokestack/High-Wage					
Low	2.1	2.0	0.9	1.5	
Middle	61.0	66.7	59.8	45.3	
Upper	36.8	31.2	39.3	53.2	
Total	3,731,932	3,690,314	3,900,669	4,080,617	9.3
Other Sectors					
Natural Resources					
Low	19.0	23.2	20.9	11.8	
Middle	64.7	64.4	56.4	62.9	
Upper	16.3	12.4	22.7	25.4	
Total	1,081,987	1,424,109	1,549,583	1,509,003	39.5
Construction					
Low	5.4	4.8	5.8	3.5	
Middle	61.6	64.8	65.1	64.5	
Upper	33.0	33.0	33.0	33.0	
Total	2,539,225	2,889,360	3,129,209	3,729,103	46.9
Personal Services					
Low	25.6	23.8	16.2	12.5	
Middle	62.9	66.4	73.8	72.7	
Upper	11.5	9.8	10.0	14.8	
Total	2,121,302	1,927,289	2,127,939	3,134,705	47.8%
All Sectors					
Low	6.6	5.8	4.9	4.7	
Middle	68.3	72.0	71.7	65.2	
Upper	25.1	22.2	23.4	30.1	
Total	46,139,784	51,258,377	58,784,560	71,135,912	54.2

Source: Calculated from CPS microdata files.

cent growth is the personal services sector, which contains workers in the hotel industry, the automobile repair and services industry, the amusements industry, and the household industry. While still one of the smallest sectors, this one grew more than 47% between 1967 and 1987, with the growth occurring entirely in the middle- and upper-earner segments. While somewhat puzzling, the upward shift in the earnings distribution of the personal services sector seems most likely to be attributable to two factors (Levy 1987). The first factor is the general trend toward growing productivity in services, as new technologies allow for the substitution of capital for labor; some estimates indicate that the level of capital per worker in the service sector is now on a par with that in the goods production sector. The second factor is that the price paid for personal services, which is primarily labor costs, has been rising in real terms and relative to the other goods-producing sectors. This upward shift has been made possible by the productivity increases in the goods and services-producing sectors across the rest of the economy.

The following sections present the smaller sectoral analyses that reflect the areas of industrial restructuring receiving wide attention and speculation as to their impact on economic development and income change.

Full-Time Workers' Distribution of Earnings in High-Technology and Defense Sectors

High-Technology Sector

The high-technology sector has experienced a dramatic upward shift in its earnings distribution over the last two decades from a position that was already highly skewed to the upper end. By 1987, 44.5% of the high-tech workers were upper earners. The greatest shift upward occurred in the 1979 to 1987 period (Tables 4.6A and 4.6B).

As a source of high-income jobs, focusing economic development efforts on the high-tech sector may seem logical. However, high tech's share of full-time employment has remained around 8% for the last twenty years. Further, of the nearly twenty-five million full-time earners added to the economy between 1967 and 1987,

TABLE 4.6A

Full-Time Workers' Distribution of Earnings by High-Technology
and Defense Sectors, 1967–1973–1979–1987 (Percent)

Industry Group	Earnings Group	1967	1973	1979	1987
High Technology	Lower	2.9	1.7	1.2	1.3
	Middle	60.9	70.4	68.8	54.3
	Upper	36.2	27.9	30.0	44.5
	Total	4,013,334	4,129,322	4,730,133	5,904,214
		100.0	100.0	100.0	100.0
Defense	Lower	1.9	1.9	0.8	1.3
	Middle	55.4	66.6	61.4	46.1
	Upper	42.6	31.5	37.8	52.6
	Total	1,575,558	1,545,061	1,617,072	2,611,237
		100.0	100.0	100.0	100.0

TABLE 4.6B

High-Technology and Defense Sectors' Shares of Full-Time
Employment, 1967–1973–1979–1987 (Percent)

Percent of Employment	1967	1973	1979	1987
High Technology	8.7	8.1	8.1	8.3
Defense	3.4	3.0	2.8	3.7

Source: Calculated from CPS microdata files.

less than two million were in the high-tech sector. Thus, this high-paying sector has not been a source of major job growth in the past. In addition, it is unlikely to be a major source of future employment growth. The majority of the industries within this sector have projected *negative* annual rates of change between 1986 and the year 2000 (Table 4.7).

Defense Sector

The defense sector is characterized by its geographic concentration; thus, government defense policy is also de facto regional policy. In chapter 5, the implications of this spatial concentration

TABLE 4.7

High-Technology Employment: Projected Annual Rate of Change,
1986 to 2000

High-Tech Industry	SIC	Percent Change
Engines and Turbines	351	−0.6
Farm and Garden Machinery	352	−1.0
Construction Machinery	3531	−0.4
Materials Handling Machinery and Equipment	3534, 5, 6, 7	0.7
Metalworking Machinery	354	−0.6
Special Industry Machinery	355	−0.9
General Industry Machinery	356	0.3
Electronic Computing Equipment	3573	1.3
Office and Accounting Machines	3572, 4, 6, 9	−0.7
Refrigeration and Service Industry Machinery	358	−0.2
Miscellaneous Nonelectrical Machinery	359	0.7
Electrical Industrial Apparatus	362	−0.5
Electric Lighting and Wiring Equipment	364	−0.4
Radio and TV Communication Equipment	3662	0.5
Electronic Tubes	3671, 2, 3	−1.1
Semiconductors and Related Devices	3674	0.5
Miscellaneous Electronic Components	3675, 6, 7, 8, 9	0.6
Aircraft	3721	−1.5
Instruments and Related Products	38	0.6
Chemicals and Allied Products	28	−0.5
Total Industry	----	1.3

Source: Derived from U.S. Congress, Office of Technology Assessment, *Technology and the American economic transition: choices for the future* (May 1988): Table 8.4, and from Projections 2000: industry output and employment through the end of the century, *Monthly Labor Review* (September 1987): Table 6.

will be explored. In the meantime, in considering economic conversion policies or efforts to whittle down the defense sector in response to budget deficits, the analysis in this section shows what type of earnings distribution would be given up.

The defense sector employs a very small percent of full-time earners—less than 4% (see Table 4.6B)—and its distribution is even more highly upward skewed than that of high technology's. The 1970s were a period when the distribution shifted downward for both the high-technology and the defense sectors, but more so for defense. However, defense earners more than recovered in the 1980s. Nearly 53% were upper earners in 1987, 10% more than those in 1967.

The extreme upward-skewed distribution of the defense sector can be explained by two factors. First, the defense sector employs a disproportionately high percentage of the economy's most-educated workers—particularly scientists and engineers. While in the manufacturing sector as a whole, engineers, engineering technicians, computer scientists, life and physical scientists, and mathematicians are less than 6% of employees, they range from 19% to 41% of employees in specific industries within the defense sector (Markusen 1985a).

Second, the nonmarket structure of the defense subeconomy gives defense employers less incentive to control costs, including labor costs. Defense employers have a protected market, they do not face international competition, and they have unique price-setting procedures such that, although they are not efficient controllers of production costs, their profit levels are higher than that of all durable goods producers combined: 13.5% compared to 10.7% (Leitenberg and Ball 1983).

Shrinkage of the defense industry, either due to economic conversion or as part of a federal restructuring, would lead to the loss of some of the economy's highest-paid employment. It could be expected that a portion of the higher earners displaced from defense would end up in other parts of the high-technology sector. Overall, however, the defense sector is such a small employer that its shrinkage would have little impact on the national economy. This may not be the case for specific regional economies of the United States, though, and this issue will be explored in chapter 6.

In general, the industries that make up the defense sector do not just produce defense-related output. Nevertheless, industries have been defined as defense-dependent and part of the sector if defense accounts for more than 10% of their output. In the latter part of the 1970s and the first half of the 1980s, defense dependency of industries already within the defense sector was found to have increased dramatically due to rising defense demand—the Reagan buildup—and to weak commercial demand. For example, defense dependency in the metal cutting-type of machine tool industry increased from 3% to 34% between 1977 and 1985 while it increased from 35% to 50% for radio and TV communication equipment and from 12% to 26% for electron tubes (Browne 1988). The

weak commercial demand that has led to increased defense dependency is a by-product of the deteriorating U.S. international trade
position that is discussed in the following section.

Industries Gaining or Losing Trade Advantage

To determine the influence of the changing U.S. international trade
position on the distribution of earnings, full-time earners were
placed into three broad industry groupings—Gainers, Losers, and
Holders of apparent trade advantage—by cross-referencing the
CPS industry codes with those used by OTA.[7] The results do not
paint a positive picture.

From Table 4.8A, it can be seen that earners in the Holders
group are essentially split between the middle and upper segments,
which looks quite positive until it is noted (from Table 4.8B) that
Holders have been less than 5% of full-time earners for each of the
four points in time and they dropped to less than 2% in 1987. The
Gainers group had a much higher percentage of middle earners,
almost 63.0%, but upper earners were still a substantial 32.2%.
Still, Table 4.8B shows that Gainers as a percentage of total full-
time earners were less than 10% in 1967 and less than 9% by 1987.

Full-time workers in the Losers group have the largest proportion of middle earners and, conversely, the smallest proportion of
upper earners. Over the twenty-year period of analysis, the Losers
group has experienced the smallest upward shift in its distribution.
At the same time, looking at Table 4.8B, it can be seen that *more
than three-quarters* of full-time earners are employed in industries
within the Losers group. Further, an examination of fringe benefit
recipiency for the Losers group indicates that significant decreases
in levels of recipiency occurred between 1979 and 1987 (no earlier
data are available). Those full-time earners in the Losers group who
were included in an employer's pension plan declined from 53% to
42% and those included in an employer's group health plan declined from 69% to 58%.[8]

It is clear from the OTA analyses that the United States has
lost its long-standing comparative advantage. Our analysis of
earners indicates the vast majority were in the vulnerable position
of being employed by industries that are decreasingly competitive

TABLE 4.8A

Full-Time Workers' Distribution of Earnings in Industries Gaining or Losing Trade Advantage, 1967–1973–1979–1987

Industry Group	Earnings Group	1967	1973	1979	1987
Gainers	Lower %	8.0	8.7	7.9	4.9
	Middle %	68.3	70.6	66.1	62.8
	Upper %	23.6	20.7	26.1	32.2
	Total	4,540,837	5,440,302	5,632,627	6,110,751
Losers	Lower %	6.6	5.1	4.5	5.0
	Middle %	69.2	72.8	72.8	66.4
	Upper %	24.2	22.2	22.7	28.6
	Total	32,356,896	42,386,180	49,684,195	54,701,939
Holders	Lower %	2.3	3.7	3.1	1.3
	Middle %	65.6	65.7	62.4	50.4
	Upper %	32.1	30.6	34.5	48.3
	Total	1,194,401	2,365,360	2,459,725	1,349,997

TABLE 4.8B

Full-Time Workers in Industries Gaining or Losing Trade Advantage, 1967–1973–1979–1987

Industry Group	1967	1973	1979	1987
Gainers %	9.8	10.6	9.6	8.6
Losers %	70.1	82.7	84.5	76.9
Holders %	2.6	4.6	4.2	1.9
Subtotal*	38,092,134	50,191,842	57,776,547	62,162,687
%	82.6	97.9	98.3	87.4
Total	46,139,784	51,258,377	58,784,561	71,135,912
%	100.0	100.0	100.0	100.0

Note: Gainer, Loser, or Holder industry status was made by cross-referencing to the Office of Technology Assessment's (OTA) classification where industries are categorized as gaining or losing apparent advantage in trade by measuring change in the ratio of the value-added gained due to exports to the value-added lost due to imports between 1972 and 1984.

*Not all CPS industry codes could be placed in the three OTA groups; the subtotal indicates the percent of all full-time workers who could be placed into one of the three groups and that the percentage that could be placed varied over the points of analysis from almost 83% to more than 98%.

Source: Calculated from CPS microdata files.

in the international economy. Unless the comparative advantage of these industries is restored, the future earnings and total compensation picture for workers in these industries appear bleak. In addition, while workers may still be shifting upward along the earnings distribution, the drop in levels of fringe benefit recipiency indicates that total compensation is slipping. It was noted previously that benefits as a percentage of total compensation increased 6% between 1970 and 1986; thus, the importance of fringe benefits relative to earnings within total compensation has increased at the same time that fewer workers are receiving them (Employee Benefit Research Institute 1988a).

The process by which comparative advantage is restored will have significant implications for the workers in the Loser industries. Will it be restored by lowering labor costs, which results in a declining living standard for existing workers and eliminates opportunities for good jobs for future workers? Or will these industries successfully transform themselves so that they become exporters of products and services that are technologically sophisticated and that generate well-paying domestic jobs?

It is the poor performance of the manufacturing sector that was primarily responsible for the United States' overall declining comparative advantage in international trade. Many of the goods the United States imports are not produced in our own markets; however, an estimated 70% of the goods manufactured in the United States are also manufactured abroad and therefore are subject to foreign competition (U.S. Department of Commerce, International Trade Administration 1988).

Foreign competition and imports have already, in the post-1973 period, pushed U.S. producers to improve efficiency, to quicken the pace of adaptation and structural change, and to resist wage and price increases. American workers can expect more of the same from their employers who are seriously engaged in an effort to regain comparative advantage.

Conclusion

The position of full-time workers improved relative to part-time workers between 1967 and 1987. The position of the full-time worker has shifted upward without exception. The shares of the part-time distribution held by low, middle, and upper earnings remained the same but male earners shifted downward along the distribution. Further, that the percentage of part-time workers who would rather be working full-time rose from 9% to 20% provides additional support that postindustrialism has created a growing disparity between part- and full-time earners.[9]

Breaking down the twenty-year trend into subperiods in this chapter's analysis has illuminated new areas of concern for the standard of living arising from changes in the earnings distribution. While 1973 has been identified as the turning point year by many researchers, the analysis here indicates that the greatest shifts in the earnings distributions for both part- and full-time workers have come since 1979. Full-time earners experienced their greatest upward shifts since 1979 while part-time earners experienced the greatest downward shifts. Further, earnings inequality for full-time workers declined from 1967 to 1979 and then increased sharply between 1979 and 1987.

In this chapter, we also asked what might the earnings distribution have looked like without the 1973 turning point in the economy, the point at which it began to deteriorate. The analysis conducted here showed that there was a lag in the impact of the economy's turning point on the earnings distribution. From 1973 to 1979, very little movement occurred in the overall earnings distribution for either part- or full-time workers, but, subsequently, there was an upward shift in the full-time earner distribution and a downward shift in the part-time earner distribution. Inequality among full-time earners increased as well.

Is the post-1973 phase—and, of greater significance for the earnings distribution, the post-1979 phase—temporary or does it represent a fundamental, structural shift in the pattern of earnings and compensation and, thus, in the ability to purchase the middle standard of living? Levy (1987) likened the post-1973 change to that of the Great Depression and suggested that government action along with short-run sacrifices on the part of labor could turn things around.

A key difference, though, between the economy in the post-1973 period and that of the depression era is its openness. The Great Depression did not result in the United States losing its international comparative advantage; the post-1973 period has had that effect. Thus, in the depression era, the United States could still exert more easily direct control over its economic path.

In actuality, the short-run sacrifices Levy had in mind, and which, in fact, are already being exacted, do not appear to be short-run. Edsall (1984) noted that federal legislative acts of the Reagan era aimed at stimulating the economy instead undermined or undid thirty years of social legislation. Further, a half-century-long trend was abandoned that had tilted tax legislation toward low- and middle-income workers. These trends, combined with the interrelated ones of declining unionization, the growth of secondary employment or contingent labor, increasing earnings inequality, and rule changes between employers and employees, are fundamental and long-lasting.

The industrial restructuring observed in this chapter does not portend a very optimistic picture of the last decade of this century for the American economy and its workers. The 1967 to 1987 period was characterized by deindustrialization and a rapid shift in sources of employment from manufacturing to services. However, the service sector's rapid and inefficient expansion came to a halt in the 1990s. The first-ever national services recession made its appearance in 1991, but despite the intensification of restructuring, and now the general recognition that real structural change has occurred in the postwar economy, no major government intervention to counteract its negative impacts has been forthcoming. The calls for government intervention and, specifically, for the development of strategic industrial policy have become insistent.[10] If these calls go unheeded, then the pattern of change in the earnings distribution that is identified in this chapter, particularly those occurring after 1973, may very well be our best indicator of the pattern that will characterize the remainder of this century.

When combined with the undoing of much of the social legislation that previously had an equalizing effect on the structure of earnings, income, and opportunity, the failure to enact supportive policies for working families and their children suggests American workers will experience still further erosion in their living standards. Moreover, the structural crisis of American capitalism and the end to the postwar growth period appear to be manifesting themselves in a growing *tolerance* for inequality within the labor force and across society.

Appendix 4.A

A Nine-Sector Production Classification

A. *High-Growth Sectors*

1. *Transportation and Trade* are clustered because together they form much of the overhead associated with the physical movement of products. These activities are increasingly tied to manufacturing through sophisticated inventory control and dispatching networks. New technologies in transportation will be essential to systemwide improvements in efficiency—not so much from innovations in specific kinds of transportation or retailing equipment but through advances in information flows that connect production with the marketplace more closely. While many of these technologies are difficult to trace, it appears that dramatic changes may occur in the near future.

2. *Transactional Activities* deliver financial and information services to businesses. The activities are clustered because, taken together, they are the most rapidly growing sector in the U.S. economy in terms of output and employment and are associated with activities in which productivity improvements due to new information technologies could be enormous.

3. *Social Infrastructure* follows a unique logic because of the involvement of the government. With the exception of government "overhead" functions, most of the activities in this sector, such as public and private healthcare and education, are delivered directly to consumers; in effect, they are services that support a human infrastructure.

B. *Manufacturing Sectors*

There has been growing concern over the future role of manufacturing activities in the U.S. economy. Significant direct and indirect linkages exist between manufacturing and the other parts of the economy. Manufacturing traditionally was the major source of U.S. productivity growth, increasing at twice the rate of the economy as a whole between 1960 and 1983. It is also likely that wage increases in other industries can be traced to productivity growth in manufacturing.

4. *Low-Wage Manufacturing* is clustered in the traditional apparel, footwear, and furniture industries.

5. *Medium-Wage Manufacturing* contains most enterprises recently tagged as "high technology" because these firms conduct significant amounts of research and employ relatively large numbers of engineers and scientists. It includes industries such as electrical equipment, communications equipment, scientific instruments, and computers and less technology-intensive industries such as food and kindred products.

6. *High-Wage Manufacturing* is dominated by traditional "smokestack" industries, such as those that produce motor vehicles, iron and steel, construction machinery, and glass. However, the high-wage category also includes such technologically sophisticated industries as chemical production and aircraft manufacturing.

C. Other Sectors

7. *Natural Resources* includes the production of raw materials and energy of all kinds, including the generation of electricity. These industries were singled out to measure the impact of different kinds of economic activity on depletable natural resources, many of which are imported, and at the same time to trace the impact of substitutes for strategic raw materials.

8. *Construction* is given its own category because of the unique nature and large size of construction activities and in view of the critical role construction plays in renewing infrastructure and improving productivity throughout the economy. The highly cyclical nature of construction activities also sets this category aside from other business activities.

9. *Personal Services* are selected because, with the exception of retailing, they contain most activities traditionally associated with the "service sectors" of the economy: hotels, beauty parlors, and dry cleaning, for example. They also contain most activities associated with recreation and leisure, a sector that has grown rapidly in response to the rising affluence among many consumers.

Source: Adapted from U.S. Congress, Office of Technology Assessment (1988).

APPENDIX 4.B

Full-Time Workers' Percent Distribution of Earnings by Production Sectors and Gender, 1967–1973–1979–1987

Production Sector	Earnings Group	Females				Males			
		1967	1973	1979	1987	1967	1973	1979	1987
High-Growth Sectors									
Transportation and Trade	Low	17.1	14.4	11.2	12.5	3.4	3.7	3.8	4.1
	Middle	80.8	84.1	85.0	78.6	66.3	68.0	66.4	60.0
	Upper	2.2	1.5	3.8	8.8	30.3	28.3	29.8	35.9
Transactional Activities	Low	6.3	5.0	4.3	3.2	3.6	3.2	2.8	2.9
	Middle	90.6	91.9	90.0	80.2	49.9	54.9	54.5	63.4
	Upper	3.1	3.2	5.7	16.2	46.6	41.9	42.7	33.7
Social Infrastructure	Low	9.9	7.2	5.2	4.5	3.2	2.1	2.6	2.7
	Middle	81.7	86.2	88.8	79.5	57.8	62.6	62.5	50.5
	Upper	8.4	6.6	6.0	16.1	39.0	35.3	34.8	46.9
Manufacturing Sectors									
Traditional/Low-Wage	Low	8.9	18.3	6.9	3.8	8.0	7.5	4.5	4.7
	Middle	86.7	81.7	89.0	93.6	76.9	78.1	79.5	78.9
	Upper	4.4	0.0	4.2	2.7	15.2	14.4	16.0	16.4
High-Tech/Medium-Wage	Low	9.4	7.5	4.7	5.8	2.2	1.9	1.9	1.8
	Middle	89.1	90.8	92.9	84.9	63.9	69.7	63.1	57.4
	Upper	1.5	1.7	2.4	9.2	33.9	28.5	35.0	40.8

APPENDIX 4.B (continued)

Full-Time Workers' Percent Distribution of Earnings by Production Sectors and Gender, 1967–1973–1979–1987

Production Sector	Earnings Group	Females				Males			
		1967	1973	1979	1987	1967	1973	1979	1987
High-Growth Sectors									
Smokestack/High-Wage	Low	5.9	5.2	1.9	2.2	1.4	1.5	0.7	1.3
	Middle	89.8	89.2	90.6	72.5	55.5	62.9	53.3	37.5
	Upper	4.3	5.6	7.5	25.3	43.1	35.7	46.0	61.2
Other Sectors									
Natural Resources	Low	24.5	14.9	19.6	12.1	18.7	23.9	21.0	11.7
	Middle	73.5	83.7	79.2	75.6	64.1	62.8	53.7	59.8
	Upper	2.0	1.3	1.1	12.3	17.2	13.3	25.3	28.5
Construction	Low	13.8	7.2	5.8	2.4	4.9	4.7	5.8	3.6
	Middle	84.5	90.3	90.6	88.7	60.2	63.6	63.2	62.4
	Upper	1.7	2.4	3.6	8.9	34.9	31.8	31.0	34.0
Personal Services	Low	46.4	42.3	27.5	20.6	6.3	10.2	9.8	6.6
	Middle	52.7	56.2	70.1	74.2	72.5	73.8	75.9	71.7
	Upper	1.0	1.5	2.4	5.2	21.3	16.0	14.3	21.8
All Sectors	Low	13.3	10.1	7.0	6.8	3.7	3.8	3.8	3.3
	Middle	82.5	86.0	88.3	80.0	62.0	65.7	62.7	55.3
	Upper	4.2	3.9	4.7	13.3	34.3	30.5	33.5	41.4

Source: Calculated from CPS microdata files. Figures may not total to 100% due to rounding.

5

The Rural and Urban Distinction in Industrial Restructuring

Introduction

A common regional division for understanding the development pattern of the United States is that of rural and urban. The terms nonmetropolitan and metropolitan are often used interchangeably with rural and urban, as they are in this chapter. The criteria by which metropolitan areas are designated include a large population nucleus—fifty thousand inhabitants—plus any adjacent counties with which there is high economic and social integration. Nonmetropolitan areas can contain purely rural land or small urban centers. At the end of the 1980s, there were close to 270 metropolitan areas designated in the United States.

While increasing development and urbanization go hand in hand, there is a continuing rationale for the presence of rural economies. Certain economic activities are found almost exclusively in the rural economy, such as natural resource extraction and farming, and other activities that do not require proximity to large urban areas locate in nonmetropolitan areas to take advantage of the lower costs of production generally associated with rural economies. Further, there is always a segment of the population and labor force that either prefers rural or small-town life or cannot overcome the migration barriers to relocating in urban areas. Additionally, new advances in communications technologies and evolving patterns of production in response to industrial restructuring alter the decision rationales for residents and industries choosing between rural or urban locations and can increase the attraction of rural locations.

In light of the development distinctions of rural and urban areas, the research presented here examines how changes in their respective earnings distributions fit within the context of whether the middle class is shrinking. The research presented illuminates how changes in the rural earnings distribution have differed from those of the urban and looks for evidence of how change in the ability to achieve a middle standard of living has varied between the two regions.

The Rural Context

The postwar period of growth in the U.S. economy has been one of overall decline for rural areas, which consequently became a persistent focus of concern for economic development policy. Paradoxically, as the postwar boom period was ending, the rural portion of the economy experienced what has been labeled the "rural turnaround," which represented a long-term reversal of rural population and employment declines. The substantial attention it elicited ran the gamut from optimism to skepticism.

The rural turnaround phenomenon, however, was only associated with the decade of the 1970s. Since 1980, rural areas have again been characterized by economic dislocation and stress. Brown and Deavers (1987) noted that the growth and vitality of the rural economy in the 1970s had been replaced by structural change and dislocation in the 1980s. Industrial restructuring in the rural economy has led to increased reliance on low-wage, low-skill manufacturing and service industries and made it vulnerable to production technology shifts. The authors note further:

> [T]he rural economy has become more closely tied with national and global economies, making it more sensitive to changes in macro economic policy, business cycles, and global competition. These events, combined with longstanding weaknesses in the rural economy, have led to significant problems in some areas, raising questions about the ability of rural areas to adapt.

The 1990s have the potential to bring a major new challenge to rural areas that would hit them precisely where they have been able to hold on to their manufacturing strength. Implementation of the North American Free Trade Agreement (NAFTA), which extends the phased elimination of tariff and nontariff barriers between the United States and Canada to Mexico, may make it easy for rural U.S. manufacturers to shift their production activity to Mexican locations, where labor costs are a fraction of those currently paid; other costs there, with the exception, perhaps, of distribution, are lower as well.

Manufacturing was one of the sources of employment growth associated with the rural turnaround; the other was services. Both served to lessen rural areas' historic dependence on the natural resources sector as the primary generator of rural jobs. The employment generated in the manufacturing sector can largely be attributed to the decentralization of production activity in the mature stages of industry product cycles. Essentially, expansion to the rural areas was a stopgap measure in American manufacturing's effort to remain internationally competitive on its homeland. Rising international competition and continued advances in global communications, such as the use of satellites for transferring production information, though, shifted the impetus for production siting beyond national borders.

Bloomquist (1987) found that industries at the top of their product cycle—distinguished by their demand for technically skilled labor—were underrepresented in rural areas and that urban areas' specialization in top-of-the-cycle industries increased substantially between 1969 and 1984. During the same period, rural areas' specialization in bottom-of-the-cycle industries—distinguished by their demand for relatively low-skilled and low-cost labor—and resource-based manufacturing industries increased.[1]

Growing international competition in the manufacturing sector provided further incentive to locate manufacturing activity in lower-cost nonmetro areas, but the effectiveness of this urban-to-rural shift in manufacturing activity was temporary. During the 1980s, even the lower cost of rural manufacturing activity was unable to successfully compete with international manufacturing activity.

For the twenty-year period of 1967 to 1987, the service sector was the largest source of employment growth for rural labor markets and almost the exclusive source for urban labor markets. While service employment growth overall has been attributed to changes in demography, household income, consumer tastes, and technology, these influences have had different weights in urban and rural areas. At least until the early 1990s, urban areas' service employment growth has been observed to have a "life of its own," with a continuing expansion of producer services despite downturns in the business cycle.

In contrast, Miller and Bluestone (1987) observed that rural services employment is primarily linked to local consumption or to the traditional rural economic base of natural resource and manufacturing industries. Slower growth in producer and distributive services is linked to the decline in this traditional export base due to shrinking world markets for agriculture and energy-related products, as well as foreign competition for low-wage, labor-intensive manufacturing.

Shifting Employment Composition and the Earnings Distribution

Historically, rural areas have had lower median incomes and wages and lower per capita incomes than urban areas. While these have been associated with lower rural levels of industrialization and lower costs of living, differences have narrowed as rural areas have become more industrialized—with the bulk of new manufacturing employment going to rural areas since the early 1970s—and their costs of living have increased.

At the same time, the level of rural employment growth in manufacturing has been exceeded by growth in trade, services, and government employment, but has this employment growth resulted in a more equal distribution of earnings? Has there been an increase in the percentage of nonmetropolitan residents who are middle earners or has the economic growth in rural areas exacerbated the within-region—urban and rural—income disparities among and within the part- and full-time earner groups? Further, has the narrowing of the median income differences between the rural and urban areas been, in any way, a result of declining proportions of middle-level earners in the urban areas? These are the questions we address in this chapter in addition to examining the power of rural earnings to purchase a middle standard of living. Using housing costs as a proxy for the cost of a middle standard of living, we will look for differences in the attainability of the middle standard of living among rural and urban earners.

Rural and Urban Change in Industrial Composition

Total population in both urban and rural areas in the United States increased 19% between 1970 and 1986, with the metro share remaining around 77% and the nonmetro share 23% (U.S. Department of Commerce, Bureau of the Census 1988). As the earlier reference to the rural turnaround implies, though, the rate of growth within the two areas has not been consistent. In metro counties, population growth per one thousand per year was 10.1 during the 1970s and 11.5 since; in the nonmetro counties, it was 13.5 during the 1970s and 7.4 since (Brown and Deavers 1987).

Trends in the numbers of earners in urban and rural areas do not correspond closely to trends in population growth. The number of urban earners grew from 1967 to 1987 while the number of rural earners declined slightly (Table 5.1). The urban full-time earner group increased nearly 80% while the rural group declined almost 7%, with the rural decline occurring after 1979.

During the same two-decade period, growth in the urban part-time labor force was more than 72%, whereas the more than 14% decline in the rural part-time labor force was slightly more than double the decline in the rural full-time labor force. However, the rural part-time labor force has recouped close to 40% of its losses since 1973.[2] Between 1967 and 1973, the decline was nearly 23%.

In the distribution of earners among production sectors, in 1967, more than 34% of the full-time earners in both the rural and the urban economies were employed in manufacturing (Table 5.2). By 1987, the proportion had declined to more than 22% in the urban economy and to almost 27% in the rural economy. Thus, while manufacturing's presence in the rural economy has lessened, manufacturing has become relatively more important in the rural than in the urban economy.

TABLE 5.1

Rural and Urban Change in the Number of Part- and Full-Time Earners, 1967–1973–1979–1987

Earner Group	1967	1973	1979	1987	1967–87
Rural Full-Time					
Number of Earners	13,958,943	14,422,983	14,963,651	13,043,207	—
Change Number	—	464,040	540,668	−1,920,444	−915,736
%	—	3.3	3.7	−12.8	−6.6
Rural Part-Time					
Number of Earners	11,876,126	9,161,847	9,640,706	10,206,903	—
Change Number	—	−2,714,279	478,859	566,197	−1,669,223
%	—	−22.9	5.2	5.9	−14.1
Urban Full-Time					
Number of Earners	32,180,841	36,835,394	40,408,067	57,599,336	—
Change Number	—	4,654,553	3,572,673	17,191,269	25,418,495
%	—	14.5	9.7	42.5	79.0
Urban Part-Time					
Number of Earners	21,264,290	19,814,820	23,867,821	36,643,709	—
Change Number	—	−1,449,470	4,053,001	12,775,888	15,379,419
%	—	−6.8	20.5	53.5	72.3

Source: Calculated from Current Population Survey (CPS) microdata files.

TABLE 5.2

Production Sectors' Shares of Rural and Urban Full-Time Earners, 1967–1973–1979–1987 (Percent)

Production Sector	Rural				Urban			
	1967	1973	1979	1987	1967	1973	1979	1987
Construction	6.9	6.9	6.2	2.0	4.9	5.1	4.9	0.4
Natural Resources	5.1	6.4	5.6	10.4	1.2	1.4	1.3	6.6
Personal Services	4.1	3.5	2.7	9.8	4.8	3.9	3.9	10.0
Traditional/Low-Wage Manufacturing	3.0	3.1	2.6	2.2	1.0	0.9	0.8	1.4
High-Tech/Medium-Wage Manufacturing	24.4	23.0	21.9	19.2	24.3	21.3	20.9	14.8
Smokestack/High-Wage Manufacturing	6.7	6.4	6.1	5.4	8.7	7.5	7.0	6.0
Social Infrastructure	21.8	23.3	26.3	19.1	20.5	26.1	27.4	19.1
Transactional Activities	5.6	6.4	7.3	5.4	10.1	10.9	12.0	8.3
Transportation and Trade	22.5	21.2	21.3	26.6	24.5	22.8	22.7	33.4
Total	13,958,943	14,422,983	14,963,651	13,043,207	32,180,841	36,835,394	40,408,067	57,599,336
%	100.0	100.0	100.0	100.0	100.0	100.0	100.0	100.0

Source: Calculated from CPS microdata files.

Manufacturing shares in the high-tech/medium-wage and smokestack/high-wage sectors have declined in both the urban and rural economies. In the rural economy, the declines were steady in traditional/low-wage manufacturing as well. However, the percentage of full-time earners the urban economy employed in the traditional/low-wage manufacturing sector increased slightly—less than 1%—between 1979 and 1987. This increase represents the addition of more than one-half million traditional/low-wage full-time earners in the traditional/low-wage sector of the urban economy during the 1980s at the same time that the rural economy lost more than one hundred thousand full-time earners in this sector.

The data on the growth of the traditional/low-wage manufacturing sector in the urban labor market are, at first glance, surprising. They do not correlate well with notions of the growing service economy and urban centers' increasingly specialized roles in it. Why has there been an "urban turnaround" in the location of the traditional/low-wage manufacturing sector, a sector that has long been identified with rural employment growth?

An explanation can be found in the work of Sassen (1988) and others who have been researching manufacturing activity in association with immigrant workers in the United States. She sees recent immigrant growth in cities providing labor for an expanding and downgraded manufacturing sector made up, in part, of declining industries that need cheap labor to survive, as well as growing electronics industries with bifurcated skill and occupational distributions. Sassen uses the term "downgraded manufacturing" to refer to production processes with social reorganization in the form of expanding sweatshops and industrial homework; technological transformations that are downgrading a range of jobs; and/or low-wage production jobs in high-technology industries. As part of this overall downgrading trend, she writes that:

> . . . the large availability of an immigrant workforce in combination with changes in the consumption structure are inducing a reconcentration of small-scale, labor-intensive manufacturing in large cities. . . . There has been an expansion in the demand for customized, highly priced goods and services. And there has been an increase in the demand for extremely cheap goods and services. The first has brought about an increase in small manufacturing shops catering to

specific clienteles [which] need to be located in large cities. . . . In the case of the growing demand for extremely cheap items, what we are seeing is that the existence of a critical mass of workers willing to work at home or in sweatshops has made cities like New York and Los Angeles competitive with Hong Kong or Taiwan as locations for the production of extremely cheap garments, footwear, bedding, toys, and a range of household items. . . . The expansion of small, labor-intensive shops relying heavily on immigrant workers . . . makes large cities in a highly industrialized country like the United States a competitive location for certain types of labor-intensive manufacturing.

The growth in urban traditional/low-wage manufacturing employment supports Sassen's hypothesis. New immigrant labor in the urban economy can be even cheaper than rural labor. Further, the urban areas, in which 77% of the total U.S. population resides, are the sites of the market niches for specialty manufactured products. NAFTA's implementation may alter this trend. While we might expect the specialty manufacturing shops' activity to continue, it may be that the manufacturing activity of the cheapest goods and services will shift out of America's central city sweatshops to sites south of the border.

Figure 5.1A graphs rural manufacturing changes in terms of absolute numbers of full-time earners. It can be seen that, from 1979 on, significant losses in absolute employment have occurred in the high-tech/medium-wage and smokestack/high-wage sectors, whereas the much smaller traditional/low-wage sector has been gradually shrinking.

Returning to Table 5.2 to look at changes in what, overall, have been the high-growth sectors, we see that the period from 1979 to 1987 brought a reversal of growth trends for social infrastructure and transactional activities in both the rural and the urban economies. Those two sectors had been losing their shares of employment while the third high-growth sector, transportation and trade, has gained a substantial share of all full-time earners in the rural economy, more than 5%, and an even greater share in the urban economy, almost 11%. The other two sectors gaining substantial shares in both the rural and urban economies are natural resources and personal services. The personal services sector includes workers in the hotel industry, the automobile repair and services industry, the amusements industry,

FIGURE 5.1A

Rural Full-Time Manufacturing Trends, 1967–1987

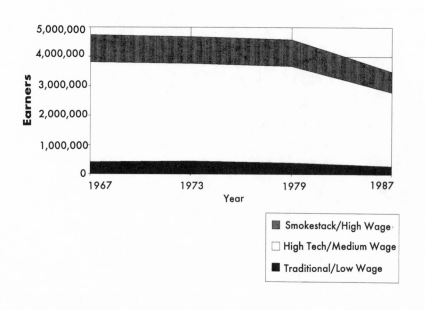

Source: Calculated from CPS microdata files.

and the household industry. The natural resources sector contains employees in agriculture, forestry, and fishing; mining; and petroleum and natural gas production. The increased shares accounted for by natural resources and personal services are not simply a result of the manufacturing sector having lost employment. Only the high-tech/medium-wage sector has lost absolute employment in the range of seven hundred thousand employees, but personal services and natural resources have each added more than seven million employees between 1979 and 1987.

Table 5.3 gives the changing production distribution picture for part-time earners. The high-growth sector, transportation and trade, is overwhelmingly the largest employer in both the rural and urban economies. It gained its greatest shares prior to 1973 and after 1979. Both the social infrastructure and the high-tech/medium-wage sectors

TABLE 5.3

Production Sectors' Shares of Rural and Urban Part-Time Earners, 1967–1973–1979–1987 (Percent)

Production Sector	Rural				Urban			
	1967	1973	1979	1987	1967	1973	1979	1987
Construction	7.0	9.1	8.9	1.7	5.4	6.8	7.1	0.3
Natural Resources	11.6	7.8	6.6	13.8	2.4	1.9	2.0	9.3
Personal Services	14.9	10.4	7.7	10.2	14.5	10.4	8.2	10.5
Traditional/Low-Wage Manufacturing	2.0	2.6	2.1	1.1	0.7	0.8	0.6	0.7
High-Tech/Medium-Wage Manufacturing	15.4	15.1	15.2	11.1	16.1	14.3	12.9	8.4
Smokestack/High-Wage Manufacturing	2.7	2.6	3.2	1.8	4.2	3.1	3.0	2.1
Social Infrastructure	19.0	20.3	24.1	17.7	20.5	22.6	25.4	17.8
Transactional Activities	3.3	4.8	4.6	9.9	7.2	8.7	8.9	12.1
Transportation and Trade	24.1	27.2	27.5	32.7	29.0	31.4	32.0	39.0
Total	11,876,126	9,161,847	9,640,706	10,206,903	21,264,290	19,814,820	23,867,821	36,643,709
%	100.0	100.0	100.0	100.0	100.0	100.0	100.0	100.0

Source: Calculated from CPS microdata files.

have experienced significant drops in their shares of employment since 1979 while the natural resources sector has gained more than a 7% share in both the rural and urban economies.

Part-time rural manufacturing employment in the traditional/low-wage sector shows a gradual decline from 1967 to 1987, the period when the rural turnaround's influence was felt in the high-tech/medium-wage and smokestack/high-wage sectors (Figure 5.1B). However, the gains of the 1970s from the turnaround were more than lost in the 1980s.

Changes in the Pattern of Female Labor Force Participation

In this chapter, particular attention is paid to the distinctions between rural and urban female labor force participation because the two-decade period of analysis was one in which the females entered the labor force in unprecedented numbers. Historically, though, rural women have been more occupied with farm and domestic work for which they did not receive individual earnings. We seek to determine here whether industrial restructuring has altered the traditional distinctions between the rural and urban female labor force and, further, to determine whether this alters the implications of middle-class status found at the national level.

In 1967, the proportions of female rural and urban full-time earners were close to the same, around 30% (Figure 5.2A). By 1973, however, a gap appeared that remained through 1987. While the percentage of female full-time earners in both the rural and the urban economies has steadily increased, in 1987, women made up a greater percentage of full-time earners in the urban sector, exceeding 40%.

Unlike the situation among full-time earners, the percentage of part-time earners who are females is basically the same in the urban and rural economies (Figure 5.2B). While the data cannot explain the difference between rural and urban female full-time employment patterns, several possibilities seem worthy of further exploration. There may be greater barriers to full-time labor force participation for rural females, such as the limited availability of child care. Alternatively, the lower cost of living in rural areas may decrease pressures on rural females to seek full-time employment.

FIGURE 5.1B

Rural Part-Time Manufacturing Trends, 1967–1987

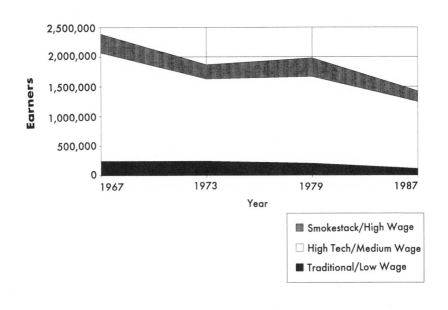

Source: Calculated from CPS microdata files.

There is also a possibility of distinctions in urban and rural employers' propensity to hire full-time female labor.

Evidence to support the last possibility is that rural and urban production sectors employ females in different proportions (Table 5.4). In 1967, three sectors employed higher proportions of females in the urban economy: social infrastructure, high-tech/medium-wage manufacturing, and personal services. Twenty years later, females employed in the smokestack/high-wage manufacturing sector had grown by more than 6% in urban areas but only 3% in rural areas; urban females employed in personal services declined by less than 4% while rural females in this sector shrank by nearly 12%. Throughout the two decades, urban females have been employed in significantly higher proportions than rural females in the smokestack/high-wage manufacturing, traditional/low-wage

FIGURE 5.2A

Females as Percent of Full-Time Earners, Rural and Urban,
1967–1973–1979–1987

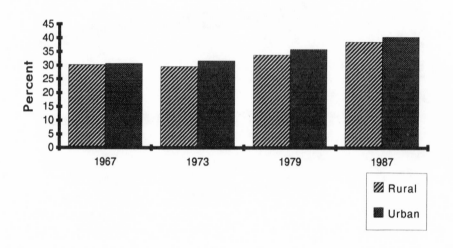

Source: Calculated from CPS microdata files.

manufacturing, and natural resources sectors. An examination of
the causes and policy implications of the higher proportions of females employed in certain rural industries may be warranted.

With the general picture of changes in the distribution of
workers among sectors of production activity established, we can
now examine changes in the distribution of earnings.

Change in the Distribution of Earnings within the Rural and Urban Economies, 1967–1973–1979–1987

By Earnings Group

The overall industrial restructuring of the last two decades, in
combination with the rural turnaround of the 1970s, has had different impacts on the earnings distributions in the rural and urban

FIGURE 5.2B

Females as Percent of Part-Time Earners, Rural and Urban,
1967–1973–1979–1987

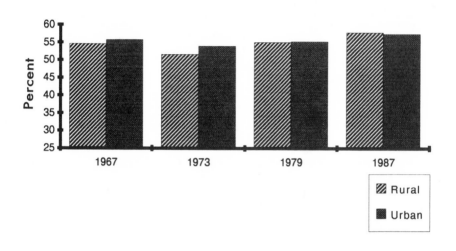

Source: Calculated from CPS microdata files.

economies. In 1967, the two full-time distributions had different proportions of lower, middle, and upper earners; by 1987, these differences had increased somewhat. In the interim, which involved the rural turnaround, the differences narrowed, only to be more than restored during the 1980s.[3] From Table 5.5, it can be seen that the rural earnings distribution has consistently had a larger proportion of lower and middle earners and a smaller proportion of upper earners. The urban distribution's downward shift to the middle segment was greater than that for the rural distribution between 1967 and 1973 as it shrank by 3.5% (from 28.7% to 25.2%) compared to the rural upper group shrinking by 2.4% (from 16.8% to 14.4%). During the 1973 to 1979 period, the shift back to the upper-earner segment was three times larger in the rural distribution (2.7%) than in the urban distribution (0.8%). However,

TABLE 5.4

Rural and Urban Females as Percent of Full-Time Earners, by
Production Sectors, 1967 and 1987

Production Sector	1967 Urban	1967 Rural	1987 Urban	1987 Rural
Construction	7.05	3.52	8.48	5.23
Smokestack/High-Wage Mfg.	16.65	14.98	23.26	17.65
Traditional/Low-Wage Mfg.	18.92	13.08	24.36	16.84
High-Tech/Med.-Wage Mfg.	25.33	31.59	31.89	37.92
Natural Resources	9.78	3.98	23.31	14.01
Personal Services	45.23	56.19	41.65	44.26
Social Infrastructure	47.99	49.61	55.70	57.94
Transactional Activities	42.46	40.25	53.35	52.58
Transportation and Trade	25.07	23.97	33.55	32.88
Total	9,883,264	4,230,216	23,298,516	5,048,177

Source: Calculated from CPS microdata files.

between 1979 and 1987, the urban distribution's shift upward was
almost three times greater (6.6%) than the rural distribution's
(2.3%); hence, the rural earnings picture deteriorated relative to
that of the urban picture during the 1980s.

Shifts in Inequality

We have noted the concerns over the increased inequality in earnings and income distribution that have accompanied analyses of
recent industrial restructuring. Displacement of middle-level
earners, whether to the upper or lower segments or to both, implies
that the inequality of the distribution is growing. In this section,
trends in inequality are examined for full-time earners in the urban
and rural economies.

The data in Table 5.6 indicate that inequality among rural full-
time earners has consistently been higher than that among urban
full-time earners. Further, and rather surprising, during the rural
turnaround of the 1970s, the level of inequality doubled in the rural economy while increasing only about one-third in the urban
economy. These results are surprising because the rising inequality

TABLE 5.5

Distribution of Rural and Urban Full-Time Earners, 1967–1973–1979–1987 (Percent)

	Low Rural	Low Urban	Middle Rural	Middle Urban	Upper Rural	Upper Urban	Rural	Total (%)	Urban	Total (%)
1967	9.1	5.5	74.1	65.7	16.8	28.7	13,958,943	100.0	32,180,841	100.0
1973	8.8	4.6	76.7	70.2	14.4	25.2	14,422,983	100.0	36,835,394	100.0
1979	7.3	3.9	75.6	70.2	17.1	26.0	14,963,651	100.0	40,408,067	100.0
1987	3.0	1.7	57.5	42.9	39.5	55.4	13,043,207	100.0	57,599,336	100.0

Source: Calculated from CPS microdata files.

TABLE 5.6

Theil Indexes of Inequality for Rural and Urban Full-Time
Earners, 1967–1973–1979–1987

Year	Rural Theil*	Urban Theil*
1987	0.0104	0.0099
1979	0.0196	0.0127
1973	0.0207	0.0137
1967	0.0103	0.0095

Note: Theil indexes have been standardized to fall within the range of zero to one following the formula $T^* = T/(\log n - T)$; see Allison (1978).

Source: Calculated from CPS microdata files.

occurred at a time when the middle segment of the earnings distribution was growing, a trend generally associated with growing
equality. The most plausible explanation for this phenomenon is
that the way in which the middle segment was growing was at its
tails, and more so in the upper tail than in the lower tail.

After 1979, the level of inequality among full-time earners in
both the rural and urban economies dropped sharply, returning
almost to its 1967 levels. A more detailed analysis than is warranted within the scope of this research might be able to explain
precisely what caused the unleveling, and then the leveling, among
full-time earners in the 1970s and 1980s. It would seem, though,
that while the direction is the same for both the rural and urban
economies, the rural and urban trends may be attributable to different influences. The increasing *rural* inequality could be explained along the lines of Kuznet's observations on income inequality trends in developing countries (Kindleberger and Herrick
1977). That is, the compressed wages of the traditional natural resources sector are replaced by a greater range of wages among
manufacturing and services sectors—increasing inequality occurs
without lowering anyone's earnings. Kuznet's observations, however, would not apply to increasing inequality among full-time
earners in the urban economy, with its much greater or advanced
level of industrialization. What would appear plausible in this case

is that the not mutually exclusive declines of unionized, manufacturing, and primary labor market employment have meant decreases in the proportion of jobs that pay middle-level earnings.

Finally, we might want to speculate as to why during the 1980s the level of inequality for both the rural and the urban full-time earners' distributions has decreased, and so much so for the rural distribution that its level is now almost the same as that in the urban economy: the leveling effect on full-time earnings in both economic regions of slow macroeconomic growth, combined with the loss of high-wage manufacturing and/or unionized urban jobs, could have evened the playing field.

Gender and Race Distinctions in the Rural and Urban Earnings Distributions

Full-Time Earners

To get a sense of what distinctions in gender and race have been present over the period of analysis, we will look first at the 1967 and 1987 full-time earner distributions for four gender and race groups: white males, white females, black males, and black females (Tables 5.7A and 5.7B).

During the twenty-year period, urban white males had the highest percentage of upper earners, which grew almost 5% as a result of an upward shift from the middle-earner group. Rural white males experienced the same trend, although the percentage of rural white male upper earners was substantially lower.

Rural white females have experienced the least change in earnings distribution. The proportion of middle earners remained virtually the same over the twenty-year period at more than 83%. Shifts have occurred in the tails of the rural white female distribution: low earners declined almost 3%—to become 11.5% in 1987— while upper earners grew more than 3%—to become 5.4% in 1987.

Among the black population, rural males and females and urban females have experienced significant upward shifts from the low- to the middle-earner segments while urban males shifted from the middle to the upper segments. The low-earner group among rural black males was 12.6% in 1987, reflecting a more than 10%

TABLE 5.7A

Urban Full-Time Earners' Distribution, by Gender and Race, 1967 and 1987 (Percent)

		Earnings		
Earners	*Year*	*Lower*	*Middle*	*Upper*
Black Females	1967	25.02	72.02	2.96
	1987	7.43	82.36	10.21
Black Males	1967	7.83	82.68	9.49
	1987	6.38	70.73	22.89
White Females	1967	9.56	85.06	5.37
	1987	5.29	79.18	15.54
White Males	1967	2.36	55.32	42.32
	1987	2.61	50.59	46.80
Total	1967	5.5	65.7	28.3
	1987	4.0	63.4	32.6

TABLE 5.7B

Rural Full-Time Earners' Distribution, by Gender and Race, 1967 and 1987 (Percent)

		Earnings		
Earners	*Year*	*Lower*	*Middle*	*Upper*
Black Females	1967	48.3	51.4	0.3
	1987	21.5	76.5	2.1
Black Males	1967	22.8	75.0	2.2
	1987	12.6	80.4	7.1
White Females	1967	14.3	83.3	2.3
	1987	11.5	83.1	5.4
White Males	1967	4.1	71.0	24.9
	1987	2.1	65.9	30.0
Total	1967	9.1	74.1	16.8
	1987	7.7	72.9	19.4

Source: Calculated from CPS microdata files.

decrease in size over the twenty-year period. The decline in the low-earner group resulted in 5% increases—to become 80.4% and 7.1%, respectively—in the middle and upper segments of the rural black males' earnings distribution.

Relatively little change occurred in the proportion of urban black males who were low earners, but this group experienced a large upward shift out of the middle segment. Urban black males who were middle earners declined almost 12% between 1967 and 1987 while those who were upper earners grew more than 13%.

Rural black females made the greatest gains over the two decades studied. Almost half were low earners in 1967, but by 1987, more than three-quarters were middle earners. Urban black females also fared well. The proportion who were middle earners grew more than 10%—to become more than 82% in 1987—while the proportion who were upper earners tripled, increasing from almost 3% to more than 10% in twenty years.

To summarize the trends among full-time workers between 1967 and 1987: in general, the full-time earnings distributions of rural white females and black males have come to resemble each other much more closely while the distributions of urban white and black females became much more alike. Thus, in the rural economy, the greatest differences in the earnings distributions were between black females and white males; in the urban economy, the greatest differences were between white and black males.

Part-Time Earners

The earnings distribution among part-time rural workers changed very little between 1967 and 1987. Lower earners continued to be a much higher proportion of the rural than the urban distribution (Tables 5.8A and 5.8B). However, the differences between the sizes of the rural and urban lower segments narrowed as a result of a downward shift among urban earners. In 1987, around 72% of rural part-time earners were in the low-earners group, compared to 64% of urban part-time earners.[4]

Growing proportions of both rural and urban white males are low earners. Urban and rural white males in this group increased by 8.5% and 7.0%, respectively, between 1967 and 1987. In contrast, urban and rural white females experienced small upward

TABLE 5.8A

Urban Part-Time Earners' Distribution, by Gender and Race, 1967 and 1987 (Percent)

		Earnings		
Earners	*Year*	*Lower*	*Middle*	*Upper*
Black Females	1967	74.1	25.7	0.2
	1987	73.7	24.4	2.0
Black Males	1967	51.8	45.5	2.7
	1987	69.1	27.3	2.6
White Females	1967	68.9	30.3	0.8
	1987	67.2	30.9	1.9
White Males	1967	49.0	43.7	7.3
	1987	57.5	35.6	6.9
Total	1967	60.6	36.0	3.4
	1987	64.1	32.1	3.8

TABLE 5.8B

Rural Part-Time Earners' Distribution, by Gender and Race, 1967 and 1987 (Percent)

		Earnings		
Earners	*Year*	*Lower*	*Middle*	*Upper*
Black Females	1967	92.2	7.6	0.2
	1987	84.5	15.5	0.0
Black Males	1967	76.5	23.1	0.3
	1987	75.5	23.7	0.8
White Females	1967	79.2	20.6	0.2
	1987	75.9	23.6	0.5
White Males	1967	57.4	38.0	4.6
	1987	64.4	31.8	3.8
Total	1967	71.2	26.8	1.9
	1987	72.1	26.2	1.7

Source: Calculated from CPS microdata files.

shifts from the lower segment. Nevertheless, almost 76% of rural white female part-time workers were low earners in 1987.

The rural black male earnings distribution has remained virtually the same, with 75.5% in the low-earner group, while the urban black male distribution experienced a very large downward shift over the last twenty years. Almost 46% were in the middle group in 1967 while almost 52% were in the low group; by 1987, only 27.3% were in the middle group while 69.1% had become low earners. The downward shift for urban part-time black males is the most extreme of any earnings group, part- or full-time, rural or urban, and signals increasing marginalization of this group.

While rural black female part-time earners still have the least advantaged position in the overall earnings picture, their position is becoming less marginalized. Between 1967 and 1987, their earnings distribution shifted upward, although it remained the most downward-skewed of any group. More than 92% were low earners in 1967. By 1987, almost 85% were low earners and the remaining 15.5% were middle earners. Urban black females saw little change in their earnings distribution: almost three-quarters were low earners and almost one-quarter were middle earners.

Fringe Benefit Recipiency among Full-Time Rural and Urban Earners, 1979 and 1987

The financial security that employee benefits provide can be critical to an individual's and a household's ability to attain—and retain—a middle standard of living. In the data presented thus far on earned compensation between urban and rural workers, we have seen that urban earners have higher levels of compensation. In this section, we look to see if urban earners also have higher levels of fringe benefits.

Rural full-time earners have somewhat lower levels of benefit recipiency than their urban counterparts (Table 5.9). The 1987 levels of benefit recipiency were lower than 1979 levels. Over the eight-year period, the decline in the percentage of workers included in employers' pension plans, as well as in the percentage whose employers paid all of their group health costs, was greater for full-time urban earners than it was for full-time rural earners.

TABLE 5.9

Rural and Urban Full-Time Earners with Benefit Recipiency, by Gender, 1979 and 1987

Benefit	Year	(1) Rural % Males	(2) Rural % Females	(3) Urban % Males	(4) Urban % Females	(5) Rural % with Benefit	(6) Urban % with Benefit	(7) Rural % Full-Time Earners	(8) Urban % Full-Time Earners
Included in Pension Plan	1979	62.7	56.6	66.5	59.2	60.6	63.8	27.0	73.0
	1987	56.6	51.5	58.3	54.1	54.6	56.6	18.5	81.5
	Change	−6.1	−5.1	−8.2	−5.1	−6.0	−7.2	−8.5	8.5
Included in Group Health	1979	81.9	72.5	85.9	77.2	78.7	82.8	27.0	73.0
	1987	76.9	66.0	79.7	72.7	72.7	76.9	18.5	81.5
	Change	−5.0	−6.5	−6.2	−4.5	−6.0	−5.9	−8.6	8.6
Employer Helped Pay for Group Health	1979	76.4	66.5	81.7	73.0	73.0	78.6	27.0	73.0
	1987	72.9	62.9	76.6	69.7	69.1	73.4	18.5	81.5
	Change	−3.5	−3.6	−5.1	−3.3	−3.9	−5.2	−8.6	8.6

Source: Calculated from CPS microdata files.

These declines have coincided with a shift in the proportion of the nation's full-time earners to urban areas.

When levels of benefit recipiency are cross-tabulated for male and female earners in rural and urban areas, the differences become more striking (see columns 1 through 4 in Table 5.9). Urban earners have higher levels of fringe benefits than rural earners, but the experience of the 1980s has served to lessen their differences. Between 1979 and 1987, urban males had the highest levels of benefit recipiency, followed by rural males, urban females, and rural females. In each group, the percentage of employers who paid all health insurance costs declined more than 40%, and for rural and urban males the decline was close to 50%. Still, a greater percentage of urban males and females had employer-paid healthcare during the period. Rural and urban females had the lowest levels of pension and group health benefit recipiency, but urban males experienced the greatest declines in benefit recipiency during the 1980s, making their position more similar to that of urban females and rural males and females.

Change in the Rural and Urban Full-Time Earnings Distributions by Production Sector

This section examines whether and how overall industrial restructuring at the national level has differentially affected full-time workers in rural and urban areas, using the nine-sector production classification introduced earlier.

The social infrastructure sector of the high-growth group of production sectors (Table 5.10) experienced downward shifts in both the urban and rural earnings distributions during the 1970s and then upward shifts since. While both the rural and the urban distributions have shifted upward, the urban shift has been greater. Thirty-two percent of urban earners are in the upper group, compared to 18% of rural earners.

The smallest percentage of urban upper earners in a high-growth sector is found in transportation and trade. In addition, this sector employs the largest percentage of middle urban earners. Among rural workers in this sector, the percentage who are low

TABLE 5.10

Rural and Urban Full-Time Workers in High-Growth Sectors, Percent Distribution of Earnings, 1967–1973–1979–1987

Production Sector	Earnings Group	1967 Rural	1967 Urban	1973 Rural	1973 Urban	1979 Rural	1979 Urban	1987 Rural	1987 Urban
Transportation and Trade	Low	9.4	5.8	9.1	5.4	9.8	4.6	11.4	6.0
	Middle	74.0	68.3	76.4	70.4	72.8	71.4	69.7	65.6
	Upper	16.6	26.0	14.5	24.2	17.4	24.1	18.9	28.5
Transactional Activities	Low	4.0	4.9	4.3	3.9	3.5	3.4	4.7	2.7
	Middle	72.3	65.7	75.1	69.3	71.5	72.5	71.0	62.5
	Upper	23.7	29.4	20.7	26.8	25.0	24.2	24.3	34.8
Social Infrastructure	Low	7.9	5.8	6.0	4.1	5.9	3.1	6.7	3.0
	Middle	75.5	66.5	80.1	72.0	81.5	74.0	75.4	64.8
	Upper	16.6	27.7	14.0	23.9	12.5	22.8	17.9	32.3
All Sectors	Low	9.1	5.5	8.8	4.6	7.3	3.9	7.7	4.0
	Middle	74.1	65.7	76.7	70.2	75.6	70.2	72.9	63.4
	Upper	16.8	28.7	14.4	25.2	17.1	26.0	19.4	32.6

Source: Calculated from CPS microdata files.

earners has increased since 1979 and exceeds the average for all full-time earners.

In the final high-growth sector, transactional activities, the rural earnings distribution stayed relatively the same during the 1980s while the urban distribution made a significant upward shift. Urban upper earners in transactional activities increased by more than 10%.

In each of the three manufacturing sectors, earnings distributions for rural and urban full-time workers shifted downward between 1967 and 1973; since then, they have shifted upward (Table 5.11). By 1987, the distributions of rural and urban earners in traditional/low-wage manufacturing looked the most alike. The high-tech/medium-wage and smokestack/high-wage manufacturing sectors in both urban and rural areas experienced sharp upward shifts. In particular, the smokestack/high-wage manufacturing sector saw increases of more than 12% in upper earners in both the urban and rural economies. Further research is needed to explain why the distribution of earnings in the smokestack sector—whose impending extinction has been much discussed—continues to be the most upwardly skewed. One possible explanation is downsizing, with the least experienced and least expensive workers being laid off. Another possibility is that productivity increases achieved in a successful effort to meet international competition have translated into rising earnings.

Data for the third major production sector grouping are presented in Table 5.12. In the natural resources sector, there was a narrowing of differences in the proportions of rural and urban earners in the low-earners segment, accompanied by a widening of differences in the middle and upper segments. The rural upper distribution shifted dramatically upward during the 1970s, from 9.2% to 21.3%; then it shifted inward from both tails, leading to a 9.3% increase in the middle segment between 1979 and 1987.

In construction, both the rural and urban earnings distributions experienced large downward shifts over the decade. For the urban distribution, this was a continuation of trends since 1967. However, in the 1980s, the rural sector saw a reversal of the previous decade's upward trend. In the 1980s, the rural construction sector was very much a middle-earner group.

Both the urban and the rural distributions experienced up-

TABLE 5.11

Rural and Urban Full-Time Workers in Manufacturing Sectors, Percent Distribution of Earnings, 1967–1973–1979–1987

Production Sector	Earnings Group	1967 Rural	1967 Urban	1973 Rural	1973 Urban	1979 Rural	1979 Urban	1987 Rural	1987 Urban
Traditional/Low-Wage Manufacturing	Low	10.1	5.6	11.1	6.5	6.0	4.4	4.9	4.2
	Middle	81.4	74.6	81.3	75.2	85.7	79.2	85.0	80.2
	Upper	8.6	19.9	7.7	18.4	8.3	16.4	10.1	15.6
High-Tech/Medium-Wage Manufacturing	Low	4.9	3.8	5.1	2.7	3.4	2.4	4.2	2.8
	Middle	79.5	67.0	82.1	72.5	81.0	68.4	77.8	63.2
	Upper	15.6	29.2	12.8	24.8	15.6	29.2	18.0	34.0
Smokestack/High-Wage Manufacturing	Low	2.5	2.0	3.2	1.6	0.9	0.9	3.4	1.1
	Middle	70.3	57.9	73.5	64.5	69.1	56.5	53.1	43.8
	Upper	27.3	40.0	23.3	33.9	30.0	42.6	43.5	55.1
All Sectors	Low	9.1	5.5	8.8	4.6	7.3	3.9	7.7	4.0
	Middle	74.1	65.7	76.7	70.2	75.6	70.2	72.9	63.4
	Upper	16.8	28.7	14.4	25.2	17.1	26.0	19.4	32.6

Source: Calculated from CPS microdata files.

TABLE 5.12

Rural and Urban Full-Time Workers in Other Sectors, Percent Distribution of Earnings, 1967–1973–1979–1987

Production Sector	Earnings Group	1967 Rural	1967 Urban	1973 Rural	1973 Urban	1979 Rural	1979 Urban	1987 Rural	1987 Urban
Natural Resources	Low	23.2	11.3	28.4	13.7	24.2	13.7	15.8	8.7
	Middle	65.2	63.7	62.5	68.0	54.6	59.3	63.9	63.0
	Upper	11.6	25.1	9.2	18.3	21.3	27.1	20.3	28.3
Construction	Low	7.8	3.9	7.1	3.5	6.3	5.7	4.6	3.2
	Middle	72.3	55.1	73.3	60.3	70.1	62.1	78.9	60.8
	Upper	20.0	41.1	19.6	36.2	23.6	32.2	16.5	36.0
Personal Services	Low	40.6	20.0	35.8	19.6	26.0	14.2	18.3	11.3
	Middle	52.4	66.8	58.4	69.2	68.0	74.8	72.1	72.9
	Upper	7.0	13.2	5.9	11.2	6.0	11.0	9.6	15.8
All Sectors	Low	9.1	5.5	8.8	4.6	7.3	3.9	7.7	4.0
	Middle	74.1	65.7	76.7	70.2	75.6	70.2	72.9	63.4
	Upper	16.8	28.7	14.4	25.2	17.1	26.0	19.4	32.6

Source: Calculated from CPS microdata files.

ward shifts in the personal services sector during the 1980s. Over the last twenty years, the rural earnings distribution in personal services has made the most dramatic upward shift from the low to the middle group of any distribution. While low earners were almost 41% in 1967, they were only 18.3% in 1987. In parallel with the trends in the natural resources sector, though, the 1980s have brought a widening gap between urban and rural earners in the personal services' middle- and upper-earners groups. The proportion of urban earners in the upper group grew to exceed by 6% that of the rural upper group.

Rural and Urban Full-Time Earners in High Technology and Defense

For more than a decade, the primary focus of economic development policy and practice has been the creation of high-technology industry and jobs. Both the rural and the urban economies experienced growth in the number of full-time earners in the high-technology sector from 1967 until 1979. The number of rural earners was roughly one-third that of urban earners. However, between 1979 and 1987, the rural economy lost more than 130,000 full-time high-tech earners while the urban economy gained close to 1.5 million in this group.

In 1987, 15% of all high-technology earners worked in the rural economy. Almost 70% of these workers were middle earners; another 28.7% were urban earners (Table 5.13). While the upper-earner group of rural high-tech workers grew 7.6% during the 1980s, the increase was considerably less than the 14.4% growth in urban high-tech workers. In 1987, 47.2% of urban high-tech earners were in the upper group.

Table 5.14 indicates that there has been little change in the shares that either the high-technology or the defense sector holds of rural or urban full-time employment. High technology in 1987 makes up around 7% of rural and around 9% of urban, full-time civilian employment. The defense sector constituted almost 2% of rural and more than 4% of urban, full-time employment in 1987.

While there is considerable overlap between the defense and high-technology sectors, we previously made the case that separate

TABLE 5.13

Rural and Urban Full-Time Workers' Distribution of Earnings by High-Technology and Defense Sectors, 1967–1973–1979–1987 (Percent)

Industry Group	Earnings Group	Rural 1967	Urban 1967	Rural 1973	Urban 1973	Rural 1979	Urban 1979	Rural 1987	Urban 1987
High Technology	Lower	3.5	2.8	3.0	1.3	1.2	1.2	1.5	1.2
	Middle	71.2	57.7	76.3	68.6	77.8	66.0	69.8	51.5
	Upper	25.4	39.6	20.7	30.1	21.1	32.8	28.7	47.2
	Total	962,105	3,051,228	977,769	3,151,553	1,010,761	3,562,673	877,755	5,005,976
	%	100.0	100.0	100.0	100.0	100.0	100.0	100.0	100.0
Defense	Lower	2.6	1.7	4.3	1.4	2.7	0.5	3.7	1.2
	Middle	65.5	53.0	75.8	64.9	66.2	60.4	63.1	44.7
	Upper	31.9	45.3	19.9	33.8	31.0	39.0	33.2	54.2
	Total	308,772	1,266,786	248,130	1,296,932	201,884	1,350,302	202,134	2,399,365
	%	100.0	100.0	100.0	100.0	100.0	100.0	100.0	100.0

Source: Calculated from CPS microdata files.

TABLE 5.14

High-Technology and Defense Sectors' Shares of Rural and Urban Full-Time Employment,
1967–1973–1979–1987

Percent of Employment	Rural 1967	Urban 1967	Rural 1973	Urban 1973	Rural 1979	Urban 1979	Rural 1987	Urban 1987
High Technology	6.9	9.5	6.8	8.6	6.8	8.8	6.7	8.7
Defense	2.2	3.9	1.7	3.5	1.4	3.3	1.6	4.2

Note: High-technology CPS codes were identified through cross-referencing with those identified in U.S. Congress, Office of Technology Assessment (1988), Table 8-4. The defense CPS codes were designated through an adaptation of the approach used by Markusen (1985b). The CPS defense group is not as extensive as that of Markusen's due to the limitation of CPS industries being identified only to the three-digit level. As a result, the CPS-identified defense group's size is likely to be underestimated.

Source: Calculated from CPS microdata files.

analysis of the defense sector is warranted because of its unique characteristics: it has a nonmarket character; its products are public goods; and it has a monopsonistic buyer, the federal government.

In contrast to the rural high-tech sector, which gained nearly 49,000 full-time earners, the rural defense sector lost close to 107,000 earners between 1967 and 1979. The defense sector's earnings distribution in both the rural and the urban economy is more upwardly skewed than high technology's (see Table 5.13). Since then, the rural distribution has regained its overall shape, whereas the urban distribution has shifted significantly upward. In 1987, 54.2% of full-time urban defense workers were upper earners, compared to 33.2% of rural defense workers.

Rural and Urban Earnings Distributions in Industries Gaining or Losing Trade Advantage

The final sectoral classification of industry employed in this examination of the impact of structural change on rural and urban earnings distributions has been selected to allow for an assessment of the influence of U.S. industry's changing international trade position.

Full-time earners for rural and urban distributions of earnings were placed into three broad industry groupings—Gainers, Losers, and Holders of apparent trade advantage—that were previously discussed in chapter 4. The primary difference that emerges is that the percentage of low earners in rural industries gaining trade advantage has been at least twice as great as that in rural industries either losing or maintaining their trade positions between 1967 and 1987 (Table 5.15). Such is not the case with urban industries.

In both urban and rural areas, close to 90% of full-time earners are in industries losing their comparative trade advantage (Table 5.16). Further, the distribution of the Loser group in both rural and urban areas is the most equal; that is, middle earners are more than 70% of the rural earner group and more than 60% of the urban earner group (see Table 5.15). Should declining employment levels in industries of the Loser group be one of the results of continued

TABLE 5.15

Rural and Urban Full-Time Workers by Distribution of Earnings in Industries Gaining or Losing Trade Advantage, 1967–1973–1979–1987

Rural Industry Group	Earnings Group	Rural 1967	Rural 1973	Rural 1979	Rural 1987
Gainers	Lower %	13.2	16.0	13.3	9.9
	Middle %	72.1	72.1	68.9	70.4
	Upper %	14.7	11.9	17.8	19.8
	Total	1,735,766	2,176,324	1,918,451	1,629,534
Losers	Lower %	8.5	6.9	6.2	7.8
	Middle %	75.4	78.3	77.3	73.9
	Upper %	16.1	14.8	16.6	18.3
	Total	9,644,760	11,317,067	12,204,084	9,758,030
Holders	Lower %	1.2	7.7	7.1	1.8
	Middle %	68.2	73.3	64.6	60.2
	Upper %	30.7	19.1	28.4	38.0
	Total	287,792	574,914	546,950	186,593

Urban Industry Group	Earnings Group	Urban 1967	Urban 1973	Urban 1979	Urban 1987
Gainers	Lower %	4.8	3.9	4.1	3.1
	Middle %	66.0	69.6	64.5	60.1
	Upper %	29.2	26.5	31.4	36.9
	Total	2,805,071	3,263,978	3,215,663	4,434,977
Losers	Lower %	5.8	4.4	3.8	4.4
	Middle %	66.6	70.7	71.1	64.7
	Upper %	27.6	24.9	25.1	30.8
	Total	22,712,137	31,069,113	34,738,737	44,582,512
Holders	Lower %	2.7	2.4	2.0	1.2
	Middle %	64.8	63.2	62.0	49.1
	Upper %	32.6	34.4	36.1	49.7
	Total	906,610	1,790,446	1,782,546	1,156,075

Note: Placement of CPS industry codes into Gainer, Loser, or Holder groups was made by cross-referencing CPS codes to the industries identified in U.S. Congress, Office of Technology Assessment (1988), Table 8-4, where industries are categorized as gaining or losing apparent advantage in trade by measuring change in the ratio of the value-added gained due to exports to the value-added lost due to imports between 1972 and 1984.

Source: Calculated from CPS microdata files.

TABLE 5.16

Distribution of Rural and Urban Full-Time Workers in Industries Gaining or Losing Trade Advantage, 1967–1973–1979–1987

Rural	Industry Group	Rural 1967	Rural 1973	Rural 1979	Rural 1987
	Gainers %	12.4	15.1	12.8	12.5
	Losers %	69.1	78.5	81.6	74.8
	Holders %	2.6	4.0	3.7	1.4
Trade Analyzed* Earners		11,668,318	14,068,305	14,669,485	11,574,157
% of Region		83.6	97.5	98.0	88.7
% of Nation		25.3	27.4	25.0	16.4

Urban	Industry Group	Urban 1967	Urban 1973	Urban 1979	Urban 1987
	Gainers %	8.7	8.9	8.0	7.7
	Losers %	70.6	84.4	86.0	77.4
	Holders %	3.4	5.0	4.5	2.3
Trade Analyzed* Earners		26,423,818	36,123,537	39,736,946	50,173,564
% of Region		82.1	98.1	98.3	87.1
% of Nation		57.3	70.5	67.6	71.0

Note: Placement of CPS industry codes into Gainer, Loser, or Holder groups was made by cross-referencing CPS codes to the industries identified in U.S. Congress, Office of Technology Assessment (1988), Table 8-4, where industries are categorized as gaining or losing apparent advantage in trade by measuring change in the ratio of the value-added gained due to exports to the value-added lost due to imports between 1972 and 1984.

*Not all CPS industry codes could be placed in the three OTA groups; the "percent of region" under the "Trade Analyzed Earners" row indicates the percent of full-time earners that could be placed into one of the three groups.

Source: Calculated from CPS microdata files.

loser status, we can expect movement toward less equality in the overall full-time earnings distributions of the rural and urban economies.

Conclusion

This comparative analysis of change in the rural economy vis-à-vis the urban economy from 1967 to 1987 has been made to determine, in a broad sense, where the rural economy fits into the national debate over disappearing middle-earnings opportunities and, more specifically, how industrial restructuring and shifting population patterns have differentially affected rural and urban earners. In analyzing the rural earnings distribution, we have looked for the influence of the "rural turnaround" of the 1970s decade.

A wide range of differences between rural and urban earnings patterns were found during a period in which the proportion of the nation's population residing in urban and rural areas did not change. Overall, the number of urban full- and part-time earners increased substantially, whereas the number of full- and part-time earners in the rural economy experienced small declines. During the 1980s, though, the number of rural part-time earners began to increase. The rural economy has a lower percentage of full-time earners who are female, but its percentage of female part-time earners is the same as that of the urban economy.

Between 1979 and 1987, urban white males had the most upwardly skewed earnings distribution, and among full-time earners, rural black females had the most downwardly skewed. Overall, the full-time earnings distributions for the four groups—white males, white females, black males, and black females—in both the urban and rural economies have shifted upward. In contrast, the proportions of low, middle, and upper earners in the rural part-time distribution did not change, whereas the urban part-time distribution shifted downward. Within the rural part-time distribution, only the earnings of white males shifted downward; in urban areas, white and black males' earnings shifted down the earnings distribution.

In 1987, urban full-time earners (and white males, in particular) had higher levels of benefit recipiency than their rural counterparts, but the experience of the 1980s served to lessen the differences.

In the analysis of trends by production sectors, changes in the earnings distributions of the high-growth sectors presented a rather mixed picture. While there was an upward shift in the urban and rural distributions in social infrastructure, the percentage of total employment in that sector began declining in the 1980s, and there was a widening of the earnings gap between the rural and urban areas. The earnings distribution for the largest sector, transportation and trade, most closely resembled the overall full-time earnings distribution, but in the rural economy, this sector has a higher percentage of low earners. The earnings distribution of the transactional activities sector shows a bifurcating trend for urban earners and a downward shift for rural earners.

Despite either low growth or absolute declines in employment, all three of the manufacturing sectors showed upward shifts in the rural and urban economies between 1967 and 1987. The natural resource and personal services sectors became high-growth sectors during the 1980s in both rural and urban areas. The earnings distribution of the rural natural resources sector showed a remarkable shifting toward the middle from both of its tails. In personal services, there was a dramatic upward shift from the low to the middle segment among rural full-time earners.

Of the nearly 5.9 million full-time high-technology earners in 1987, nearly 878,000, or 15%, were rural. Approximately 8% of all full-time civilian defense earners were rural, but they made up only 2% of all 1987 full-time rural employment. Thus, we can predict that changes in these two highly visible sectors would have relatively little effect on the rural economy.[5]

In considering the impact of international trade on the rural earnings structure, it appears that rural industries that gained comparative trade advantage have relied more heavily on low earners than have either urban industries or rural industries that are either holding or losing their trade positions. Further, in both the urban and the rural economies, industries assessed as losing their comparative trade advantage are the largest sources of middle-level jobs.

The rural turnaround of the 1970s lessened the overall differences in the earnings distributions between the rural and urban economies, but it increased inequality in the rural full-time earners distribution. The experience of the 1980s reversed both of these trends, resulting in a level of inequality among rural full-time earners that is almost the same as that of urban full-time earners. In addition, the gaps in levels of unearned compensation in the form of health and pension benefits have narrowed between rural and urban full-time earners.

An important question for economic development policy concerns how the ability of rural and urban full-time earners to purchase the middle standard of living might have changed over two recent decades. Can we assume that the overall cost of the middle

standard of living is lower in the rural areas and, thus, that lower
earnings in the rural areas do not mean lower consumption of the
middle standard in comparison to the urban areas? Not necessarily.

Let us first consider changes in the market basket reflecting a
middle standard of living since 1967. There is little doubt that the
basket has come to include a greater range of goods and services:
two cars instead of one, microwave ovens in addition to stoves, and
televisions plus VCRs. Furthermore, we can argue that greater proportions of the basket must now be purchased in the national marketplace at standardized prices and that an increasing number of
items are not, or cannot be, produced in the rural areas at all, let
alone at a lower cost. Therefore, goods cannot be purchased more
cheaply in the rural areas. However, this may be less true for the
service components of the middle standard of living: rural consumers may be at an advantage because of the lower labor costs fac-
tored into the price of services in their areas.

There should be differences in the cost of the largest and single
most important consumption item of the middle standard of living—home ownership. While we have only limited aggregate rural
data to compare to aggregate urban data on the cost of houses, they
support the common perception—and observations from micro rural and urban housing markets—that differences do exist. The median price of a new home in nonmetropolitan areas was 83% of that
in metropolitan areas in 1967 and 81% in 1987.[6]

It would also be fair to argue that greater variations in the cost
of owning the intermediate- or middle-range house have developed
since 1967, particularly within metropolitan areas. The combination of population and industry shifts, continued urbanization, the
maturing and nest-building of the baby boomers, and smaller
household sizes has led to a more differentiated metropolitan economic and spatial geography. Within this metropolitan geography,
it has become much more difficult to purchase a home in cities
like San Francisco and Los Angeles while it is relatively more easy
in cities like Rochester, New York, or Raleigh, North Carolina.

Still, even the cost of the intermediate- or middle-range house
in the aggregate rural housing market can be said to have become
more differentiated. While rural spatial geography might have
shrunk over the last two decades, rural economic geography has

become more complex, with the development of retirement and recreational communities, the reduction in agricultural lands, and increases in industrial, office, and commercial development. To make the monthly mortgage payments, individuals still depend on a financial institution for mortgage loans. There have been concerns over whether deregulation of the nation's financial system in the 1980s led to redlining in rural areas. In this sense, a rural full-time earner's ability to become a homeowner may be lower than that of an urban full-time earner in an identical position.

A final point to consider in this discussion of rural and urban full-time earners' abilities to purchase homes relates to our earlier observation about the percentage of rural female full-time earners. Nationwide, the ability to purchase a home with the earnings of one full-time worker has significantly decreased since the late 1960s. Some of the rise in traditional households with two full-time earners has to be attributable to this factor. Could it be that the lower percentage of female full-time earners in the rural areas is at least partly due to the fact that in rural areas it is easier to purchase a home and the middle standard of living with the earnings of one full-time worker? Even if this is the case today, trends suggest that this comparative advantage in purchasing the single most important consumption item of the middle standard of living may be eroding for rural earners.

6

The Regional Implications of Industrial Restructuring

Introduction

The national economic landscape is not, of course, a homogenous plane. Planners and policymakers have long been concerned with the uneven pattern of development among regions and the resulting differences in standards of living among the population. The origins of this unevenness are many, including historical differences in the timing of when specific regions were developed; differences in the natural resource and industrial mix; differences in population characteristics, such as age structure; and differences in labor force characteristics, such as educational levels and participation rates among different demographic groups.

While there is a significant variation in the national economic geography, there has been, until recently, consensus that a long-run trend toward income convergence was occurring among the nation's regions. The income measures over which this consensus has developed are that of regional per capita earnings and income. The trends observed for these measures across regions in the period between 1929 and the late 1970s indicated a convergence attributed to two factors: within-region shifts in employment—for example, from low-wage agricultural employment to higher-wage industrial employment—and the increased mobility of workers who traveled between regions in search of higher returns on their labor.[1]

Since the late 1970s, divergence has been observed in regional per capita earnings. Carlino (1992) suggests, however, that the trend toward convergence has not reversed but rather that there has been a short-run adjustment to a long-run equilibrium in per capita earnings among regions.

This chapter considers the issue of regional income convergence by looking at the *distribution* of earnings rather than at per capita earnings. Differences in the distribution of earnings between the urban and rural regions, which were considered in chapter 5, are valuable because of long-standing economic development policy concern over income inequality between those two broad regions. Because of the national significance of shifts in the overall distribution of earnings, the regional variations in the trend should command our attention as well.

The choice of which regional configurations to analyze is not as clear-cut as in the urban/rural configuration. Regional analysts have focused on different groupings of states to reflect their particular economic and geographic concerns, depending on data availability. Discussion of industrial restructuring over the past few decades has often been phrased in terms of shifts between two major regions—from the Rustbelt (alternatively called the Snowbelt or Frostbelt) to the Sunbelt. Essentially, the Rustbelt label encompasses the Northeast and Midwest while the Sunbelt label applies to the South and West. These four regions—Northeast, Midwest, South, and West—are the major U.S. Census Bureau regions. The nation has also been divided into nine census divisions that are commonly employed in regional analyses and especially in per capita income analyses.

Instead of using these nine census divisions, we will here examine regional shifts in the earnings distribution between 1967 and 1987 within the four major census regions and in the most populous state of each region. This regional approach allows us to take a closer look at trends in some of the nation's most important states. Further, in this country, most economic development policy-making takes place at the state level. The state examined in the Northeast is New York, which ranks second in population nationwide. In the Midwest, the chosen state is the nation's sixth most populated, Illinois. In the South, the nation's third-largest state, Texas, is examined. In the West, we examine the nation's largest state, California. The mid-1980s population ranks of these four states were all different from the 1960s ranks, and they reflected the regional shifts in the nation's population that occurred over two decades. In 1960, New York was the top-ranking state, California was second, Illinois was fourth, and Texas was sixth.[2]

In general, population shifts follow employment and industry shifts. Many analysts have characterized the shifts in population and economic activity shifts, from states like New York in the Northeast and Illinois in the Midwest to states like Texas in the South and California in the West, as simply movement between the two larger regions: from the Rustbelt to the Sunbelt. The problem with such an approach is that it can obscure the existence of what may be quite different reasons for migrations out of the Rustbelt and into the Sunbelt, which in turn can have different outcomes in terms of employment and earnings patterns for each region. It can also obscure the differences in the consequences of migration for the regions from which migration took place.

The economic boom of the 1960s, in which income growth throughout the nation was narrowing regional income differences, obscured the emerging evidence of regional weaknesses resulting from the shifts in the industrial base to the South and West. For example, Levy (1987) noted that manufacturing employment increased 20% nationwide in the 1960s but not at all in the Middle Atlantic states and only 12% in the Great Lakes states. States in the Far West were the primary recipients of this employment increase. Furthermore, Crandall (1988) observed that while regional per capita income differences narrowed, the shift of manufacturing activity did not narrow regional manufacturing wage differences; in fact, wages in the Great Lakes states of the Midwest continued to climb even when these states were losing market shares in their manufacturing industries. In addition, manufacturing wages in the Pacific states of the West region generally fell in industries gaining shares of relative employment.

What may best explain these trends and others to be considered shortly is the notion of profit squeeze, together with corporate response to unionization in the face of profit squeeze. The term *profit squeeze* is used to describe the position American corporations found themselves in due to their lack of preparation for heightened international competition, which began in the late 1960s and was spawned, to a significant degree, by American international development assistance in the postwar period. The incidence of unionization is not evenly distributed across the nation; for example, the rate of unionization for the four states analyzed here varied between 15% and 50% in 1987.[3]

Shifts in regional development in response to profit squeeze can be viewed as functions of profit cycles.[4] Essentially, the theory of profit cycles suggests that industry response to changing sources of profitability affects employment growth within regions, as well as production and employment relocation between regions.

In the profit cycle, as an industry sector matures, it passes stages of profitability, ranging from zero, when the product is just being developed, to "superprofits," when, for example, an industry is offering a new product for which there may at first be a high demand and no substitutes, then to normal profits, and, ultimately, to negative profits. The impetus for regional shifts in production comes in the post-superprofit stages, when corporations—whose dominance in a market is eroding from delayed but eventual entry of competitors, changing consumer tastes, substitute commodities, and/or, as in the case of the late 1960s, increasing international competition—seek to lower their costs of production.

Labor costs continue to be dominant in industrial production (Storper 1982). As a result, shifts in a regional earnings distribution may occur when a significant number of industries find themselves on the waning side of the profit cycle and seek to reduce labor costs. Given the tendency toward sticky wages, that is, strong resistance to wage cuts, shifting profit cycles may be more apparent in the regional pattern of fringe benefit recipiency: industries may find it easier to cut labor costs by lowering levels of fringe benefit recipiency, which do not have visible, fixed prices attached to them.

When the element of unionization is added to the picture, attempts to adjust to labor costs can have very different effects on the earnings distributions in the regions from which and to which industries are migrating. When industry is leaving a region, there may be a downward shift in the overall earnings distribution, to the extent that job growth takes place in nonunionized industries.[5] In the unionized industries, on the one hand, union response to the threat of job loss could result in wage and benefit concessions, which would show up as downward shifts in the industries' earnings distribution and as lower incidences of benefit recipiency. On the other hand, if unions believe that job loss will occur despite concessions, they may continue to bargain hard for wage increases for those whose jobs remain; this could appear as upward-shifting earnings distributions in industries whose employee numbers are declining (Kaufman and Martinez-Vasquez 1987; Linneman and Wachter 1988).

In the regions to which profit-squeezed industry migrates, earnings distributions could shift upward depending on the extent to which labor costs were lower than in the previous region. Furthermore, since the regional migration may result in more employers bidding for the pool of available labor, wages could be bid up across industries.

Some of the regional implications of profit cycles are that regions can become overdeveloped and weighted with mature industries. When this occurs, there will be industry out-migration to less-developed regions with lower labor costs and costs of living (Markusen 1985a). As a result, regional convergence in distributions of earnings can occur as a result of the dedevelopment of certain regions. This is a different phenomenon than regional convergence of per capita income that can result when, in the course of aggregate national growth, the standards of less-developed regions are raised.

In the analysis that follows, we look for inferential evidence of profit cycles at the subnational level between 1967 and 1987, as we focus primarily on full-time earners, whose earnings should have been able to purchase the middle standard of living for themselves and their households. Given the four-by-four structure of the analysis—that is, four regions and four states—the selection of factors to be analyzed will be narrower than in the preceding chapters. At the regional level, change in the full-time distribution of earnings is analyzed by earnings segment, the nine production sectors, and the two separate smaller sectoral analyses, the high-tech/defense and trade-affected sectors. Fringe benefit recipiency is analyzed at the regional and at the state levels. The level of educational attainment is also analyzed at the state level, the level at which any policy action would be instigated. Finally, to make some determination of change in the attainability of the middle standard of living, we will examine patterns of home ownership.

Regional Distributions of Earnings

Beginning with change *between* regions, the regional shares of the nation's full-time earners changed between 1967 and 1987, just as regional shares of population changed. However, the ranks of the regions stayed the same: the South ranked first in full-time earners, followed by the Midwest, the Northeast, and the West. Over the two decades, the South's and the West's shares of full-time earners grew at the expense of the Northeast and the Midwest. The South's share of full-time earners increased from 29% to 34%, the Midwest's share shrank from 28% to 24%, the Northeast's share shrank from 27% to 22%, and the West's share increased from 16% to 20% (Figure 6.1).

The South's disproportionately large share, 44%, of the nation's low earners remained unchanged despite regional economic growth. Further, even though the Northeast and Midwest experienced economic decline during the same period, their shares of the nation's low earners actually shrunk while the share of the growing West increased substantially by 8%.

The Midwest's and the Northeast's shares of middle earners declined over the last two decades, to the benefit of the South and the West, which had equal proportions of upper earners in 1967, 21%, and their shares were significantly lower than the Northeast's, at 28%, and the Midwest's, at 30%. By 1987, the Northeast and Midwest lost shares of upper earners. Their shares and the West's were nearly equal while the South's 29% share was substantially larger.

Focusing on shifts in the earnings distribution *within* each of the four major regions, we find that for the Northeast, the middle-earner segment grew at the expense of the lower and upper segments between 1967 and 1979 (Table 6.1). After 1979, the distribution made a significant shift upward: the upper-earner group gained almost 10% of the Northeast's full-time earners, increasing from 23.5% to 33.3%.

The patterns in the three other regions were similar, but in none of the other three regions did the upper-earner group increase by as much as 10%. The earnings distribution in the West showed the least change overall, with the 1987 distribution looking almost identical to that for 1987. Thus, while the West had the highest earnings distribution of the four regions in 1967 by a significant degree, in 1987, its distribution closely resembled that of the Northeast. Further, there was a trend toward convergence in the shapes of the regions' distributions.

Let us next examine the fringe benefit portion of total compensation for full-time earners *across regions*. Table 6.2 shows the percentage of full-time earners in each region who were included in pension and group health plans, as well as the percentage whose

FIGURE 6.1

Regional Distribution of Full-Time Earners, 1967 and 1987

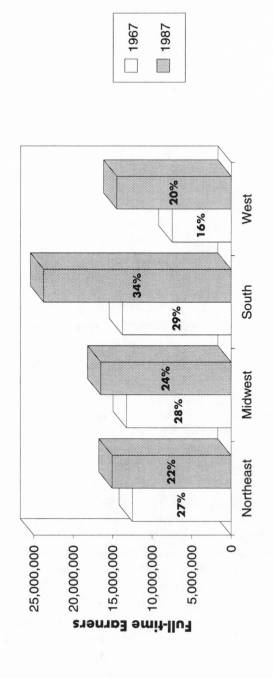

Note: n: 1967 = 46,139,783; 1987 = 71,135,910.

Source: Calculated from Current Population Survey (CPS) microdata files.

TABLE 6.1

Distribution of Full-Time Earnings by Region, 1967–1973–1979–1987

Region	Earnings Group	Year			
		1967	*1973*	*1979*	*1987*
Northeast	Low %	5.1	4.1	3.1	3.1
	Middle %	69.3	71.5	73.4	63.6
	Upper %	25.6	24.4	23.5	33.3
	Total	12,558,792	12,518,126	13,351,713	15,652,849
Midwest	Low %	5.9	5.5	4.8	4.4
	Middle %	66.4	70.4	70.0	65.6
	Upper %	27.7	24.0	25.2	30.1
	Total	12,698,495	14,417,454	15,474,409	17,048,732
South	Low %	9.8	7.7	6.4	6.1
	Middle %	72.3	75.6	74.5	68.3
	Upper %	17.9	16.7	19.1	25.6
	Total	13,581,788	15,915,705	19,138,792	24,408,813
West	Low %	4.5	5.1	4.6	4.4
	Middle %	62.2	68.7	67.2	61.1
	Upper %	33.2	26.2	28.2	34.5
	Total	7,300,708	8,407,091	10,819,649	14,025,516

Source: Calculated from CPS microdata files.

employers helped pay for group healthcare. In 1979, the Northeast had the highest levels of benefit recipiency in all three categories examined. It was followed by the Midwest, the West, and the South. All regions have experienced drops in the levels of benefit recipiency for full-time earners during the 1980s; however, the Northeast experienced the largest decline in the percentage of full-time earners included in a pension plan. As a result, by 1987, the Midwest region ranked first in benefit recipiency.

The South and the West have had substantially smaller percentages of employees receiving benefits, but more of the West's full-time earners received health-related benefits in 1979 than did those in the South. Still, of the four regions, the West experienced the greatest decreases in the proportion of earners included in group health plans and in employer assistance in paying for group health plans.

TABLE 6.2

Change in the Percent of Full-Time Earners with Benefit
Recipiency by Region and State between 1979 and 1987

| | | By Region | | | |
Benefit	Year	Northeast	Midwest	South	West
Included in Pension Plan	1979	67.1	66.6	58.5	59.7
	1987	58.8	60.6	53.3	53.2
	Change	−8.3	−6.0	−5.2	−6.5
Included in Group Health	1979	84.4	83.9	78.4	80.3
	1987	79.6	78.6	73.5	73.8
	Change	−4.7	−5.3	−4.9	−6.5
Employer Helped Pay for	1979	80.6	80.4	71.8	76.6
Group Health	1987	77.4	75.9	69.0	71.2
	Change	−3.2	−4.5	−2.8	−5.4

| | | By State | | | |
Benefit	Year	New York	Illinois	Texas	California
Included in Pension Plan	1979	66.4	68.5	55.7	58.6
	1987	59.0	60.3	54.5	50.9
	Change	−7.5	−8.3	−1.2	−7.7
Included in Group Health	1979	84.0	85.7	76.6	80.7
	1987	77.5	79.5	72.9	72.3
	Change	−6.4	−6.2	−3.7	−8.4
Employer Helped Pay for	1979	80.0	81.6	70.1	77.3
Group Health	1987	75.2	76.4	67.5	70.1
	Change	−4.8	−5.2	−2.7	−7.1

Source: Calculated from CPS microdata files.

Regional Change in Industrial Composition

The Northeast and the Midwest showed declines in the number of
full-time earners within major production sectors between 1967
and 1987. These declines occurred in the manufacturing sectors,
precisely the ones we might expect according to profit-cycle theory. Decline in the Midwest was slight, though, compared to that in
the Northeast, which saw absolute declines in all three of its man-

ufacturing sectors and which supports the argument that we need to distinguish between these two Rustbelt regions in our analysis (Table 6.3). The Northeast's largest decline, 22.6%, was in the high-tech/medium-wage sector. This was also the sector in which the Midwest experienced its only decline, 6.4%. In contrast, the South and the West gained more than 900,000 and 750,000 full-time workers, respectively, during the same period in this sector.

The Midwest had the largest number of full-time earners in the smokestack/high-wage industry in 1967 and continued to do so in 1987. However, that region experienced only a 2.2% increase in smokestack/high-wage earners in this sector over the last two decades while the South's increase was nearly 20% and the West's was close to 43%. Clearly, there was a major regional shift in manufacturing employment between 1967 and 1987, and we will see shortly what has happened to the earnings distributions of full-time workers in the manufacturing sectors as these sectors have shifted the regional location of their work forces.

TABLE 6.3

Regional Shares of Full-Time Earners in Major Goods-Producing and Distribution Sectors, 1967 and 1987

Production Sector	Year	Northeast	Midwest	South	West
Transportation and Trade	1967	2,791,198	3,069,544	3,336,983	1,826,769
	1987	3,497,656	4,196,225	6,103,140	3,350,398
	% Change	25.3	36.7	82.9	83.4
Traditional/Low-Wage Manufacturing	1967	147,038	149,288	277,106	154,018
	1987	127,792	198,904	429,762	205,146
	% Change	−13.1	33.2	55.1	33.2
High-Tech/Medium-Wage Manufacturing	1967	3,789,225	3,551,104	2,633,366	1,258,427
	1987	2,933,542	3,322,609	3,535,772	2,026,866
	% Change	−22.6	−6.4	34.3	61.1
Smokestack/High-Wage Manufacturing	1967	871,450	1,312,249	986,129	562,013
	1987	759,717	1,341,149	1,178,352	801,397
	% Change	−12.8	2.2	19.5	42.6

Note: Production Sector is based on an adaptation of the Office of Technology Assessment's industry classification.

Source: Calculated from CPS microdata files.

The high-growth sectors were true to their label in all of the four regions. The largest percentage increases of full-time earners occurred in the transactional activities sector, particularly in the South, 196%, and in the West, 167%. The social infrastructure and the transportation and trade sectors, though, showed larger gains in actual numbers of earners and were significantly larger sectors. Increased employment in many of the industries within these high-growth sectors is more directly related to general population growth than was the case for the manufacturing sectors. Thus, it is not surprising that the largest employment increases in these sectors occurred in the South and the West, where population growth was greatest.

Natural resource workers were predominantly found in the South, followed by the West. In comparison to the three other regions, there was little growth in the percentage of full-time construction workers in the Midwest, only 6.5%. In contrast, the Northeast saw a more than 40% increase in construction workers, suggesting that far more building activity took place in that area of the Rustbelt. The increases in the South and West were considerably greater, more than 60% and 80%, respectively, as might be expected.

We begin our examination of the distribution of earnings within each production sector for the four regions with the picture for 1967 (Table 6.4). In that year, the West had the largest percentage of upper earners in eight of the nine sectors. The percent of full-time workers who were low earners was smaller in almost every sector than it was for either the Midwest or the South. For every sector, the distribution of earnings was lowest in the South, in that the proportion of upper earners was significantly smaller than in the other regions while the proportion of lower earners was much greater. For example, the South's percentage of low earners in the personal services sector, 39%, was more than twice that of any of the other regions. In the Midwest, the smokestack/high-wage and construction sectors had the highest distributions of earnings. In 1967, the Northeast and Midwest distributions of earnings tended to be the most similar of the four regions, although in the two largest production sectors—transportation and trade and high-tech/medium-wage manufacturing—the Midwest's distributions were more highly skewed to the upper end.

TABLE 6.4

Regional Distribution of Earnings by Production Sectors, 1967 (Percent)

Production Sector	Earnings Group	Northeast	Midwest	South	West
High-Growth Sectors					
Transportation and Trade	Low	5.6	6.5	8.8	5.3
	Middle	71.0	66.8	74.1	65.7
	Upper	23.4	26.7	17.0	29.0
	Total	2,791,198	3,069,544	3,336,983	1,826,769
Transactional Activities	Low	5.7	4.5	4.7	3.4
	Middle	65.6	67.4	69.6	65.0
	Upper	28.7	28.1	25.7	31.6
	Total	1,268,685	935,586	1,071,267	753,020
Social Infrastructure	Low	4.8	8.3	8.1	3.8
	Middle	69.0	68.6	72.9	64.6
	Upper	26.2	23.1	19.0	31.6
	Total	2,501,594	2,322,531	3,072,960	1,755,632
Manufacturing Sectors					
Traditional/Low-Wage Manufacturing	Low	0.0	8.4	15.7	2.0
	Middle	81.4	74.7	78.5	79.4
	Upper	18.6	16.9	5.8	18.6
	Total	146,038	149,288	277,107	154,018
High-Tech/Medium-Wage Manufacturing	Low	4.1	3.1	5.8	3.2
	Middle	71.3	68.7	79.3	57.4
	Upper	24.6	28.2	14.8	39.4
	Total	3,789,225	3,551,103	2,633,365	1,258,426
Smokestack/High-Wage Manufacturing	Low	1.6	2.4	2.9	1.1
	Middle	64.8	59.1	66.5	50.1
	Upper	33.6	38.6	30.6	48.8
	Total	871,540	1,312,249	986,129	562,013
Other Sectors					
Natural Resources	Low	14.9	16.2	25.8	8.2
	Middle	65.7	68.2	60.4	71.1
	Upper	19.4	15.6	13.9	20.8
	Total	139,440	199,671	523,874	219,002
Construction	Low	2.4	5.6	8.3	2.6
	Middle	62.6	55.6	72.6	45.7
	Upper	35.0	38.9	19.1	51.7
	Total	558,365	709,424	890,675	380,761
Personal Services	Low	16.6	19.4	39.0	16.8
	Middle	69.3	66.9	54.5	67.4
	Upper	14.1	13.7	6.5	15.8
	Total	491,707	449,098	789,430	391,067

Source: Calculated from CPS microdata files.

When we examine the regional earnings distributions for production sectors in 1987 (Table 6.5) and compare them with those for 1967 (Table 6.4), the trend toward a convergence in earnings distributions across regions is clearly evident. The difference in size between the West's upper-earner groups and those of the three other regions has lessened in almost all sectors. Further, the South's earnings distributions have shifted upward so that they look more like those of the other regions. The South even has a higher percentage of upper earners in one sector—natural resources.

The biggest regional discrepancy in the earnings distribution occurs in the high-tech/medium-wage sector, which has more than twice as many full-time earners as the other two manufacturing sectors combined. Upper earners are only 21.9% of the South's distribution, compared to more than 33% for the same sector in each of the other regions.

We have seen that there were declines in the number of full-time earners in high-tech/medium-wage manufacturing between 1967 and 1987 in both the Northeast and the Midwest. Combined, these two regions' declines were more than one million in the twenty-year period. While the South had fewer earners in this sector in 1967 than either the Northeast or the Midwest, it added more than nine hundred thousand full-time workers over the next two decades and became the region with the greatest number of high-tech/medium-wage workers.

We might infer that this shift of high-tech/medium-wage manufacturing to the South was motivated by employers' desires to pay lower wages because the distribution of earnings in regions where employment is growing is much lower than the distribution in the regions where employment is leaving the sector. Such an inference could be taken as indirect evidence of profit cycles at work in specific industries within the broader high-tech/medium-wage manufacturing sector.

Evidence that the construction sector is becoming a middle-earner sector is found again in the Midwest and the West. In both regions, the tails of the construction earnings distributions have shrunk while the middle segment has grown.

To sum up, despite the fact that the Northeast and the Midwest have actually lost full-time earners in one or more sectors over the

TABLE 6.5

Regional Distribution of Earnings by Production Sectors, 1987
(Percent)

Production Sector	Earnings Group	Northeast	Midwest	South	West
High-Growth Sectors					
Transportation and Trade	Low	5.2	6.8	8.4	6.1
	Middle	64.9	68.1	66.6	64.5
	Upper	29.9	25.1	25.0	29.4
	Total	3,497,655	4,196,225	6,103,139	3,350,397
Transactional Activities	Low	1.6	2.7	4.1	2.8
	Middle	61.1	65.0	66.4	59.9
	Upper	37.3	32.3	29.4	37.2
	Total	2,481,881	1,961,573	3,174,743	2,008,184
Social Infrastructure	Low	2.6	4.4	4.8	2.0
	Middle	64.3	68.6	70.4	60.8
	Upper	33.1	27.0	24.8	37.2
	Total	4,267,132	4,404,450	6,715,247	3,741,462
Manufacturing Sectors					
Traditional/Low-Wage	Low	1.4	3.1	5.9	4.8
Manufacturing	Middle	83.8	78.8	83.1	81.8
	Upper	14.8	18.1	11.0	13.4
	Total	127,792	198,904	429,762	205,146
High-Tech/Medium-Wage	Low	2.2	1.6	4.2	5.0
Manufacturing	Middle	64.5	65.1	73.9	59.2
	Upper	33.3	33.3	21.9	35.8
	Total	2,933,542	3,322,609	3,535,772	2,026,866
Smokestack/High-Wage	Low	0.3	1.1	2.0	2.5
Manufacturing	Middle	51.1	44.9	44.2	42.4
	Upper	48.6	54.0	53.9	55.1
	Total	759,718	1,341,150	1,178,353	801,397
Other Sectors					
Natural Resources	Low	8.8	19.3	11.2	8.9
	Middle	70.8	59.3	60.0	67.9
	Upper	20.4	21.4	28.9	23.2
	Total	137,557	254,546	729,124	387,776
Construction	Low	2.7	1.6	5.3	2.5
	Middle	58.1	64.2	71.0	58.4
	Upper	39.2	34.2	23.7	39.0
	Total	803,577	755,520	1,467,692	702,314
Personal Services	Low	8.9	12.5	14.4	12.6
	Middle	73.0	75.6	74.3	68.2
	Upper	18.2	11.8	11.2	19.2
	Total	643,995	613,756	1,074,981	801,974

Source: Calculated from CPS microdata files.

1967 to 1987 period, and that the addition of full-time earners in those regions has been much lower than in either the South or the West,[6] the earnings distributions for the production sectors in these regions have shifted upward. The middles of the regional distributions of earnings have been declining, but the same pattern observed at the national level is evident regionally: the declining middle is due to a growing upper-earner group. We will consider to what extent this upward-shifting trend can be related to differences in unionization levels when we look at the pattern in each of the regions' largest states.

Changing Earnings Distributions in New York, Illinois, Texas, and California

New York

Although it is one of nine states in the Northeast region, New York employs more than one-third of the region's full-time earners. As a result, much of the economic decline generally associated with the Northeast can be traced to trends within the state of New York.

The state experienced absolute losses of full-time earners in seven of its nine production sectors between 1967 and 1973, resulting in a 6.2% decline in the number of full-time earners. Transactional activities and social infrastructure were the only two sectors that did not lose full-time earners (Table 6.6).

While the 1967 to 1973 net change in the number of full-time earners in the state was close to a 290,000 loss, one sector—high-tech/medium-wage manufacturing—lost by itself nearly 390,000 earners. During this period, though, the sector's middle-earner group grew by almost 5%, primarily as a result of low earners moving upward.

By 1979, New York had slightly more than recovered from the employment losses observed in 1973. However, the earnings distribution significantly shifted downward to the middle from the upper segment during these six years (see Table 6.6). Every sector reversed its declining employment trend except the smokestack/high-wage manufacturing sector. Interestingly enough, this was the

TABLE 6.6

NEW YORK

Full-Time Workers' Distribution of Earnings by Production
Sectors, 1967–1973–1979–1987 (Percent)

Production Sector	Earnings Group	1967	1973	1979	1987
High-Growth Sectors					
Transportation and Trade	Low	5.2	3.1	3.8	5.4
	Middle	68.5	72.3	73.8	64.0
	Upper	26.3	24.6	22.4	30.6
	Total	1,037,427	1,025,275	1,054,315	1,187,578
Transactional Activities	Low	6.4	3.8	1.6	1.7
	Middle	67.2	69.8	74.8	61.3
	Upper	26.3	26.4	23.6	36.9
	Total	585,555	620,527	640,588	1,000,309
Social Infrastructure	Low	4.1	3.3	1.3	2.2
	Middle	66.3	65.8	78.2	62.5
	Upper	29.6	30.9	20.5	35.3
	Total	982,093	1,196,831	1,351,563	1,615,615
Manufacturing Sectors					
Traditional/Low-Wage Manufacturing	Low	0.0	0.0	0.0	0.0
	Middle	76.1	69.7	82.5	93.4
	Upper	23.9	30.3	17.5	6.6
	Total	37,260	30,801	33,651	33,141
High-Tech/Medium-Wage Manufacturing	Low	5.1	1.7	1.8	2.0
	Middle	66.3	71.1	72.6	62.3
	Upper	28.7	27.1	25.6	35.7
	Total	1,299,138	912,151	998,683	829,718
Smokestack/High-Wage Manufacturing	Low	2.6	1.1	1.5	0.0
	Middle	65.5	67.9	61.3	55.9
	Upper	31.8	30.9	37.2	44.1
	Total	250,621	230,704	204,766	165,721
Other Sectors					
Natural Resources	Low	26.3	37.0	29.6	17.9
	Middle	54.0	57.2	66.0	73.3
	Upper	19.6	5.8	4.5	8.9
	Total	27,919	23,043	38,325	39,087
Construction	Low	0.6	0.9	6.8	4.2
	Middle	59.3	61.8	74.5	56.8
	Upper	40.1	37.3	18.8	39.0
	Total	183,693	174,029	152,739	268,592
Personal Services	Low	17.0	12.3	16.7	9.6
	Middle	66.7	72.3	72.4	70.1
	Upper	16.2	15.4	10.8	20.3
	Total	251,308	153,352	189,393	237,922
All Sectors					
	Low	5.5	3.3	3.0	3.2
	Middle	66.6	69.2	74.4	62.7
	Upper	27.9	27.6	22.6	34.1
	Total	4,655,015	4,366,712	4,664,024	5,377,682

Source: Calculated from CPS microdata files.

only sector whose earnings distribution continued to shift upward: 6% of the middle-earner group shifted to the upper group. Insight into this trend might be gained by examining patterns of union bargaining in this sector. The first glance raises the question of whether the predominant union strategy might have been to sacrifice employment for wage increases.

More than half, nearly 155,000, of the full-time earners added to New York State between 1973 and 1979 were found in one sector—social infrastructure. At the same time that this sector experienced a 13% increase in full-time earners, its earnings distribution shifted downward by more than 10%. Among possible explanations for this trend might be the increasing numbers of women and minorities entering the labor market, and this segment in particular, as well as the growth of paraprofessional positions in fields such as medicine and law that are included in the social infrastructure sector.

While the overall performance of New York State's economy was below the national average for the 1970s and the state seemed to be experiencing secular decline, trends of the 1980s suggested the worst was over. That the state made a comeback could be seen in New York's unemployment rate, which was 130% of the national rate during the 1975 recession but only 85% of the national rate during the 1982 recession. Further, the state's share of the total national value of new building contracts rose and, in parallel, full-time construction employment grew substantially between 1979 and 1987: the more than 268,000 construction earners employed in 1987 represented a 76% increase from 1979 (Gurwitz 1983).

New York's full-time earners increased 15% overall between 1979 and 1987 while employment declined in all three manufacturing sectors. The greatest sources of employment increases occurred in what we have previously identified as high-growth sectors. In particular, social infrastructure contributed 37% of the growth while transactional activities contributed more than 50%. The overall earnings distribution shifted upward from the middle segment by 11% during this period and the shifts were greater in the two largest growing sectors: transactional activities shifted upward by more than 13% while social infrastructure shifted upward more than 15%.

The high-tech/medium-wage and smokestack/high-wage man-

ufacturing sectors also saw their earnings distributions shift upward, even though they experienced absolute employment declines
of approximately 20% each. In contrast, the traditional/low-wage
manufacturing sector's employment declined less than 2%. Its distribution shifted downward from the upper segment by nearly 11%:
middle earners were more than 93% of this sector. New York's 50%
unionization rate in manufacturing was the highest of the four
states analyzed and second highest in the nation. While specific
unionization rates are not available for the three manufacturing
sectors analyzed, trends suggest a union strategy of trading off employment for wage increases in the high-tech/medium-wage and
smokestack/high-wage sectors.

By taking a slightly different view of selected industry sectors
in Tables 6.7A and 6.7B, we can obtain a sense of how important
two sectors that are often the focus of economic development efforts—high technology and defense—are to New York State's economy. Just as is true nationally, the earnings distributions for these
sectors are more upwardly distributed than both the overall New
York full-time worker distribution and the distribution for most of
the nine sectors listed in Table 6.6. High-technology and defense
distributions slid backward during the 1970s and sharply reversed
themselves after 1979. High technology accounted for more than
10% of all of New York's full-time earners in 1967 and less than 8%
by 1987. The high-technology and defense sectors represented a
small as well as declining source of rising earnings. Further, New
York's earnings distributions in high technology and defense were
not nearly as upwardly shifted as those in Illinois, its sister state in
the Rustbelt.

When we look at the distribution of New York's full-time
earners by industries gaining, losing, or holding their comparative
advantage in international trade (Tables 6.8A and 6.8B), we find
that the state has the smallest proportion of earners in our study's
"Gainers" group, 5.6% in 1987, and less than the overall national
proportion discussed in chapter 4. In addition, while the distribution of earnings for the New York Gainers group has followed the
national trend, shifting upward since 1979, it has done so to a
much lesser extent than in Illinois, Texas, or California. Although
nationwide there was an increase in absolute employment numbers in the Gainers group, New York experienced a decrease. New

TABLE 6.7A

Full-Time Workers' Distribution of Earnings by High-Technology
and Defense Sectors, 1967–1973–1979–1987 (Percent)

Industry Group	Earnings Group	1967	1973	1979	1987
High Technology	Lower	2.6	0.8	1.4	0.9
	Middle	60.2	67.7	69.7	55.2
	Upper	37.2	31.5	28.9	43.9
	Total	488,891	362,330	453,429	414,981
		100.0	100.0	100.0	100.0
Defense	Lower	2.2	1.2	0.0	0.0
	Middle	54.3	57.8	65.7	52.2
	Upper	43.5	41.0	34.4	47.8
	Total	185,445	122,393	83,081	139,431
		100.0	100.0	100.0	100.0

TABLE 6.7B

High-Technology and Defense Sectors' Shares of New York State's
Full-Time Employment, 1967–1973–1979–1987

Percent of Employment	1967	1973	1979	1987
High Technology	10.5	8.3	9.7	7.7
Defense	4.0	2.8	1.8	2.6

Note: High-technology CPS codes were identified through cross-referencing with those identified in U.S. Congress, Office of Technology Assessment (1988), Table 8-4. The defense CPS codes were designated through an adaptation of the approach used by Markusen (1985b). The CPS defense group is not as extensive as that of Markusen's due to the limitation of CPS industries being identified only to the three-digit level. As a result, the CPS-identified defense group's size is likely to be underestimated.

Source: Calculated from CPS microdata files.

TABLE 6.8A

NEW YORK STATE

Full-Time Workers by Distribution of Earnings in Industries
Gaining or Losing Trade Advantage, 1967–1973–1979–1987

Industry Group	Earnings Group	1967	1973	1979	1987
Gainers	Lower %	6.8	3.6	7.4	4.3
	Middle %	63.8	70.5	68.0	63.6
	Upper %	29.5	25.8	24.7	32.1
	Total	403,040	319,701	303,335	301,052
Losers	Lower %	5.6	3.0	2.6	3.3
	Middle %	68.4	69.5	75.0	64.0
	Upper %	26.0	27.5	22.4	32.7
	Total	3,323,370	3,736,412	4,074,962	4,298,085
Holders	Lower %	5.2	13.6	1.0	1.5
	Middle %	57.8	62.4	74.7	55.0
	Upper %	36.9	36.2	24.2	43.5
	Total	130,314	242,459	231,849	111,447

TABLE 6.8B

Distribution of New York State's Full-Time Workers in Industries
Gaining or Losing Trade Advantage, 1967–1973–1979–1987

Industry Group	1967	1973	1979	1987
Gainers %	8.7	7.3	6.5	5.6
Losers %	71.4	85.6	87.4	79.9
Holders %	2.8	5.6	5.0	2.1

Note: Placement of CPS industry codes into Gainer, Loser, or Holder groups was made by cross-referencing CPS codes to the industries identified in U.S. Congress, Office of Technology Assessment (1988), Table 8-4, where industries are categorized as gaining or losing apparent advantage in trade by measuring change in the ratio of the value-added gained due to exports to the value-added lost due to imports between 1972 and 1984.

Source: Calculated from CPS microdata files.

York's Loser group has been growing, however, and that group's earnings distribution has shifted upward by more than 10% since 1979. Middle earners are now 64% of the distribution while upper earners are 33%.

Examining the 1967 to 1987 change in the relationship between levels of educational attainment and levels of earnings for New York State, we find that the earnings distribution for full-time earners with less than a high school education has shifted upward from the lower to the middle segment (Table 6.9). Among high school graduates, the earnings distribution has shifted between the lower and upper segments of the tails. For those with some college training or a bachelor degree, the distribution has shifted downward significantly from the upper to the middle group. Finally, the distribution of earnings for full-time workers with postgraduate training has remained very much the same, although postgraduate training does not appear to provide as great a return to earnings in New York as it does in California or Illinois.

Illinois

Like New York, Illinois experienced population out-migration, severe manufacturing employment losses, and overall economic performances beneath the national average during the 1967 to 1987 period. There are, though, important distinctions between the economic development path followed by the midwestern state of Illinois and that of New York in the Northeast.

Much of New York's worst economic performance had ended by the early 1980s. Such was not the case for Illinois, which did not benefit from the United States' overall bicoastal shift in growth. Illinois has been an integral part of an aging industrial heartland. The north-central portion of the Midwest, which encompasses Illinois, was the only group of states to experience net job losses in the 1980s (Markusen and Carlson 1989). Furthermore, while New York State's premier urban center—New York City—continued to gain national and international predominance over the period of analysis, Illinois's premier city—Chicago—lost status as a major urban center. Because New York City is a major international center for the movement and storage of goods, as well as for the planning, financing, accounting, and marketing of trade, its primary position has strengthened in the increasingly integrated world economy, as have the major urban centers in California (Markusen and Carlson 1989). In contrast, Chicago's status peaked during the era when the nation's growth was predominantly generated internally.

During the 1980s, Illinois did experience increases in the number of workers who were wage and salary civilian employees. The number of full-time wage and salary earners increased 12.3% while the number of part-time wage and salary earners increased 9.3%.

Four production sectors lost full-time workers between 1979 and 1987—the three manufacturing sectors and the natural resources sector (Table 6.10). Combined, the manufacturing sectors lost more than 20%, or 212,000, of their full-time wage and salary earners. The three high-growth sectors—transportation and trade, transactional activities, and social infrastructure—more than made up for the loss. They gained more than one-half million full-time earners, which represented a nearly 30% increase from 1979. After the three high-growth sectors, the personal services sector experienced the largest increase in the number of full-time earners, close to 66,000.

Illinois's middle earners increased between 1967 and 1979, but during the 1980s, a 6% increase in upper earners occurred in sectors with slow or even declining employment growth. The earnings distributions in two of the high-growth sectors—social infrastructure and transportation and trade—are lower than those for all earners combined. Only the transactional activities sector, which is the smallest of the three high-growth sectors, has a higher percentage of upper earners than average. Despite declines in the numbers of earners, the manufacturing sectors experienced larger than average shifts upward during the 1980s. The two largest manufacturing sectors, high-tech/medium-wage manufacturing and smokestack/high-wage manufacturing, each saw more than a 10% shift in earners from the middle- to the upper-earner groups, again raising the question of what role unions might have played in shifting earnings distributions.

Turning to consider how Illinois's full-time earners have fared in the high-technology and defense sectors, we can see from Tables 6.11A and 6.11B that, since 1973, the state experienced a gradual

TABLE 6.9

Full-Time Workers' Level of Educational Attainment by Level of Earnings in New York, Illinois, Texas, and California, 1967 and 1987 (Percent)

Earnings Group	Year	Educational Attainment							
		Less Than High School				High School Graduates			
		New York	Illinois	Texas	California	New York	Illinois	Texas	California
Lower	1967	8.5	7.5	13.8	7.2	5.2	4.0	7.0	3.5
	1987	6.4	7.3	13.4	13.6	3.5	3.3	7.0	3.4
Middle	1967	77.7	76.5	78.1	69.3	71.5	67.9	77.1	66.7
	1987	80.9	71.6	78.0	76.9	71.1	73.2	74.5	71.1
Upper	1967	13.9	16.0	8.1	23.5	23.3	28.1	15.9	29.8
	1987	12.7	21.0	8.6	9.5	25.4	23.5	18.5	25.5
Region	1967	34.6	35.6	37.0	25.9	36.4	35.9	32.0	33.4
Totals	1987	12.5	10.2	15.0	13.7	36.0	36.6	31.7	27.9

Educational Attainment

Earnings Group	Year	Some College				College Graduate				Postgraduate			
		New York	Illinois	Texas	California	New York	Illinois	Texas	California	New York	Illinois	Texas	California
Lower	1967	3.0	5.3	6.2	5.0	2.3	3.9	4.7	2.9	1.2	1.3	1.6	1.9
	1987	2.8	3.3	5.8	2.0	1.7	2.1	2.1	2.0	2.2	0.5	0.0	1.4
Middle	1967	59.0	56.1	66.3	58.9	41.6	44.2	54.4	32.3	33.0	29.6	47.0	21.5
	1987	67.4	63.9	67.0	62.5	48.7	54.2	54.7	42.6	33.0	34.3	37.4	25.6
Upper	1967	38.0	38.7	27.6	36.1	56.1	51.9	40.9	64.8	65.8	69.2	51.4	76.6
	1987	29.9	32.8	27.3	35.5	49.7	43.8	43.2	55.4	64.8	65.2	62.6	73.0
Region	1967	13.1	15.2	14.7	22.8	8.3	9.1	9.7	9.7	7.6	4.2	6.6	8.3
Totals	1987	21.8	25.4	25.8	28.9	16.1	15.5	15.9	16.2	13.7	12.3	11.6	13.3

Source: Calculated from CPS microdata files.

TABLE 6.10

ILLINOIS

Full-Time Workers' Distribution of Earnings by Production Sectors, 1967–1973–1979–1987 (Percent)

Production Sector	Earnings Group	1967	1973	1979	1987
High-Growth Sectors					
Transportation and Trade	Low	5.8	6.3	4.0	4.8
	Middle	65.2	64.4	72.3	66.2
	Upper	29.0	29.3	23.7	29.0
	Total	627,792	695,435	714,869	846,022
Transactional Activities	Low	3.0	3.7	2.5	1.0
	Middle	66.9	69.9	70.0	58.7
	Upper	30.2	26.3	27.5	40.3
	Total	243,703	274,851	315,330	506,602
Social Infrastructure	Low	7.3	3.5	5.0	4.1
	Middle	67.2	71.1	70.5	66.5
	Upper	25.4	25.3	24.5	29.4
	Total	486,822	669,960	737,701	921,882
Manufacturing Sectors					
Traditional/Low-Wage Manufacturing	Low	0.0	16.2	0.0	9.8
	Middle	60.0	69.5	88.1	44.3
	Upper	40.0	14.3	11.9	45.9
	Total	21,971	23,329	20,712	18,414
High-Tech/Medium-Wage Manufacturing	Low	3.3	2.6	1.2	0.9
	Middle	67.8	67.2	67.6	58.5
	Upper	28.9	30.2	31.2	40.6
	Total	884,888	847,664	826,299	677,008
Smokestack/High-Wage Manufacturing	Low	6.3	0.7	1.4	0.8
	Middle	58.2	69.0	64.3	54.2
	Upper	35.5	30.3	34.3	45.0
	Total	165,002	185,531	201,163	140,824
Other Sectors					
Natural Resources	Low	4.0	29.4	18.7	3.6
	Middle	79.7	55.8	49.6	54.5
	Upper	16.3	14.8	31.7	41.9
	Total	30,488	41,703	48,472	47,177
Construction	Low	6.4	4.0	4.6	0.0
	Middle	48.8	44.7	49.9	53.5
	Upper	44.8	51.3	45.5	46.5
	Total	130,780	122,715	148,851	169,739
Personal Services	Low	14.3	15.7	18.3	11.6
	Middle	64.0	69.8	71.0	81.0
	Upper	21.8	14.4	10.6	7.4
	Total	99,074	73,432	79,976	145,531
All Sectors	Low	5.3	4.5	3.8	3.2
	Middle	65.4	66.8	68.5	62.9
	Upper	29.3	28.7	27.7	33.9
	Total	2,689,711	2,934,621	3,093,374	3,473,199

Source: Calculated from CPS microdata files.

TABLE 6.11A

ILLINOIS

Full-Time Workers' Distribution of Earnings
by High-Technology and Defense Sectors, 1967–1973–1979–1987
(Percent)

Industry Group	Earnings Group	1967	1973	1979	1987
High Technology	Lower	6.2	1.2	0.0	1.1
	Middle	66.7	69.8	64.0	47.8
	Upper	27.1	29.0	36.0	51.1
	Total	306,982	355,633	349,533	343,510
		100.0	100.0	100.0	100.0
Defense	Lower	3.1	0.0	0.0	2.1
	Middle	70.7	70.4	48.8	44.9
	Upper	26.1	29.7	51.2	53.0
	Total	39,595	96,408	83,014	86,252
		100.0	100.0	100.0	100.0

TABLE 6.11B

High-Technology and Defense Sectors' Shares of
Illinois Full-Time Employment, 1967–1973–1979–1987

Percent of Employment	1967	1973	1979	1987
High Technology	11.4	12.1	11.3	9.9
Defense	1.5	3.3	2.7	2.5

Note: High-technology CPS codes were identified through cross-referencing with those identified in U.S. Congress, Office of Technology Assessment (1988), Table 8-4. The defense CPS codes were designated through an adaptation of the approach used by Markusen (1985b). The CPS defense group is not as extensive as that of Markusen's due to the limitation of CPS industries being identified only to the three-digit level. As a result, the CPS-identified defense group's size is likely to be underestimated.

Source: Calculated from CPS microdata files.

but steady decline in these sectors' proportions of full-time wage
and salary employment. Markusen and Carlson (1989) explained
that the defense sector's decline was due to the changing nature of
weapons production. Weaponry is increasingly made up of guidance systems, communications equipment, and scientific instruments, which are predominantly produced in states along the East,
South, and West coasts, the nation's defense perimeter.[7] The materials and machine-made parts components produced in the Midwest represent a decreasing share of weaponry.

Significant change occurred in Illinois's defense sector during
the 1970s. More than 20% of the middle-earner group shifted to the
upper-earner group; after 1979, the upper group made up more
than half of the distribution. However, the defense sector's upward
shift in Illinois was much lower than what was observed for New
York, Texas, and California. Illinois's high-technology sector experienced absolute declines since 1973, but its earnings distribution
was steadily shifting upward during the process.

Aggregating Illinois's full-time earners into sectors to assess
the impact of trade, we find the number of full-time earners employed in the Gainer group was declining since 1973 (Tables 6.12A
and 6.12B). By 1987, it was below the 1967 level. Between 1979
and 1987, there was a 24% decline in the number of full-time
earners found in industries gaining trade advantage. While New
York State also experienced declines in the number of earners in
its Gainer group, Illinois's losses were much greater. (We will see
shortly that both Texas and California have added earners to their
Gainers group during the same period.) Illinois's Loser industries
employed more than ten times as many full-time earners as did the
Gainers in 1987. The Loser group grew 6% during the 1980s. The
Holder group, made up of those industries neither gaining nor losing trade advantage, has consistently been smaller than the Loser
and Gainer groups, and the number of earners in this group declined by almost one-half, 47%, between 1979 and 1987. Earners
in the Loser group had the lowest earnings distribution, and although it shifted upward since 1979, the degree of movement was
somewhat less than that of the other two groups. It can be seen,
then, that although Illinois generally outperformed the Midwest region, its economic performance was not up to the level of even its
co-Rustbelt state, New York.

TABLE 6.12A

ILLINOIS

Full-Time Workers by Distribution of Earnings in Industries Gaining or Losing Trade Advantage, 1967–1973–1979–1987

Industry Group	Earnings Group	1967	1973	1979	1987
Gainers	Lower %	3.7	5.4	4.4	1.4
	Middle %	66.7	65.3	63.4	59.5
	Upper %	29.7	29.4	32.2	39.2
	Total	281,108	344,775	342,671	260,672
Losers	Lower %	6.3	4.3	3.6	3.5
	Middle %	66.1	67.6	69.7	64.4
	Upper %	27.6	28.2	26.7	32.1
	Total	1,823,104	2,334,638	2,534,550	2,689,439
Holders	Lower %	1.4	4.4	2.0	1.5
	Middle %	68.0	61.1	60.8	48.1
	Upper %	30.6	34.5	37.2	50.4
	Total	102,931	203,586	171,211	79,666

TABLE 6.12B

Distribution of Illinois Full-Time Workers in Industries Gaining or Losing Trade Advantage, 1967–1973–1979–1987

Industry Group	1967	1973	1979	1987
Gainers %	10.5	11.8	11.1	7.5
Losers %	67.8	79.6	81.9	77.4
Holders %	3.8	6.9	5.5	2.3

Note: Placement of CPS industry codes into Gainer, Loser, or Holder groups was made by cross-referencing CPS codes to the industries identified in U.S. Congress, Office of Technology Assessment (1988), Table 8-4, where industries are categorized as gaining or losing apparent advantage in trade by measuring change in the ratio of the value-added gained due to exports to the value-added lost due to imports between 1972 and 1984.

Source: Calculated from CPS microdata files.

The percentage of full-time earners in Illinois who lacked a high school degree in 1967 was lower than that in Texas but higher than New York's or California's percentages (see Table 6.9). By 1987, Illinois had the lowest percentage of the four states. Nevertheless, the percentage of high school dropouts who were upper earners increased 5% over the two-decade period, to 21%, a proportion more than 8% higher than any of the other three states. For the four other levels of educational attainment—high school graduate, some college, college graduate, and postgraduate training—the middle-earner segment grew between 1967 and 1987 primarily as a result of earners shifting out of the upper group. Thus, full-time earners in Illinois seemed to have been in the unique position of receiving lower returns to education over the two-decade period.

Texas

Texas is like an attractive, troublesome, and immature person who gets an inheritance—ranching—and then gets a second one—oil—and now has to grow up and get to work.[8]

Joe B. Frantz

As the above quote implies, natural resources have long been an important component of the Texas economy. In particular, oil was the driving force of the state's economy, taking the state on a roller coaster ride throughout the 1970s and 1980s.

The oil industry—and the growth of the construction industry when oil was on the upswing—attracted many migrants from the industrial heartland to Texas. Overall, the state's population growth between 1970 and the later 1980s was much higher than the national average and even that of the nation's largest state, California. During the 1970s, Texas's population grew 27%, compared to 18.5% for California. Between 1980 and 1986, the percentage increase fell to 17%, but this figure was still higher than California's at 14%.[9] In-migration accounted for 49% of Texas's population growth during the 1970s and 54% in the 1980 to 1986 period.

While Texas's earnings distribution for full-time earners was consistently higher than the rest of the South's, it was generally lower than that for New York, Illinois, or Chicago. In 1987, Texas was the only one of the four states in which upper earners were not at least 30% of full-time workers. Furthermore, low earners made up a larger percentage of the earnings distribution in Texas than in the other states. Still, the economic growth and change Texas experienced in the 1970s and 1980s led to a narrowing in the difference between the sizes of the low, middle, and upper segments of the earnings distribution in Texas and the sizes of the other state distributions.

Only one production sector, traditional/low-wage manufacturing, experienced a decline in number of earners in Texas (Table 6.13). Whereas the earnings distribution for the traditional/low-wage manufacturing sector is quite low, the sector made up an increasingly negligible portion of all full-time earners in Texas. In contrast, the sector with the second lowest earnings distribution, personal services, grew 26% during the 1980s. Low earners made up almost 15% of this sector.

The nationally identified high-growth sectors were also significant sources of growth for full-time earners in Texas. Transportation and trade, social infrastructure, and transactional activities were, respectively, the state's largest employing sectors. The earnings distributions for these three sectors tended to be lower than that of the state overall. In fact, nearly 9% of full-time workers in the largest sector, transportation and trade, were low earners in 1987, compared to 6% for the state as a whole. Transportation and trade and social infrastructure each employed more than one-quarter of the state's full-time earners. Social infrastructure provided the major source of jobs with middle-level earnings. The sector experienced an upward shift primarily from the middle to the upper segment, but its upper segment was still almost 5% smaller than the average of all sectors in the state.

The next largest sector after the high-growth sectors was high-tech/medium-wage manufacturing. In Texas, this sector was almost three times larger than the smokestack/high-wage manufacturing sector. Its earnings distribution was similar to that for the state as a whole. In contrast, the small and very slow growing smokestack/high-wage manufacturing sector has seen dramatic upward shifts in its distribution of earnings since 1973, and by 1987, nearly two-thirds of its full-time earners were in the upper group. The Texas earners in this sector appear to be elite: their distribution of earnings was substantially higher than that of any sector in any of the four states.

TABLE 6.13

TEXAS

Full-Time Workers' Distribution of Earnings by Production Sectors, 1967–1973–1979–1987

Production Sector	Earnings Group	1967	1973	1979	1987
High-Growth Sectors					
Transportation and Trade	Low	8.4	6.5	6.5	8.6
	Middle	77.0	76.4	69.9	64.5
	Upper	14.6	17.1	23.5	26.9
	Total	620,182	778,210	818,469	1,236,014
Transactional Activities	Low	6.3	3.8	3.9	5.2
	Middle	67.5	74.6	71.2	65.7
	Upper	26.2	21.6	24.9	29.1
	Total	210,265	292,310	426,447	697,806
Social Infrastructure	Low	9.6	7.1	5.2	4.9
	Middle	74.7	77.0	75.8	71.5
	Upper	15.8	15.9	19.0	23.6
	Total	522,530	774,062	945,431	1,209,822
Manufacturing Sectors					
Traditional/Low-Wage Manufacturing	Low	4.7	16.7	11.2	8.7
	Middle	75.7	72.0	69.2	76.7
	Upper	19.6	11.2	19.6	14.6
	Total	23,148	25,972	40,900	26,119
High-Tech/Medium-Wage Manufacturing	Low	4.5	3.0	4.6	4.3
	Middle	75.6	78.0	73.0	68.3
	Upper	19.9	19.0	22.5	27.4
	Total	340,422	398,942	533,009	586,585
Smokestack/High-Wage Manufacturing	Low	0.7	1.5	1.6	0.4
	Middle	53.7	61.8	47.2	35.1
	Upper	45.6	36.7	51.3	64.5
	Total	171,486	198,053	197,167	200,852
Other Sectors					
Natural Resources	Low	17.9	16.9	9.6	6.1
	Middle	64.2	64.9	69.3	54.9
	Upper	18.0	18.2	21.2	39.0
	Total	103,776	176,367	213,995	237,570
Construction	Low	5.6	4.3	6.6	2.2
	Middle	68.9	70.1	66.8	47.5
	Upper	25.5	25.6	26.6	50.3
	Total	158,937	188,113	335,677	368,703
Personal Services	Low	30.5	33.4	13.7	14.8
	Middle	63.8	61.4	78.3	72.4
	Upper	5.7	5.2	7.9	12.8
	Total	135,176	91,015	150,809	190,588
All Sectors	Low	8.8	7.0	5.8	6.0
	Middle	71.7	74.0	70.8	65.6
	Upper	19.5	19.0	23.3	28.3
	Total	2,285,918	2,923,044	3,661,904	4,654,058

Source: Calculated from CPS microdata files.

That the 1970s were a boom era for construction in Texas is verified by the sector's full-time employment growth. Between 1973 and 1979, the sector grew 78%. The distribution of earnings within the construction sector shifted very little over this high-growth period. In contrast, during the 1980s, when overall employment growth was less than 10% and the boom and bust of the state's building industry attracted widespread national attention, the earnings distribution shifted upward quite dramatically. The upper-earner group almost doubled in size, to become more than 50%, due primarily to a nearly 20% shift out of the middle group.[10]

Our final sector to examine for Texas, natural resources, is arguably its most important. As such, the relatively small number of full-time earners that it employs may come as a surprise. Still, the number of natural resource employees in Texas was far larger than that in New York or Illinois or even California. Further, the sector more than doubled in size since 1967. While the agriculture component of the sector was a decreasing source of employment as a whole due to structural shifts in agricultural production, Glasmeier (1986) has noted that its economic importance remains substantial and that it still contributes a significant portion of the state's gross regional product. Additionally, at least 22% of nondurable manufacturing employment in Texas is associated with food processing.

The oil and mining components of the natural resources sector also generate significant numbers of durable manufacturing jobs. For example, within the nonelectrical machinery industry, it has been estimated that nearly half of the workers are employed in the production of oil field machinery.[11] Thus, the natural resources sector generates significant employment outside of its own sector.

In 1967, the natural resources sector was second to the personal services sector in having the largest proportion of low earners, almost 18%. By 1987, not only had the low-earner group shrunk by two-thirds, but its share of low earners was smaller than that of the transportation and trade sector or the traditional/low-wage manufacturing sector. Furthermore, by 1987, its percentage of upper earners was the third highest among the nine production sectors. While the natural resources earnings picture is rather rosy, Texans are rightfully concerned about what will happen "when the

well runs dry." As we all know, oil and mine resources are nonrenewable.

With Texas being one of the most aggressive states, to what
extent can the nationally much sought after sectors of high technology and defense be looked toward to meet the state's future employment needs? Tables 6.14A and 6.14B indicate that both high
technology and the defense sector within it grew significantly during the 1980s. Even so, the high-technology sector made up only
7.5% of all full-time employment in Texas, a proportion lower than
that of New York, Illinois, or California. While the earnings distributions of high technology and defense were quite high and shifted
upward by more than 10% since 1979, it does not appear that large
numbers of future Texans will be employed in these sectors.

When we consider how well Texas's full-time earners were sit-
uated given trends in international trade, we find a picture quite
similar to that of the other states (Tables 6.15A and 6.15B). The
industries assessed to be losing trade advantage employed the vast
majority of the full-time earners, and their earnings distribution
was quite parallel to the state's overall. Unlike Illinois and New
York, Texas added employees, although the number is relatively
small, to industries assessed to be gaining trade advantage and that
had a somewhat higher earnings distribution. The size of the
earner group of industries holding their own shrank, as it did elsewhere. This distribution was nearly equally split between middle
and upper earners.

The level of educational attainment among Texas's full-time
earners was fairly similar to that for the other states at the postsecondary levels and diverges below that (see Table 6.9). The state
had the highest percentage of workers without a high school degree. There was virtually no change in the earnings distribution for
high school dropouts in Texas between 1967 and 1987. Among high
school graduates, the distribution of earnings had shifted upward,
but the upper-earner group at this level was significantly smaller
than that in the other states. Workers with some college training or
a bachelor degree saw little to no change in their earnings distributions while more than 10% of those with postgraduate training
shifted from the middle- to the upper-earner group. Texas was the
only state in which a college degree or a postgraduate education

TABLE 6.14A

TEXAS

Full-Time Workers' Distribution of Earnings by High-Technology and Defense Sectors, 1967–1973–1979–1987 (Percent)

Industry Group	Earnings Group	1967	1973	1979	1987
High Technology	Lower	0.8	0.0	2.5	2.3
	Middle	54.3	71.1	61.2	47.5
	Upper	45.0	28.9	36.4	50.3
	Total	157,541	160,119	214,214	347,794
		100.0	100.0	100.0	100.0
Defense	Lower	1.6	0.0	0.0	0.0
	Middle	60.8	72.8	66.6	53.7
	Upper	37.6	27.2	33.5	46.3
	Total	75,949	62,531	70,862	132,053
		100.0	100.0	100.0	100.0

TABLE 6.14B

High-Technology and Defense Sectors' Shares of Texas Full-Time Employment, 1967–1973–1979–1987

Percent of Employment	1967	1973	1979	1987
High Technology	6.9	5.5	5.9	7.5
Defense	3.3	2.1	1.9	2.8

Note: High-technology CPS codes were identified through cross-referencing with those identified in U.S. Congress, Office of Technology Assessment (1988), Table 8-4. The defense CPS codes were designated through an adaptation of the approach used by Markusen (1985b). The CPS defense group is not as extensive as that of Markusen's due to the limitation of CPS industries being identified only to the three-digit level. As a result, the CPS-identified defense group's size is likely to be underestimated.

Source: Calculated from CPS microdata files.

TABLE 6.15A

TEXAS

Full-Time Workers by Distribution of Earnings in Industries Gaining or Losing Trade Advantage, 1967–1973–1979–1987 (Standard Definition of the Middle, 50% to 200% of All-Earner Median)

Industry Group	Earnings Group	1967	1973	1979	1987
Gainers	Lower %	9.4	10.5	7.5	5.5
	Middle %	71.3	69.2	59.9	60.8
	Upper %	19.3	20.3	32.7	33.7
	Total	234,611	380,287	373,512	376,753
Losers	Lower %	9.1	6.0	5.6	6.5
	Middle %	71.2	75.0	72.4	66.1
	Upper %	19.7	19.0	22.0	27.3
	Total	1,619,652	2,382,591	3,132,424	3,632,506
Holders	Lower %	0.0	1.6	3.6	0.0
	Middle %	72.8	79.5	64.8	51.3
	Upper %	27.2	18.9	31.6	48.7
	Total	52,016	108,480	106,236	76,339

TABLE 6.15B

Distribution of Texas Full-Time Workers in Industries Gaining or Losing Trade Advantage, 1967–1973–1979–1987

Industry Group	1967	1973	1979	1987
Gainers %	10.3	13.0	10.2	8.1
Losers %	70.9	81.5	85.5	78.1
Holders %	2.3	3.7	2.9	1.6

Note: Placement of CPS industry codes into Gainer, Loser, or Holder groups was made by cross-referencing CPS codes to the industries identified in U.S. Congress, Office of Technology Assessment (1988), Table 8-4, where industries are categorized as gaining or losing apparent advantage in trade by measuring change in the ratio of the value-added gained due to exports to the value-added lost due to imports between 1972 and 1984.

Source: Calculated from CPS microdata files.

provided increasing returns to earnings; in New York, Illinois, and California, the percentage of upper earners with postsecondary degrees declined.

California

This final section of the regional analyses of the changing earnings distribution is an in-depth analysis of the state of California. Changes in California's economy and earnings distribution are particularly relevant for understanding the relationship between the changing earnings distribution and the "debate over the disappearing middle" for several reasons. First of all, California is the nation's largest state and accounted for more than 11% of the entire population in 1987. During the 1980s, its population grew 17%—twice as fast as the national average. More than 9% of this growth was due to net in-migration, a rate four times higher than that for the nation as a whole.[12] California has, arguably, the most diverse population in the country. Ethnic minorities have become the majority.

Second, California's economy is also the largest in the country and, in fact, contributes a larger share to the gross national product—nearly 13%[13]—than it does to the nation's population. Indeed, California has been called a nation-state and one of the largest industrial economies in the world. This economy of California has always been on the leading edge of postwar industrialism. "High technology" originated in California's Silicon Valley. Not unrelated, the defense industry has always had a strong presence in the state, a presence that firmly established itself with shipbuilding and aircraft building during World War II. From its combination of population and economic growth, California projected to the rest of the nation and the world a seemingly Teflon-like ability to ride out downturns in the business cycle during the 1980s.[14]

However, as Teitz and Shapira (1989) observed in the late 1980s: "California's aggregate growth conceals great turbulence within its economy." They noted that the state was experiencing massive deindustrialization, with high levels of plant closures and worker layoffs, and its economy had become increasingly vulnerable to national and international economic and political uncertainties.

We will now consider the impacts California's population and economic growth has had on its labor force, earning opportunities, and the ability to attain a middle standard of living. Over the twenty-year period, more than 5.6 million workers were added to the California economy. In 1967, 44% of the total employment was part-time; by 1987, 40% was part-time. This decline in the percentage of all earners who are part-time workers runs counter to notions of the growth of the part-time labor force associated with industrial restructuring, that is, the shift to service-related employment, and with demographic shifts in the labor force, such as the increased participation of women. Females were 54% of California's part-time labor force in 1967 and 57% in 1987. However, they were 31% of the full-time labor force in 1967 and 40% in 1987.

Consequently, claims and expectations that the part-time labor force grew due to significant numbers of females entering the labor force over the two-decade period are not supported by the California picture. Still, claims that industrial restructuring led to the growth of the part-time labor force cannot be as easily dismissed since our data source, the U.S. Census Bureau's Current Population Survey, only tells us about workers in the formal economy.[15] If it were possible to include employment data on California's informal economy, it is quite possible that part-time employment would have increased as a proportion of all employment. Data on informal economy employment might also help to explain another anomaly about California's part-time employment. Nationwide, the percentage of part-time workers who would rather be working full-time—the involuntary part-time workers—rose from 9% to 19% between 1968 and 1987.[16] The percentage of involuntary part-time employment for the last decade, 1978 to 1988, in California has declined from 9.8% to 7.9%.[17] The much lower percentage of involuntary part-time employment in the late 1980s for California compared to that for the nation may be a result of involuntary part-time employees being displaced to the informal economy.

California workers have consistently had higher wages than those of the nation as a whole. In 1967, the state's full-time workers in the low-earner group were 5%, compared to 7% for the nation. The percentage of middle earners nationwide was higher than that for California, that is, 67%, compared to 59%. However, this was because of the state's higher percentage of upper earners: they were 37% in California, compared to 25% for the nation. Over the next two decades, California's distribution of low, middle, and upper earners changed very little. In contrast, the low-earner group nationwide decreased slightly, around 2%, while the upper-earner group increased 5% and was now 30% of full-time earners. As a result, California's full-time workers were still in a superior earning position compared to the rest of the country, but their advantage was slipping as their earnings distribution did not experience the upward-shifting trend.[18]

Part-time workers in California had a different earnings picture (see Table 6.19). We would expect the majority of part-time workers to fall into the low-earner group, and this was consistently the case; however, there was no reason a priori to expect that the part-time earnings distribution for California, as well as for the nation, would not shift upward, like that of full-time workers nationwide, or, at least, remain stable, like that of full-time workers in the state. Both part-time earnings distributions showed a bimodal trend, though. Between 1967 and 1987, the California low-earner group grew from 57% to 61% while the nation's group grew 1.5% to 66.0%. The size of the middle-earner group in California fell more than 4% while that for the nation fell 2%. The upper-earner group increased slightly among the state's and the nation's part-time workers. A trend toward bimodalism was surfacing over this period. More significantly, the part-time workers' shift to the low-earner group in California indicated that their position in the state's labor market was eroding.

Further evidence of this erosion can be found in a comparison between 1977 and 1987 of the change in the ratio of median earnings for California's part-time as well as full-time workers to that for the nation as a whole. Beginning with California's full-time workers, their median earnings figure was 45% higher than the median for the nation in 1977. By 1987, the median for California had increased to 64%.

In contrast, little change occurred in the ratio of median earnings for part-time workers overall to that of the nation. The figure was 38% in 1977 and 37% in 1987. However, significant changes occurred among different demographic groups within the part-time labor force. The ratio of California males' part-time earnings dropped from 8% to 9%, depending on the race of the male. In contrast, female part-time earners' ratios increased from 1% to 4%, depending on their race; these ratios were still lower than those for the males, just as was the case with full-time earners.

We noted earlier that the full-time workers' distribution of earnings in 1987 was very similar to that in 1967. Thus, California's full-time earners did not experience the same overall twenty-year upward movement in real terms that the nation as a whole experienced. From Table 6.16, it can be seen that the full-time earners distribution shifted downward significantly, by nearly 8%, between 1967 and 1979; then between 1979 and 1987, it returned to its overall shape of the late 1960s, in which middle earners were approximately 59% and upper earners almost 37% of all full-time earners.

The transportation and trade sector was the dominant employer of full-time earners in 1967, with 23% of the state's total. Relative to the three other largest sectors—social infrastructure, high-tech/medium-wage manufacturing, and transactional activities—it did not grow as fast over the next two decades. By 1987, it had increased 22% and had fewer earners than social infrastructure, which increased 25%. The percentage of transportation and trade workers who were middle earners grew slightly from 1967 to 1987, primarily as a result of upper earners moving down. In contrast, the entire earnings distribution of the faster-growing social infrastructure sector shifted upward, so that by 1987, the upper-earner group was 42.3%. While, in general, the earnings distributions of all the sectors shifted downward during the 1970s and then reversed their movement and shifted upward during the 1980s, the degree to which social infrastructure shifted upward was the most significant. The fourth largest sector, transactional activities, also shifted upward more than average, and upper earners are now more than 40%.

In contrast, the third largest sector, high-tech/medium-wage manufacturing, had significant downward movement in its distribution. This sector made up nearly 70% of all manufacturing employment. Smokestack/high-wage manufacturing employment comprised another 26% but declined as a share of overall employment at the same time that its earnings distribution was shifting upward. Upper earners became more than half of the distribution.

TABLE 6.16

CALIFORNIA

Full-Time Workers' Distribution of Earnings by Production Sectors, 1967–1973–1979–1987 (Percent)

Production Sector	Earnings Group	1967	1973	1979	1987
High-Growth Sectors					
Transportation and Trade	Low	5.4	5.8	4.6	5.1
	Middle	62.3	69.3	67.4	64.1
	Upper	32.3	24.9	28.0	30.8
	Total	1,060,287	1,104,204	1,428,504	1,802,393
Transactional Activities	Low	3.6	5.0	3.4	2.8
	Middle	65.0	64.9	68.1	57.0
	Upper	31.4	30.2	28.5	40.2
	Total	476,525	487,022	778,017	1,241,913
Social Infrastructure	Low	4.4	2.4	2.8	1.3
	Middle	58.1	67.5	67.3	56.4
	Upper	37.5	30.1	29.9	42.3
	Total	976,587	1,430,003	1,583,425	1,995,835
Manufacturing Sectors					
Traditional/Low-Wage Manufacturing	Low	5.6	5.7	6.3	7.9
	Middle	80.7	81.3	82.8	81.0
	Upper	13.7	13.0	10.9	11.0
	Total	55,559	83,686	47,751	86,540
High-Tech/Medium-Wage Manufacturing	Low	3.0	2.5	2.6	6.0
	Middle	56.0	70.2	68.4	57.5
	Upper	41.1	27.3	29.0	36.5
	Total	892,416	835,260	1,104,970	1,410,896
Smokestack/High-Wage Manufacturing	Low	1.3	0.8	1.0	2.1
	Middle	48.4	65.3	48.2	41.9
	Upper	50.3	33.9	50.8	55.9
	Total	382,839	379,875	384,603	516,028
Other Sectors					
Natural Resources	Low	6.2	8.2	8.6	5.8
	Middle	65.8	76.6	69.1	78.6
	Upper	28.0	15.3	22.4	15.5
	Total	109,654	110,510	136,844	179,382
Construction	Low	1.2	6.3	5.2	1.2
	Middle	40.8	46.6	56.3	56.4
	Upper	58.1	47.1	38.5	42.5
	Total	214,731	225,676	266,193	407,467

TABLE 6.16 (continued)

CALIFORNIA

Full-Time Workers' Distribution of Earnings by Production Sectors, 1967–1973–1979–1987 (Percent)

Production Sector	Earnings Group	1967	1973	1979	1987
Personal Services	Low	16.3	20.1	12.8	10.4
	Middle	63.8	65.6	76.4	66.1
	Upper	19.9	14.3	10.8	23.5
	Total	259,459	238,226	278,663	431,962
All Sectors					
	Low	4.6	4.6	3.9	3.9
	Middle	58.5	67.3	66.5	58.7
	Upper	36.9	28.1	29.6	37.4
	Total	4,428,056	4,894,462	6,008,968	8,072,414

Source: Calculated from CPS microdata files.

While quite small, the traditional/low-wage manufacturing sector deserves notice because of the erratic growth pattern it displayed. The sector grew 50% from 1967 to 1973, declined by more than 40% from 1973 to 1979, and then increased more than 80% between 1979 and 1987. The growth of this sector in the 1980s is suggestive of Sassen's (1988) observations about low-wage manufacturing employment growth, which was absorbing new immigrant labor in major metropolitan areas; California has been the foremost "absorber" of immigrants in the nation.

Next to traditional/low-wage manufacturing, the natural resources sector had the least number of full-time earners, less than 180,000, but it has shown steady gains over the last twenty years. At the same time, and demonstrating the opposite pattern of natural resources in Texas, the earnings distribution shifted downward significantly, more than 12%, from the upper to the middle group. The construction sector, which nearly doubled in size, also saw a downward shift of 16% in its distribution but was still one of the highest distributions.

When the portion of California's full-time earners who fall into the separate and smaller high-technology and defense sectors classification are examined (Tables 6.17A and 6.17B), we find that the

TABLE 6.17A

CALIFORNIA

Full-Time Workers' Distribution of Earnings by High-Technology and Defense Sectors, 1967–1973–1979–1987 (Percent)

Industry Group	Earnings Group	1967	1973	1979	1987
High Technology	Lower	1.8	1.3	1.1	3.0
	Middle	48.9	63.9	66.4	49.0
	Upper	49.3	34.9	32.5	48.0
	Total	507,994	436,691	585,234	852,819
		100.0	100.0	100.0	100.0
Defense	Lower	1.6	1.0	0.6	2.0
	Middle	44.6	59.2	50.7	39.1
	Upper	53.8	39.8	48.6	58.9
	Total	312,797	281,394	323,872	656,567
		100.0	100.0	100.0	100.0

TABLE 6.17B

High-Technology and Defense Sectors' Shares of California's Full-Time Employment, 1967–1973–1979–1987

Percent of Employment	1967	1973	1979	1987
High Technology	11.5	8.9	9.7	10.6
Defense	7.1	5.8	5.4	8.1

Note: High-technology CPS codes were identified through cross-referencing with those identified in U.S. Congress, Office of Technology Assessment (1988), Table 8-4. The defense CPS codes were designated through an adaptation of the approach used by Markusen (1985b). The CPS defense group is not as extensive as that of Markusen's due to the limitation of CPS industries being identified only to the three-digit level. As a result, the CPS-identified defense group's size is likely to be underestimated.

Source: Calculated from CPS microdata files.

high-technology sector was greater, though not by much, than that of New York State, Illinois, or Texas and that the defense sector was significantly larger, more than 5%. Both sectors' earnings distributions followed the general pattern of the state overall, shifting downward in the 1970s and then strongly reversing this movement during the 1980s. The high-technology sector was nearly evenly split between middle and upper earners in 1987 while the defense sector was almost 40% middle earners and almost 60% upper earners.

In reaggregating all of California's full-time earners to obtain a sense of how well they have fared in light of changes in international trade patterns, we find, as we did for the other states, that the vast majority—76% in 1987—were employed in industries assessed to be losing trade advantage (Tables 6.18A and 6.18B). As was the case for all full-time earners combined, the earnings distribution of this large Loser sector shifted upward significantly since 1979, only to resume its 1967 shape. Middle earners were more than 60% of the Loser group while upper earners were almost 36%. In comparison, the much smaller Gainer sector, less than 10%, had a significantly higher distribution of earnings in 1987. Further, the Gainers' distribution was above its 1967 level. Middle earners were about 54% and upper earners were more than 42%. California shared with its co-Sunbelt state the good fortune of seeing its Gainer sector grow in the number of full-time earners it employs. However, California's sector grew by more than two hundred thousand, compared to only slightly more than three thousand for Texas (see Table 6.15A). We previously saw that the Gainer sector had lost full-time workers in both New York and Illinois.

Table 6.19 presents the distribution of earnings for the nine major production sectors employing part-time workers in 1967 and 1987. We noted earlier that the part-time earnings distribution had actually shifted downward between 1967 and 1987, much of which can be attributed to the 5% movement of middle earners to the lower segment in the sector employing the largest numbers of part-time earners, transportation and trade.

However, other sectors had almost unbelievable downward shifts. For example, in 1967, the traditional/low-wage sector was made up of almost 14% low earners, more than 77% middle earners, and 9% upper earners. Two decades later, 73% of the earners were

TABLE 6.18A

CALIFORNIA

Full-Time Workers by Distribution of Earnings in Industries Gaining or Losing Trade Advantage, 1967–1973–1979–1987

Industry Group	Earnings Group	1967	1973	1979	1987
Gainers	Lower %	5.1	2.8	4.4	4.1
	Middle %	57.6	72.6	60.1	53.5
	Upper %	37.3	24.6	35.5	42.4
	Total	417,197	500,543	533,470	751,086
Losers	Lower %	4.8	4.6	3.7	4.2
	Middle %	59.6	67.1	67.6	60.1
	Upper %	35.6	28.3	28.7	35.8
	Total	3,110,847	4,130,920	5,160,101	6,138,237
Holders	Lower %	1.7	3.4	1.4	0.0
	Middle %	52.6	58.2	56.4	52.1
	Upper %	45.6	38.4	42.2	47.9
	Total	109,504	194,735	223,644	167,508

TABLE 6.18B

Distribution of California's Full-Time Workers in Industries Gaining or Losing Trade Advantage, 1967–1973–1979–1987

Industry Group	1967	1973	1979	1987
Gainers %	9.4	10.2	8.9	9.3
Losers %	70.3	84.4	85.9	76.0
Holders %	2.5	4.0	3.7	2.1

Note: Placement of CPS industry codes into Gainer, Loser, or Holder groups was made by cross-referencing CPS codes to the industries identified in U.S. Congress, Office of Technology Assessment (1988), Table 8-4, where industries are categorized as gaining or losing apparent advantage in trade by measuring change in the ratio of the value-added gained due to exports to the value-added lost due to imports between 1972 and 1984.

Source: Calculated from CPS microdata files.

TABLE 6.19

Part-Time Workers' Distribution of Earnings by Production
Sectors, 1967 and 1987 (Percent)

Production Sector	Earnings Group	1967	1987
High-Growth Sectors			
Transportation and Trade	Low	64.5	69.7
	Middle	32.8	27.7
	Upper	2.7	2.6
	Total	981,419	1,631,502
Transactional Activities	Low	49.4	58.6
	Middle	45.2	36.5
	Upper	5.4	4.9
	Total	278,267	612,897
Social Infrastructure	Low	55.4	53.6
	Middle	41.8	38.1
	Upper	2.8	8.4
	Total	729,003	1,289,169
Manufacturing Sectors			
Traditional/Low-Wage Manufacturing	Low	13.7	73.0
	Middle	77.3	27.0
	Upper	9.0	0.0
	Total	30,907	38,079
High-Tech/Medium-Wage Manufacturing	Low	45.1	50.2
	Middle	45.4	42.6
	Upper	9.5	7.2
	Total	461,067	537,695
Smokestack/High-Wage Manufacturing	Low	23.2	30.5
	Middle	67.4	65.7
	Upper	9.4	3.9
	Total	118,508	124,107
Other Sectors			
Natural Resources	Low	83.1	73.9
	Middle	16.4	24.7
	Upper	0.6	1.4
	Total	177,676	249,468
Construction	Low	6.8	45.4
	Middle	22.1	39.8
	Upper	71.1	14.8
	Total	495,517	372,968

TABLE 6.19 (continued)

CALIFORNIA

Part-Time Workers' Distribution of Earnings by Production
Sectors, 1967 and 1987 (Percent)

Production Sector	Earnings Group	1967	1987
Personal Services	Low	76.4	74.9
	Middle	19.9	19.2
	Upper	3.7	5.9
	Total	517,758	575,542
All Sectors	Low	57.3	60.9
	Middle	37.6	33.3
	Upper	5.0	5.8
	Total	3,473,754	5,431,428

Source: Calculated from CPS microdata files.

in the low group and the remaining 27% were in the middle group. In the construction sector in 1967, almost 7% of the earners were in the low group, more than 22% were in the middle group, and more than 71% were in the upper group. By 1987, more than 45% in part-time construction were low earners, almost 40% were middle earners, and almost 15% were upper earners. Part-time workers can be workers who work full-time hours—thirty-five hours or more per week—but not year-round or who work year-round—fifty weeks or more—but not full-time hours or who work some combination of these two factors. It is not possible to say to what extent the extreme downward shifts in these two sectors were due to less hours of work or lower wages received per hours worked, but what we can determine is that the use of part-time labor in these sectors changed so much so that construction and traditional manufacturing offered much lower earnings opportunities.

Turning now to consider the relationship between earnings levels and levels of educational attainment among California's workers, we can look back to Table 6.9 to see that full-time earners in the state had higher levels of postsecondary education than in New York, Illinois, or Texas, which was primarily due to the much larger proportion of earners in the category of "some college but not a bachelor degree." Between 1967 and 1987, the earnings distribution for full-time workers without a high school degree dramatically shifted downward. More than 23.0% of this group were upper earners in 1967 but now only 9.5% are; the percentage of low earners has increased from more than 7% to almost 14%. The earnings distribution of full-time earners who are college graduates has also shifted downward substantially. Almost 65% of college graduates were upper earners in 1967, compared to more than 55% in 1987. California's full-time earners with postgraduate training had the highest levels of earnings out of the states analyzed; nearly three-quarters were in the upper-earner group.

Examining the relationship between levels of educational attainment and earnings and production sectors for the last ten years, Table 6.20 indicates that the significant upward shift in earnings of workers in the social infrastructure sector was accompanied by parallel shifts in educational attainment. Education and earnings levels shifted upward for full-time workers in the transportation and trade sector and dramatically so for the high-tech/medium-wage manufacturing and transactional activities sectors. Two of the smaller sectors also showed similar experiences: smokestack/high-wage manufacturing and, surprisingly, personal services. Workers in the remaining three sectors—natural resources, construction, and traditional/low-wage manufacturing—were characterized by declining educational attainment levels and declines in the percentages who are upper earners.

Among the part-time labor force, the downward shift in the earnings distribution of the largest sector, transportation and trade—70% were low earners in 1987, compared to 65% in 1977—was accompanied by a decline in the level of educational attainment of its workers. Its percentage of part-time workers with less than a high school degree increased from more than 27% to 32%, with corresponding decreases in the percentage of workers with high school degrees and college-level training.

The social infrastructure sector showed the opposite trend. Part-time workers improved their already high levels of educational attainment: 70% had postsecondary training. Their higher level of educational attainment has been accompanied by an upward shift in the earnings distribution. Upper earners among part-time social infrastructure workers were 4% in 1977 and 8% in 1987.

TABLE 6.20

CALIFORNIA

Full- and Part-Time Workers by Level of Educational Attainment, 1977 and 1987 (Percent)

Production Sector	Full 1977	Full 1987	Part 1977	Part 1987
High-Growth Sectors				
Transportation and Trade				
Less than High School Degree	18.7	14.6	27.1	32.0
High School Degree	34.0	33.3	28.4	26.6
Some College	33.3	33.6	35.0	32.9
Four Years College	10.0	14.6	6.0	5.7
Graduate School	4.0	3.9	3.5	2.9
Transactional Activities				
Less than High School Degree	4.8	5.7	15.7	10.2
High School Degree	32.0	26.5	28.5	32.4
Some College	40.5	32.3	36.6	36.7
Four Years College	16.0	22.5	9.6	15.1
Graduate School	6.6	12.9	9.7	5.6
Social Infrastructure				
Less than High School Degree	7.1	3.6	12.9	10.4
High School Degree	21.0	19.6	20.4	20.0
Some College	28.7	29.9	32.7	33.6
Four Years College	13.3	17.8	10.5	14.0
Graduate School	29.9	29.1	23.4	22.0
Manufacturing Sectors				
Traditional/Low-Wage Manufacturing				
Less than High School Degree	45.4	66.7	50.2	46.3
High School Degree	37.4	30.7	42.5	37.6
Some College	11.1	2.6	3.6	13.6
Four Years College	1.9	0.0	3.7	2.6
Graduate School	4.2	0.0	0.0	0.0
High-Tech/Medium-Wage Manufacturing				
Less than High School Degree	24.2	23.6	38.7	32.3
High School Degree	33.0	28.9	27.8	26.7
Some College	27.7	21.0	24.3	28.1
Four Years College	8.4	16.1	6.1	7.7
Graduate School	6.7	10.4	3.1	5.1
Smokestack/High-Wage Manufacturing				
Less than High School Degree	20.1	12.4	17.9	15.4
High School Degree	25.4	27.0	42.9	20.6
Some College	32.7	25.9	33.1	38.9
Four Years College	10.6	18.9	0.0	11.4
Graduate School	11.3	15.8	6.1	13.8

TABLE 6.20 (continued)

CALIFORNIA

Full- and Part-Time Workers by Level of Educational Attainment, 1977 and 1987 (Percent)

Production Sector	Full 1977	Full 1987	Part 1977	Part 1987
Other Sectors				
Natural Resources				
Less than High School Degree	36.7	37.7	72.7	72.4
High School Degree	34.9	29.5	14.1	12.0
Some College	18.7	24.3	9.4	12.2
Four Years College	6.9	2.6	1.2	1.7
Graduate School	2.9	5.9	2.7	1.7
Construction				
Less than High School Degree	16.2	20.2	25.3	41.9
High School Degree	32.8	40.1	40.1	32.5
Some College	34.1	29.8	28.3	18.3
Four Years College	7.7	9.1	5.0	6.6
Graduate School	9.2	0.9	1.3	0.7
Personal Services				
Less than High School Degree	24.1	22.2	42.8	34.5
High School Degree	32.1	32.3	22.3	27.4
Some College	1.9	30.8	27.2	26.5
Four Years College	9.2	9.7	6.0	9.2
Graduate School	2.6	5.1	1.8	2.3
Total				
Less than High School Degree	15.8	13.7	27.0	27.0
High School Degree	29.4	27.9	26.7	25.5
Some College	31.3	28.9	30.8	30.4
Four Years College	11.1	16.2	6.9	9.3
Graduate School	12.5	13.3	8.6	7.9

Source: Calculated from CPS microdata files.

What do the trends in earnings levels, sectoral shifts, and levels of educational attainment mean for the state of California? The trends of the second decade appear to bolster the U.S. Congress, Office of Technology Assessment's (1988) prediction for the nation that: "Inequality in education may well become the most significant source of wage inequality." Full-time workers' levels of educational attainment increased significantly and so did their earnings. Part-time workers' overall levels of educational attainment improved somewhat, but not in all sectors. Further, the percentage of part-time workers without high school degrees was twice as high as that for full-time workers, and the part-time earnings distribution actually shifted downward.

The U.S. Department of Labor's (DOL) projections to the year 2000 for occupational employment also support the idea that levels of educational attainment are becoming increasingly important. DOL projects that the share of total employment held by occupations requiring the highest education levels is expected to increase through the end of the twentieth century while the share for occupations requiring the least amount of education will decline.

For example, each of the three broad occupational groups with the most highly trained workers in terms of educational attainment—executive, administrative, and managerial workers; professional workers; and technicians and related support workers—is projected to continue to grow more rapidly than the average for total employment. Collectively, these three groups, which accounted for 25% of the total employment in 1986, are expected to account for almost 40% of the total job growth between 1986 and 2000. In contrast, many factors, such as office and factory automation, changes in consumer demand, and import substitution, are expected to lead to relatively slow growth or a decline for occupational groups requiring less education, such as administrative support workers, including clerical; farming, forestry, and fishing workers; and operators, fabricators, and laborers.[19]

In the late 1980s, the DOL attempted to determine the implications of its projections for blacks and Hispanics in the labor force, and its findings are especially pertinent to California given the large and growing percentage of workers who are ethnic minorities. The DOL's data showed that, nationwide, blacks and Hispanics accounted for a greater proportion of persons employed in occupations projected to grow more slowly or to actually decline. These are the occupations with the lowest education requirements. In parallel, blacks and Hispanics were underrepresented in the occupations projected to grow the fastest and that also require the greatest amount of education. The implication of the DOL's analyses is that blacks and Hispanics, both nationwide and in the state of California, must increase their levels of educational attainment so that they can pursue the most favorable job opportunities. If they do not, their primary source of employment will be increasingly in the service worker group.[20]

The earnings data for California's full-time workers showed that they had the highest level or most upward skewed distribution of earnings of all the geographic categories analyzed in this chapter: the nation as a whole; the four main census regions; and the largest state in each census region. When, however, we look beyond earnings to how workers' pensions and healthcare are provided for, and to the ability of earnings to enable home ownership, it will quickly become evident that the position of California's full-time workers is inferior relative to the rest of the nation.

Workers' Abilities to Attain a Middle Standard of Living in New York, Illinois, Texas, and California

As we have done at other regional levels, we will now relate the pattern of fringe benefit recipiency, in this section, and costs of home ownership, in the following section, to full-time workers' abilities to attain a middle standard of living. The distinctions among the states and their regions in these components of the middle-class consumer basket are marked and provide insight into how intense development and dedevelopment affect the attainability and stability of American workers' desired standard of living.

Our data on fringe benefit recipiency, it may be recalled, cover the period of 1979 to 1987, and they indicate that there have been across-the-board declines in benefit recipiency during the 1980s. New York's full-time earners experienced a 7.5% decline in those who were included in a pension plan accompanied by smaller declines in health coverage (see Table 6.2). Illinois's full-time earners experienced the greatest decline in the percentage included in a pension plan, an 8.3% decline; even so, they had the highest percentage included in a pension plan, more than 60%, the highest percentage included in an employer's group health plan, more than 80%, and the highest percentage for whom an employer helped pay for group health, more than 76%. This is surprising given that union membership, which is generally associated with higher benefit levels, in Illinois was lower than its co-Rustbelt state, New York.[21]

In 1979, California's full-time earners ranked third in the proportion who were included in pension plans, group health plans, and whose employers helped pay for group health. The subsequent declines in the levels of pension and group health provisions were great enough for California's workers that by 1987 they ranked last of the four states.

When we look at benefit recipiency among full-time earners in Texas, we find they have done fairly well since 1979. Levels of benefit recipiency by all three categories in Table 6.2 were lowest for Texans in 1979, but the subsequent declines in recipiency were the smallest of the four states. As a result, California now has lower percentages of full-time earners included in pension and group health plans than does Texas.

Further examination of California has shown that the across-the-board declines in the pension and health benefit recipiency first observed for full-time earners from 1979 were evident for full- and part-time workers during the middle 1980s. The biggest declines occurred in the percentage of full-time workers who were included in employer group health plans for all three earnings levels. Lower earners experienced the greatest declines in coverage. Among full-time earners, the greatest declines of employers paying for *all* of the costs of group health were found among those with the lowest earnings while the reverse was true for part-time earners.

This California pattern of benefit recipiency was a more extreme version of the national pattern of benefit recipiency that has had the effect of further skewing the earnings/compensation distribution. To the extent that the California trend is a precursor to that for other states, as well as a trend that has been amplified by the growing crisis in health insurance coverage since 1987, this critical component of the middle-class consumption package was becoming less attainable and/or secure.

Regional Variations in the Preeminent Middle-Class Consumption Item: The Cost and Rate of Home Ownership

Although there was a marked trend toward convergence in the shapes of the earnings distributions of the four regions and of the production sectors within the four regions, there did not appear to

be a parallel trend toward convergence in housing prices and in the
rate of home ownership among the four regions. In fact, the trend
was just the opposite—toward divergence.

For example, the median sales price of new one-family homes
sold in each of the four regions was much more similar in 1967
than in 1987 (Table 6.21). The South consistently had the lowest
median sales price for the new one-family house while the Northeast and West traded places for the highest median price over the
decade of the seventies. However, the Northeast's price was highest
of the four regions in 1967 and 1987. In 1967, the Northeast's median house price was $6,000, or 31% higher than the South's; by
1987, it was $52,000, or 59% higher than the South's.

For those who aspire to the middle-class dream, we can look
at regional variations in the house price of the representative first
home. The South again consistently had the lowest price for this
home, but the West had the highest price in 1967 and 1979 while

TABLE 6.21

Housing Price Indexes by Region, 1967–1973–1979–1987

Housing Indicator	Year	Northeast	Midwest	South	West
Median Sales Price of New One-	1967	$25,400	$25,100	$19,400	$24,100
Family Houses Sold [1]	1973	$37,100	$32,900	$30,900	$32,400
	1979	$65,500	$63,900	$57,300	$69,600
	1987	$140,000	$95,000	$88,000	$111,000
% Increase in Price	67–73	46.1	31.1	59.3	34.4
	73–79	76.5	94.2	85.4	114.8
	79–87	113.7	48.7	53.6	59.5
House Price of Representative	1967	$17,797	$16,350	$15,206	$18,318
First Home [2]	1973	$28,157	$22,628	$21,295	$25,783
	1979	$46,657	$41,823	$38,165	$58,559
	1987	$93,844	$56,562	$55,142	$82,285
% Increase in Price	67–73	58.2	38.4	40.0	40.8
	73–79	65.7	84.8	79.2	127.1
	79–87	101.1	35.2	44.5	40.5
Home Ownership Rates of 35	1973	62.2	76.0	68.7	65.2
to 39 Year Olds (%)	1980	65.8	78.0	71.7	66.1
	1987	62.0	69.7	65.8	55.6

Sources: [1] U.S. Department of Commerce and U.S. Department of Housing and Urban
Development (annual); [2] Apgar and Brown (1988).

the Northeast had the highest price in 1973 and 1987. In 1967, the price of the representative first home in the most expensive region, the West, was $3,112, or 20% higher than one in the South; by 1987, the price in the most expensive region, the Northeast, was $38,702, or 70% higher than that of the South's.

Although the South consistently had the lowest house prices, the rate of home ownership was always highest in the Midwest. Table 6.21 also gives the rates of home ownership by region for thirty-five to thirty-nine year olds. This age group encompasses the age of the typical full-time earner in 1967 that was profiled in chapter 3. This earner was supposed to be able to provide a middle-class standard of living for a household, and the primary consumption item of this middle-class standard was home ownership. While comparable data are not available for 1967, almost 14% more thirty-five to thirty-nine year olds in the Midwest owned their own homes than did those in the Northeast in 1973. In 1987, the gap in home ownership between two regions was largest for the Midwest and the West; the gap was more than 14%. Rates of home ownership experienced similar increases of around 1% to 3% in all the regions between 1973 and 1980. However, during the 1980s, all regions had experienced a decline in home ownership rates among thirty-five to thirty-nine year olds, but the degree of decline was varied, ranging from almost 4% for the Northeast to more than 10% for the West.

Published uniform data on the median sales prices of homes are not available at the state level across the nation. In this analysis, the choice was made to use the data for the regions as a proxy for the states, with the exception of California.

While the general economic outlook of New York State improved considerably since the 1970s, and the earnings of full-time workers shifted upward significantly, the extent to which New Yorkers could as easily attain the middle standard of living in 1987 as they could in 1967, or even as easily as their counterparts in other states could in the late 1980s, depended in large part on changes in the cost of home ownership. We have seen that the increase in the sales price of new one-family homes sold in the Northeast during the 1980s was almost double that of any other region while the percentage increase in price of the representative first home was more than double that of any other region. Thus, the improved labor market position in the 1980s for New York State workers was accompanied by skyrocketing inflation, exceeding 100%, in the cost of home ownership and would seem to indicate that the middle standard of living became more difficult to attain.

In comparison, the picture for Illinoisans and midwesterners was actually bright. Since the Midwest had the lowest housing price inflation and highest home ownership rates, it would appear that attaining a middle standard of living continued to be more possible in Illinois and the Midwest in general.

Texas, as part of the South, should have had the lowest housing prices of the four states, and given that its earnings distribution and fringe benefit recipiency improved over the period of analysis, we would expect the middle standard of living to have become more attainable. Since 1987, however, the nation has become engulfed in the savings and loan (S&L) crisis, and Texas has been at the eye of this storm. Failing S&Ls means mortgage money for home purchases becomes relatively less available and more expensive and, thus, may lessen the attainability of home ownership.

California, too, is a state deeply affected by the S&L crisis. Before it surfaced, though, one might have expected that since 37% of California's full-time workers were upper earners, compared to 30% nationwide, they would have had relatively less difficulty purchasing a house than workers elsewhere in the nation; but, the housing affordability index for the state was only half that of the nation overall. In December 1988, 23% of California households had the annual income needed to purchase the median-priced, single-family home in the state. Nationwide, the figure was 47%.[22] The California sales price of this median-priced home was more than $172,000, compared to less than $90,000 nationwide. In the largest urban centers of the state, the inability to purchase a home with the earnings of a full-time worker was even more extreme. For example, the housing affordability index for the San Francisco Standard Metropolitan Statistical Area was less than 10% and the median-priced home was more than $240,000.

The irony of California's sustained high levels of population and economic growth was that it appeared to have made the middle-class dream increasingly less attainable. Spiraling housing costs around the state reflected a supply of housing that was insufficient to meet the demands of the growing population. The Bay Area Economic Forum, made up of a cross section of government, business, labor, and higher education leaders in the San Francisco region, noted:

> The skyrocketing cost of housing—especially housing close to employment centers—has driven up wages, and made it more difficult to recruit and transfer employees in all but the high compensation brackets.[23]

Regional government officials and policymakers, as well as the business sector, worried that the state's high housing costs would ultimately lead to economic decline because workers would be either unable or unwilling to live in such high-cost areas and employers would have to locate elsewhere in order to have access to labor.

Workers experience further negative impacts because the high wages they must demand in their relatively futile effort to keep up with housing costs forces employers to look for other ways to reduce labor costs, such as reducing levels of fringe benefit provision. While reductions in the levels of fringe benefits have occurred throughout the nation, we have seen that they have been the most extreme in California.

It would appear, then, that attaining a middle-class standard of living, as measured by the ability to own one's own home, became more difficult in all regions during the 1980s, but particularly so in the West. This was the case despite the fact that house prices were lower in the West than they were in the Northeast and, further, that house price inflation in the West had been close to half that of the Northeast since 1980. In addition, California's reputation as the forerunner and, indeed, the setter of national trends suggested that the prospects for attaining and retaining the middle-class standard of living did not look bright at the end of the 1980s.

7

Changing Earnings Distributions and Opportunities for Middle-Class Living: What Should Be Done?

Review of Approach

This book began by noting the alleged national economic trend of the disappearing middle class, a trend with potentially great importance to the long-run economic development of this country and to the maintenance of the population's perceived high—and widely enjoyed—standard of living. The focus of this book on the implications of a declining middle-class trend for the nation's regional economic development pattern distinguishes it from other book-length treatments on the disappearing middle class.

The first observations of the disappearing middle trend began in the early 1980s; the ensuing debate was largely muddled, as well as steeped in political and statistical controversy. Political controversy has arisen because it does not help the cause of the party in power to have the middle class of our society and economy shrinking. This group of Americans is the political majority and forms the backbone of our nation. The middle class is taken to personify democracy, equality of opportunity, and position. Further, it has historically produced and consumed most of the nation's output.

While the above seems to be broadly accepted about the middle class, no one is able to say exactly who or what the middle class is. This is true whether we try to define the middle class in sociological or economic terms. However, because the intent of this book has been to focus on issues of economic development planning, we have examined the economic aspects of the middle class, the area that raises statistical controversy.

How do we define the middle economic class? Do we say that it has to have a specific amount of income or do we say that to qualify for the label, its members must be able to purchase a certain "middle" standard of living? In the latter case, how do we account for the fact that, over time, the contents and prices of the consumer basket representing a middle standard of living have changed, as has the consumer unit purchasing the basket? This question raises a myriad of definitional and statistical problems that have had to be sorted through prior to settling on the approach taken in this book.

To briefly recapitulate, we have argued that when we ask the question, "Do we live as well-off as we used to?"—Does the middle class live as well-off as it used to?—our reference image is the Ozzie and Harriet–type household of the late 1960s in which a family or household owned its own home and was comfortably supported by the earnings of one full-time earner. Indeed, for the middle economic class, owning one's own home is the ultimate symbol of membership. The appropriate way to track the question of what is happening to the middle class from an economic development perspective is by defining the middle class based not on simply a dollar amount or range but rather on a consumer basket that provides a middle standard of living. We found, though, that while there was a government-defined consumer basket that could be taken to represent the middle standard in the late 1960s, this basket is no longer updated for use in current times.

In lieu of the ideal approach, the approach settled upon in this research had two consequences. First, a 1967 middle consumer basket, which is the same as the government-defined moderate household budget, was used to determine just how correct was our perception of a broad middle economic class, personified by the Ozzie and Harriet–type household, in the late 1960s. Second, a statistical definition was created to measure the proportion of middle-level, full-time earners who were supposed to be able to purchase the middle standard of living for themselves and their households. This definition was 50% to 200% of current-year median earnings for each year analyzed. Using this definition, we tracked changes in the percentages of earners who had middle, as well as

lower and upper, earnings. Further, we tracked changes in the ability of the median earnings figure to purchase the median-priced
house, as a means of relating the statistical definition to the cost of
the middle standard of living. The key findings of this twenty-year
analysis were as follows.

Key Findings

The analysis of distributions of earnings for the 1967 to 1987 period revealed an overall and dramatic upward shift in the distribution for full-time earners. Approximately half of all white full-time
males were upper earners; female full-time earners have been, and
remain, predominantly middle earners. Blacks, and especially
black females, saw dramatic improvements in their earnings picture over the two-decade period. Two possible explanations, or a
combination thereof, may warrant attribution for the relative improvement in black female earnings. First, it is possible that the
success of affirmative action programs has improved labor force
opportunities for black females. Second, it is also possible that
black females' relative earnings pictures have improved because
their dire economic circumstances necessitated their greater labor
force attachment, which, in turn, led to greater earnings increases.

With the consumer-basket approach to defining the middle
standard of living, we found, surprisingly, that only around half of
all full-time earners could purchase this basket in the late 1960s,
the time at which the national economy was at one of its highest
levels. The ability to purchase a middle standard of living was not
in reality as widespread as it was thought to be. Further, the media-
projected image of the middle-class family was also not as preva-
lent as one might have thought. The statistics presented in chapter
2 bear repeating: traditional families—a married couple with a
male breadwinner, children, and a wife who does not work in the
paid labor force—were no more than 8% of all households. Perhaps
we should wonder whether, in fact, this middle class, for whom
great concern over its disappearance has been expressed, is primarily a figment created by media imaginations for the purpose of
selling the goods and services of our thriving postwar economy?

Comparison of part- and full-time earners revealed that the

1967 to 1987 period created a growing disparity between the two groups. Full-time earners experienced upward shifts in their earnings, but no change occurred in the shape of part-time earners' distribution. Consequently, the gap between the median earnings of full- and part-time earners grew. In addition, the percent of part-time earners who would rather be employed full-time increased. The evidence suggests that labor market adjustments to structural change and economic decline appear to have come at the expense of part-time earners over full-time earners.

The answer to the question "Did the middle shrink?" is "yes" for full-time earners, but the reason the proportion of middle-level earners decreased was because the proportion who were upper earners increased. However, this does not mean that all was well for full-time earners. Even though they experienced improvements in their earnings levels, they saw substantial erosion in the purchasing power of those earnings. Further, from the late 1970s forward, this analysis has shown that the level of benefit recipiency for full-time earners dropped. Thus, nonwage compensation in the form of healthcare benefits and pension provision, two areas critical to the ability to attain and retain a middle standard of living, was being taken away from full-time earners.

The impact of the 1970s economic slowdown appeared to have had a lagged effect on the earnings distribution. The economy's turning point away from growth is generally characterized as occurring around 1973. Our analysis has shown that from 1973 to 1979, very little movement occurred in the overall earnings distribution for either part- or full-time workers; but since 1979, the full-time distribution has shifted upward and the part-time distribution shifted downward. As noted, since 1979, the rate of nonwage compensation fell. In addition, inequality in the distribution of earnings increased. This post-1979 lagged economic adjustment appears to represent a fundamental, structural shift in the pattern of earnings and compensation and, thus, in the ability to purchase the middle standard of living.

An important focus of this book has been on determining the regional impacts of the changing earnings distribution. The regional analysis was conducted in a three-layered approach. First, the nation was divided into metropolitan and nonmetropolitan regions to determine how industrial restructuring and shifting population patterns have differentially affected rural and urban earners' abilities to enjoy a middle standard of living. Among the more notable differences found were that rural earners' returns to education appear to be higher; there was a lower percentage of full-time female earners in the rural areas; and the lessening of differences in earnings distributions between the rural and urban areas during the 1970s was more than restored during the 1980s. That there was a lower percentage of rural females working full-time, in combination with the lower cost of home ownership in rural areas, would seem to imply that the ability to consume a middle standard of living was greater in rural than in urban areas.

In the second level of regional analysis, earners were grouped into the four major census regions: the Northeast, Midwest, South, and West. It was found that although there has been a trend toward convergence in the shapes of the regions' earnings distributions and of their production sectors over the last two decades, there was an opposite trend in the cost of housing and the rate of home ownership. Further, it was found that while attaining a middle standard of living as measured by the ability to own one's own home became more difficult in all regions during the 1980s, this was particularly the case in the West.

In the third level of regional analysis, the largest state in each of the four census regions was examined. Distinct variations in the patterns of change in the earnings distributions among New York, Illinois, Texas, and California were found that, along with variations in housing prices, generated varying abilities to attain the middle standard of living. New York State experienced large employment losses, especially in manufacturing, between 1967 and 1973. Between 1973 and 1979, it had recovered its employment losses but experienced a downward shift in the full-time earnings distribution from the upper to the middle segment. From 1979 to 1987, the number of full-time earners in New York continued to grow—in nonmanufacturing sectors—and the earnings distribution reversed its movement and shifted upward. However, New York had fewer workers employed in industries assessed to be gaining international trade advantage than the other three states analyzed while the number employed in Loser industries was growing. Also, New York State's improved labor market position of the 1980s was accompanied by skyrocketing inflation in the cost of home ownership.

While the worst of New York State's economic troubles over the two-decade period seemed to have ended by the early 1980s, the same could not be said about its co-Rustbelt state, Illinois. The number of full-time earners in manufacturing and natural resources shrank in that state, but employment additions in the high-growth sectors—transportation and trade, transactional activities, and social infrastructure—compensated for the losses. The earnings distribution among full-time earners grew only in the middle segment from 1967 to 1979 and subsequently shifted upward. Two of Illinois's greatest sources of growth, the transportation and trade sector and the social infrastructure sector, had lower earnings distributions than the state's average, though. Further, Illinois experienced a steady decline in the proportion of workers in the high-technology and defense sectors. In addition, the state had greater losses than New York in the number of earners employed in industries assessed to be gaining in international trade advantage. Housing price inflation appeared to have been much lower in Illinois than in New York; thus, attaining a middle standard of living continued to be more possible in Illinois and the Midwest, in general, than anywhere else.

Texas's percent growth in population has been higher since 1970 than the national average or even that of the nation's largest state, California. Its economic growth over the two-decade period narrowed the differences between it and the other three states analyzed. However, in 1987, Texas was the only one of the four states in which upper earners were not at least 30% of full-time workers. Natural resources were a more important source of employment, directly and indirectly, in Texas than in the other three states. This sector's earnings distribution shifted upward dramatically between 1967 and 1987, but Texans' efforts to develop other sources of employment are critical for the state's economic future, particularly since the employment in natural resources derives from production activity associated with nonrenewable factors of supply.

In the final state analyzed, California, it was found that full-time workers had the most upward-skewed earnings distribution of all the geographic categories analyzed. Changes in the state's pattern of non-wage compensation combined with its extraordinarily high housing costs, though, placed California's workers in 1987 in a much inferior position relative to the rest of the nation for trying to attain a middle standard of living for the remainder of this century. The perceived high standard of living and sources of economic opportunities long associated with the state were being challenged on a number of fronts, and these challenges have continued into the 1990s.

At a time of skyrocketing healthcare costs and the demise of many of the state's less costly providers, such as the health maintenance organizations, California's employers made the biggest cuts in the provision of health benefits of the four states analyzed. Improvements in the education levels of California's part-time workers were slight or not at all while full-time workers had significant increases in their educational levels of attainment. At the same time, the distribution of earnings for part-time workers did not improve. In the largest sector, transportation and trade, the earnings distribution actually shifted downward along with its distribution of educational attainment. In contrast, the distribution of earnings for full-time workers improved substantially. The jobs/housing imbalance in the state—that is, the insufficient supply of housing at prices affordable by area wage levels—has led to longer and longer commutes, the promotion of no-growth initiatives in smaller communities whose secondary road systems are being inappropriately used for these commutes, and increasingly voiced concerns by private industry and the public sector over the prospects of the long-term economy.

The 1990s have brought far greater levels of stress to the California population. The state's economy is in recession; it has a multibillion-dollar state budget deficit and substantial cutbacks are being made to its educational system; its largest city, Los Angeles, was subject to one of the worst riots in the nation's history in the spring of 1992; and housing prices in the state have fallen in real terms. California appears to warrant continuation of its reputation as a national trendsetter as other states have begun to experience similar fiscal and economic problems.

Planning's Unintended Consequences for the Middle Economic Class

In order to understand what kinds of policy and planning intervention are necessary to improve the prospects for the middle economic class, we must first understand how the practices of private and public planning in the United States have had an impact on the middle class. Private planning, that is, corporate planning, has its greatest impact on the income side of the middle-class equation. Through its role as an allocator of wages and benefits, which represent more than 90% of the employed's source of income, private planning contributed to the great expansion of the middle class in the postwar period and, more recently, to its subsequent decline.

Public planning, at the local level, has been a primary contributor to the creation of the middle consumption package and, now, to increasingly pricing this consumption package out of the reach of middle-level earners. This is because of its impact on the cost of owning a home. The practice of local planning has played a significant role in escalating the price of home ownership beyond the reach of an aspiring middle class.

The declining ability to purchase the middle standard of living has not been equal across all household types. Data for young married couples who were first-time home buyers indicate that 32% of their income was required to make a purchase in 1987, compared to only a 22% after-tax cash burden in 1967 (Mishel and Simon 1988). Whereas in 1967, the median earnings for a full-time worker—when using the affordability rule of two and a half times earnings—could easily buy the median-priced home, by the late 1980s this home's price was nearly 20% above what could be afforded with the median earnings. This simplistic figure does not take into account the increased cash that would need to be saved by the individual full-time earner to make the down payment on today's more expensive home.

It is no wonder that more and more home buyers are dual-earner couples; it takes more than one earner to be able to afford a home. Further, Danes and Winter (1990) found that it is the *wife's* commitment to the labor force, as measured by hours worked rather than by the amount she earns, that has the greatest impact on whether a dual-earner household will make the transition from renter to home owner.

Essentially, then, the prospects for obtaining the most important item of the middle-class dream increasingly depend on both the husband and wife working full-time. This means, of course, that where children are present, additional expenses must be incurred for child care. The cost of owning a second auto also must frequently be included to get the additional working parent to work and the children to child care. That most of these households are located in the suburbs generally rules out the option of relying on public transportation.

To some extent, dual-earner households also incur extra costs for services they purchase since both parents are working, such as cleaning services and maintenance and repair services. However, many of these household budgets are too stretched to afford purchasing such services. As a result, quality of life deteriorates when home work combined with market work creates extraordinarily long working hours. Research has shown that it is the wife whose hours are by far the longest (Hochschild 1989), but it would be fair to say that the entire family's quality of life deteriorates as a result of decreased time for parenting, family, and friends.

In households that do not have two earners, the chances of obtaining the middle standard of living's main item, home ownership, have lessened as the costs of owning one's own home have risen. At the same time, these aspiring middle-class earners represent a growing proportion of all American households and of households with children. In essence, the broad middle class has split apart, dividing increasingly into lower and upper middle segments.[1] Accompanying this split has been increasing income and social segregation.

In general, we do not think of the United States as having much in the way of public planning activity at levels higher than the local level. Still, some macroeconomic policies and national legislation represent de facto public planning at the national level that has significantly influenced the position of the middle class. Further, while there are actions that can be taken at the local planning level to alleviate the plight of those who aspire to, and of those who are trying to hold on to, a position in the middle class, the incentives for taking these actions at the local level are weak and at times negative. Thus, regional and higher levels of planning are called for.

Planning's Contributions to the Growth of Middle-Level Earners

The growth of middle-level earners in the postwar period is the result of private, corporate planning, industry structure evolution, and the tolerance of unionization set within the context of a strong economy.

Occurring throughout the twentieth century, but especially during this postwar period, the expansion techniques adopted by corporate planners created a growing layer of middle-management jobs. In addition, growing proportions of nonmanagement and non-white-collar jobs came to be compensated with equal middle-level wages and benefits and to enjoy similar job security, in large part as a result of gains achieved by unions.

The postwar relationship between U.S. corporations and their employees was a further evolution of scientific management techniques that has been labeled a system of bureaucratic control, leading to greater stratification of a firm's work force and a middle layer of employment that included craft workers, technical and professional employees, supervisors, and middle-level administrative staff. These middle layers of employment had relatively high wages, low unemployment, and secure employment (Edwards 1979).

The favorable position that many blue-collar workers enjoyed during the postwar period was in no small way due to the efforts of unions. Federal legislation—the Taft-Hartley Act—created the foundation from which unions could organize to secure high standards of living for their members, standards that kept pace with inflation through mechanisms such as cost-of-living adjustments. All workers, *unionized and nonunionized,* benefited from the standards of compensation and benefit recipiency that the unions secured for their members and that became industrywide standards. As a result, we saw the rise of a *blue-collar middle class.*

Federal support or, rather, tolerance of unions greatly waned in the last two decades. The most potent symbol of this shifting government attitude toward unions was the Reagan administration's handling of the air-traffic controllers' strike. The use of the strike as a bargaining tool was denied to the controllers, and those who struck were fired from their jobs. This shift, combined with state governments' at times seemingly desperate efforts to create good business climates, meant that existing union-represented workers were forced to give back wages and other compensation and that if closing unionized plants were replaced, it would be with nonunionized new plants. Diminished union strength is responsible for the growing inequality between skilled and unskilled workers' wages by lowering real wages for the less skilled.

The U.S. trends in corporate planning, industry structure evolution, and union tolerance promoted a strong middle economic class as long as the other major international economies were hampered by war-damaged infrastructures and relatively unsophisticated industrial structures. But nations such as Japan and Germany rebuilt their infrastructure, with considerable U.S. assistance. With explicit national planning—a tripartite effort in Germany of government, industry, and labor while Japan's effort was dominated by government and industry—they were able to outcompete the United States.[2] The lack of specific, strategic industrial planning has put the American economy, and the middle economic class, at a considerable disadvantage in the last two decades.

Planning's Contributions to Setting the Middle Standard of Living

The National Highway Act was the only *explicit* planning effort, and contributed more than any other planning effort, to the development of the postwar middle-class standard of living and life-style—the "American dream" package. The act's stated rationale was not, of course, to create the suburban sites for the postwar American dream but rather to create an interstate road system for national defense purposes. The population of the nation's urban centers needed a quick way to get out of the city in case of attack. But while a U.S. city has yet to be subject to attack from a foreign enemy, the new federal highway system encouraged many urban Americans as well as industries to make a fast exit to the suburbs.

The postwar American dream package, which was a suburban package, could not have been built without financing. National policy played a significant role in making the dream possible through the creation of federal housing programs. Not only did these programs provide a significant amount of the financing for the middle-class dream home in suburbia but they also set the standards for its remaining private financing:

> For the single-family home buyer, the federal housing programs provided insurance for the housing loan. The heart of the federal program reduced the home buyer's monthly payment to a minimum

amount. Secondly, the government required that its loans be self-liquidating. . . . The government housing programs were so effective that soon private lenders had to provide very similar terms. . . . Once this process of building affordable housing began, however, it never stopped . . . the process of building the suburbs has continued as the principal method of providing housing for this country's expanding middle class (Abeles 1989, p. 142).

National tax policy also played a significant role in making the dream possible in that the interest paid for home mortgage loans is tax deductible. Thus, homeowners get a tax break over renters that may enable them to buy their first home or buy more housing than they would have been able to otherwise.

Local-Level Planning's Influence

The primary mechanism at the local level contributing to the creation of the middle-class consumption basket was the land-use regulatory tool of zoning, which played a major role in setting the standards for the primary consumption item of the middle-class standard of living: home ownership. Once these standards were set, zoning was the primary tool for protecting this standard of consumption. It protected the middle-class dream for one segment, largely white, of the prime labor force–age population of the postwar period while excluding that era's poor—and ultimately many of white suburbia's offspring—from sharing the dream.

Postwar industry job growth occurred primarily in the suburbs. Those left behind in the city tended to be the least skilled and were faced with diminishing economic opportunities. Residential zoning restrictions prevented many of the city's industrial workers from moving to the suburbs to follow industry job growth (Abeles 1989).

Those locked into the center city were predominantly blacks. During World War II, one of the most significant demographic movements was the migration of southern rural blacks who had been agricultural workers to major cities across the United States for employment in industries engaged in war production. The subsequent postwar movement of industry to the suburbs, accompanied by restrictive residential zoning of the suburbs, had the effect of locking the black population into the nation's decaying central cities, eliminating their prospects for upward mobility. Zoning played a major role in preventing a substantial portion of the nation's black population from participating in the great postwar growth boom and ever realizing middle-class status.[3]

Abeles (1989) observed that the move from the city to the suburbs can easily require all of a household's economic resources. As a consequence, new suburbanites want to protect themselves from anything, including social and/or racial change, that could affect the economic value of their new home or neighborhood. Zoning offered the means of this protection, acting to control the housing costs of subsequent home building in the suburbanite's community. A tool such as minimum lot size could guarantee that the next subdivision would have homes priced at their same level or even higher. The label "exclusionary zoning" has been given to this practice of land regulation. In suburbia, it has meant the exclusion of multifamily units and low-cost single-family housing forms, such as mobile homes (Feagin 1989).

The "suburban squeeze," as Dowall (1984) has labeled the effects of restrictive zoning and other controls placed on housing development, affects "no longer only the poor who are hurt by overly restrictive and exclusionary land use controls, but the majority of first-time home buyers," that is, our aspiring middle class. This squeeze has contributed to the price of new housing far outpacing the rate of inflation over the last two decades. In the long run, the consequences of expensive housing include higher costs of doing business and the threat that an area will lose employers whose business is not locationally dependent. In the interim, less mobile employees who cannot relocate from the region because they are part of a dual-earner household or who have jobs in lower-skilled and lower-paying employment are forced to commute to the new suburban sources of employment from either inner-city areas or the region's outskirts, where housing costs are lower.[4]

In the most recent period of suburbanization, many communities are no longer focused on using zoning to guarantee a certain high-income-level newcomer population or environmental regulations to protect their special features. Instead, they are taking efforts to limit and control development to their most extreme by establishing a no-growth environment.

The growth these communities are seeking to control or prevent has been spurred significantly by the movement of back office and service employment functions from the city. In large part, the traffic congestion that developed during the 1980s in the suburbs is a result of the increased commuting of lower-paid office and service industry workers to their suburban places of employment. These workers commute because they cannot afford to live in their employing communities, due, in large part, to the historic exclusionary zoning traditions of these suburbs. This jobs/housing imbalance, as the above trend has been labeled, is making life difficult for would-be newcomers and old-timers of the suburbs alike. Further, it ultimately threatens the economic vitality and the standard of living of our metropolitan regions (Cervero 1989; Dowall 1984).

Prognosis for the Middle Economic Class

The 1967 to 1987 analysis of this book revealed that the prospects for attaining and retaining the middle-class standard of living did not look bright at the end of the 1980s; the first years of the 1990s appear to validate the gloomy prognosis of our twenty-year analysis on both the earnings and consumption side of the middle economic class equation. The crisis of healthcare coverage has deepened; structural dislocation in the economy continues; the nation again slipped into a recession; and, for the first time, this recession has been labeled a services recession, one that is displacing many white-collar middle- and upper-earnings workers. The differential regional impacts of the recession vary significantly from the 1980s' impacts and have led, in some states, to actual devaluing of the preeminent middle-class consumption item: single-family detached homes. Housing price deflation may suggest that some present members of the middle class suffer while aspiring middle-class members may find owning one's own home within closer reach. Given the current state of the economy and eroding earnings and benefits packages, however, it is questionable how many of those aspiring to membership in the middle class can take advantage of the deflation.

While the United States has already been substantially affected by global restructuring, the worst effects of this restructuring for the manufacturing sector may not yet have been felt. By erasing trade barriers between the United States and Mexico, the North American Free Trade Agreement (NAFTA) may facilitate the relocation of industries in the lattermost stages of their profit cycles to south-of-the-border sites where labor and most other production costs are significantly lower. This can be expected to have disproportionately negative impacts on the nation's southern and rural regions.

Throughout the nation, state and local governments are in fiscal crises, and we are beginning to hear more frequently about cities and school systems going bankrupt. Traditionally, the middle economic class has been the main bankroller of government. Although there was considerable lip service paid during the 1980s to the concept of tax relief for the middle-income group, the effective federal tax rate for all but the bottom and top income deciles changed very little under Reagan's tax reform package. The effective rate for the lowest income decile experienced the largest increase while that for the richest decile incurred the largest decrease (Mishel and Simon 1988).

Where the middle class does not pay directly through federal and local taxation, it pays indirectly through stagnating wages and declining fringe benefits due to combinations of higher premiums or copayments and lesser services. That is the earnings/income side of the middle economic class equation. What about the consumption package variable?

There appears to be little to no indication that the consumption package for the middle economic class is going to become more affordable. Perhaps, though, its cost will not rise as quickly as it has in recent years, especially since there has been a slowdown in increases in the purchase price of homes.

Many would-be buyers have not fueled the upward spiral because their budgets simply cannot stretch far enough to get into the market. Regional recessions, and the overall national recession of the early 1990s, have contributed to holding down prices and, in some areas, to prices actually falling. The savings and loan crisis has dried up mortgage money in some areas of the country, further hampering the residential sales market.

Other major consumption items, such as healthcare, automobiles, and college educations, continue to rise steeply. The cost of vehicle ownership has outpaced inflation at the same time that the necessity of private automobile travel has been growing because most new employment growth is in the suburbs, where public transportation is generally inefficient, if available at all.

In addition, the costs of services that middle-income households may want to purchase to alleviate their combined home and office work loads continue to rise. Since budgets are already stretched, these households often cannot afford to purchase such services and simply end up having less leisure time.

We have had a remarkable growth in single-headed households, and those with female heads are now 21% of all families with children. Sixty-two percent of female household heads were in the labor force in 1988, and 67% of those with children under the age of eighteen were working (Hayghe 1990, Tables 3 and 4). The prospects for these households purchasing the middle standard of living on their earnings are negligible, as is the possibility of being able to purchase services to alleviate the tremendous home and child care responsibilities these single parents face.

It is not only working couples and single parents who are having difficulty attaining the middle standard of living. The proportion of grown children living with their parents has been on the rise in recent years because declining earnings and rising housing costs, for both owners and renters, make it difficult for them to live on their own.

Recognizing the divergence between the earnings/income and consumption sides of the middle economic class equation should lead Americans to question whether achieving the middle standard of living as it is now defined and priced is worth the sacrifice in the quality of life that it requires. In correlation, we should ask how planning and public policy can help bridge the gap between the two. The concluding section of this book attempts to offer some insight into this question.

Social Infrastructure Investment, the Promotion of Economic Integration, and Strategic Industrial Policy

> The appropriate way to deal with the rise in earnings inequality is through taxation and transfer policies . . . and through public expenditures on education and training that encourage individual re-

sponses to the increased importance of education (Blackburn et al.
1990/1991, p. 43).

The above quote, representative of many proposed solutions to the
plight of the present and aspiring middle class, not only is too simplistic but does little to address the needs of the increasingly het-
erogeneous demography of the aspiring middle class at the end of
the twentieth century. The Ozzie and Harriet–type family of the
golden postwar era is a minority. Today's beleaguered middle class
is composed less and less of traditional families with only a male
breadwinner and increasingly of dual-earner families, single-par-
ent-headed households, and never-married adults.

This author would not disagree that changes in taxation and
transfer policies could be helpful in alleviating the plight of the
middle class. If we were to move back toward a more progressive
taxation structure, the middle-income group would have more income available to purchase the inflationary middle standard of living. However, in terms of attaining the middle standard of living as
it is represented by home ownership, it must be established that
the solution does not lie in changes in the labor market but rather
in the housing market. We have seen for full-time earners that their
earnings distribution has shifted upward dramatically but that the
purchasing power of their earnings has fallen. We have also discussed the mechanics of suburban land and housing development
that have significantly contributed to increases in the median costs
of home ownership, outpacing increases in median earnings levels.

Social Infrastructure Investment

The response of adding more earners to a household in order to
maintain one's standard of living can only go so far. Further real
rises in housing prices will price out even dual-earner households.
We are seriously lacking in the amount of policy attention paid to
the tremendous burdens faced by dual-earner families. The welfare
of families and children will be increasingly threatened if greater
policy efforts are not forthcoming. These should include efforts at
the local level to expand the supply of child care and to see that
the supply of child care is conveniently located en route to or on
site of parents' workplaces. At the national level, we need to establish a basic level of public funding for child care programs to ensure

that the quality of child care provision is equitably distributed across working families with varying abilities to pay for child care and to ensure that child care workers are adequately compensated for the valuable service to society that they provide. The recently adopted national family and medical leave policy, enabling working parents to care for children and other dependents, is a step in the right direction. However, since it applies only to companies with fifty or more employees, it has been estimated that half of all workers and 94% of companies are not covered under the act.

The observed trend of reductions in the level of nonwage compensation in the form of health insurance and pension benefits does not bode well for the security of the standard of living one has achieved. Taking away these paid benefits is the same as reducing a worker's salary. In the case of health insurance, planning for extreme increases in premiums over the last few years has been difficult for any one worker (and, granted, for any employer). In addition, the growing trend of self-employment among white-collar employees as corporations are restructuring and eliminating middle layers of employment means that growing numbers of workers must self-insure. All in all, rising healthcare costs have meant that employers feel a profit squeeze, workers feel an income squeeze, and workers unable to keep up with rising premiums that they must pay for out of their own pockets are placed in precarious positions in the event of catastrophic illness. At the national level, increasing attention and regulation to the healthcare and pension benefit industries appear to be warranted, as well as consideration of extending the public sector's role in ensuring that all members of society are adequately covered. At the local level, economic development authorities should consider these forms of unearned compensation when they are evaluating the economic development impact potential of various job-creation proposals.

On another note, additional public expenditures on education and training are needed. The income gap between the educated and less educated is increasing while we spend less on education per pupil than many of our advanced industrialized competitors. Inequality in education appears increasingly to be a source of earnings inequality. The supply of good-paying union jobs for uneducated workers has steadily diminished and simply cannot be counted on in the future. Not only does higher education seem to be a prerequisite for good-paying jobs but it may be the price for admission to the full-time labor market.

Economic Integration

Increased aggregate public expenditures on education, however, will not solve the problem of the unequal quality and opportunity afforded in different educational systems, the effects of which magnify throughout society and the future economy. Reich (1991) observed:

> As Americans continue to segregate according to what they earn, the shift in financing public services from the federal government to the states, and from the states to cities and towns, has functioned as another means of relieving America's wealthier citizens of the burdens of America's less fortunate.

One of the ways this has become most clear is in the financing of public school systems. We have historically funded education at the local level, but property tax revolts in certain states are creating a path of economic self-destruction. Wealthy communities within such states raise private funds to supplement inadequate public school budgets for themselves, but the mass of these states' school-age populations are being inadequately prepared for the labor force and will, therefore, be relegated to permanent marginal economic status and become permanent drags on future prosperity. In states without property tax revolts, wealthy communities fund their systems at higher levels, paying teachers premium wages and offering many enrichment programs for their students. School systems in less wealthy communities pay their teachers lower wages and are forced to provide only the basics. Attempts to limit what wealthy communities can pay for their public school systems have resulted in many parents simply removing their children from the public system and placing them in the private education system. As a consequence, these parents are less amenable to voting for local property tax increases to improve public school systems (Reich 1991).

The proposed solutions to the plight of the present and aspiring middle class generally are void of any spatial context, and yet it should be clear by now that there is indeed a spatial context to much of the problem. It is predominantly in this arena that the practice of planning, as it has been permitted in this country, can make a significant contribution to solving the plight of the middle class. Planning can do so by reversing the exclusionary zoning practices that have contributed to the creation of suburban squeeze, to communities being segregated by income and thus race, and, consequently, to inequalities in local school systems, to jobs/housing imbalances, and to increasing traffic problems.

The changes called for in the practice of local planning in order to alleviate the plight of the middle class are not new ideas. What may be new to practitioners in the field is the realization of how the practice of planning contributed to the growth of the middle economic class in the postwar era, to establishing the norms for its standard of living, and now to the plight of those who aspire to this standard.

We need to abandon the idea that the American dream—the consumption package of the middle standard of living—can only be found in the traditional suburb if we are going to be able to implement the changes required. As a consequence, planners should be promoting higher-density patterns and mixed-use developments. They need to be concerned if their community's local house prices and rents are higher than comparable communities; if the employees in their public agencies or private service sector, as well as the adult children of local families, cannot afford to live in their community; and if corporate concerns over high housing prices are preventing new economic development. Dowall (1984) states that this kind of information will allow a planner to determine the extent of his or her community's suburban squeeze; it also allows a determination of the plight of the middle class. Further, planners need to consciously recognize the racially discriminating impacts of their communities' planning practices.

Many alternative zoning tools are available for mitigating the impacts of exclusionary zoning and creating more economically integrated communities. Inclusionary zoning—joint development within master-planned projects of offices, housing, and retail services; conditional-use zoning—such as allowing a new office development only if it is located within a specified radius of an existing high-density area; zoning swaps where the classifications of two land parcels are switched—such as residential for industrial; and modification of existing single-family zoned areas to allow accessory units are some of the recent innovations that need far wider adoption (Cervero 1989). At the same time, we need greater availability of child care closer to home and work sites, which may also require modifications to current zoning legislation (Cibulskis and Ritzdorf 1989).

Public officials and planners will need to educate their communities to the barriers they help to erect for those seeking to enjoy a middle standard of living, but it may well be that NIMBYistic[5] attitudes will prevail. If so, then only regional mechanisms will force localities out of their exclusive, income-separated patterns. Tax-base sharing and fair-share housing are two legislative initiatives whose universal adoption could go a long way toward eliminating the inequalities in the standards of living among communities. With tax-base sharing, some percentage of tax revenues is pooled at the regional level and then redistributed. The idea has been developed to take away communities' incentives to zone for commercial rather than residential development (Cervero 1989). However, such tax sharing could also be employed to equalize the funding of local school systems. Setting affordable housing quotas for municipalities would undo the discrimination against low- and moderate-income families that the practice of local zoning has predominantly fostered. As Cervero (1989) has noted, though, both of these initiatives require the action of higher levels of government. Since we do not have regional metropolitan governments, it is left to the state government to be the initiator in most cases.

Perhaps the greatest support for regional governance and for changing the existing practice of local land regulation will come from within the private sector rather than the public sector. The price of the new suburban home is out of reach for many aspiring middle class families, even for two-wage-earner families. Developers are increasingly realizing that if they want to stay in business, they will need to build housing that is more affordable to a broader segment of the population, yet they are faced with resistance from many localities and an unwillingness to modify present land-use regulations. Corporations and small businesses alike are having difficulties attracting employees in many metro areas because of the mismatch between prevailing wages and housing costs.

Thus, the private sector may provide the largest impetus for movement toward economically integrated communities. The Regional Government Council of the San Francisco Bay Area recently issued a report titled "A Region at Peril." A joint product of the private sector and public agencies, it aired concerns over the region's future competitiveness due to its jobs/housing imbalances. Local and state planners should foster support for zoning reform from within the business community to help counter the inevitable resistance they will meet from residential property owners.

Public planners and officials need to be made aware of how one of their primary responsibilities—land-use planning—has played a fundamental role in setting the American standard of living in the postwar period and is now impeding movement toward a more economically integrated landscape critical to the successful resolution of this nation's major social and economic problems; and just as economic zoning resulted in de facto racial zoning, economic integration would result in greater racial integration.

This book's focus on the plight of the middle class in no way implies that the problems of the lower class do not deserve attention. What it is important to understand is that increasingly the lower and middle classes share the same problems and that a squeezed middle class means there is less chance of upward mobility for the lower class. Furthermore, the demographic composition of the participants from the lower and middle classes in the economy has changed drastically over the last twenty-five years, leading to shifts in needs for public services. Public planners and officials need to expand their awareness of the needs and obstacles nontraditional groups face in order to alleviate barriers that our current pattern of land-use development has fostered. In order to do so, they need to accept and promote the concept of an economically integrated landscape whereby housing and employment patterns permit an intermixing of different income groups, as opposed to our present patterns, which separate the lower, middle, and upper classes.

Strategic Industrial Policy

As we noted earlier, the lack of specific, strategic industrial planning in the United States has put our economy, and its middle economic class, at a considerable disadvantage relative to our advanced industrial and industrializing competitors. In many cases, the governments of our competitors targeted specific industries and provided financial assistance and other incentives to build them into international successes. In a relatively short period of time, many U.S. industries were being outcompeted by foreign industries in products and technologies the American industries had originally developed. In recent years, many U.S. industries have begun to take restructuring steps to improve their ability to compete in the international marketplace; however, they do so at a disadvantage when their international competitors continue to be the beneficiaries of strategic industrial planning. Labor-intensive U.S. industries may increasingly be siting their production facilities south of the border as NAFTA begins to be implemented. Without strategic industrial planning to support the efforts of industry trying to be more competitive, and to mitigate the impacts of industry that may site production out of the United States under agreements such as NAFTA, the American economy may continue to grow slowly, if at all, while efforts to eliminate its debtor nation status will be hampered.

Investment in social infrastructure and support for a more economically integrated landscape will be thwarted as long as the national economy experiences slow or no growth. Support for major social investment was greatest in the postwar period when the U.S. economy was at its most robust and internationally dominant. If we do not undertake the investment in social infrastructure and actions for a more economically integrated landscape that will make the middle standard of living affordable for middle-level earners, then efforts to restore our postwar growth rate may be undermined. If such efforts are successful while ignoring issues of social infrastructure and economic integration, inequality of opportunity for middle-class life can only increase, and this may threaten more than just the nation's overall standard of living.

Notes

Chapter 2: What Is Happening to Middle-Level Earners?

1. Specifically, the author has calculated from data in the U.S. Census Bureau's Current Population Survey (CPS) that wage and salary earnings ranged between 97% to 98% of total money income for the last twenty years for full-time workers. This was determined from the CPS microdata files by dividing the mean earned income figure by the mean total money income figure for 1967. The comparable published figures for the 1980s were then examined to ensure that the ratio of earnings to total money income had stayed the same.

2. Katharine L. Bradbury (1986) appears to have been the first writer to use this phrase within the context of the debate over the declining middle class.

3. The distribution of earners is based on individual annual pretax wage and salary income. Individuals reporting negative wages and salaries have been excluded from the universe.

4. The proportion of U.S. households that were "traditional" families, with a male breadwinner, children, and a wife who did not work in the paid labor force, was only 17% in 1985, and those with exactly 2 children were 4% of all households. (See Table 17, "Characteristics of Married-Couple families, by Joint Labor Force Status of the Husband and Wife, by Age of Husband: March 1985," Household and Family Characteristics: March 1985, *Current Population Reports*, Series P-20, No. 411.) This latter group is the Ozzie and Harriet family. Statistics on the size of these groups have been published only since 1980 so the exact degree of shrinkage of this group cannot be determined from published data.

5. Draper wrote this in her dissent from a special panel of the U.S. Bureau of Labor Statistics (BLS). This panel's recommendations were responsible for the BLS abandoning the lower, moderate, and higher family budget series. Had it not been abandoned, this series would have been the best proxy for a nationally defined middle consumer basket, taken from the moderate family budget (Watts 1980).

6. These percents were calculated from Table B-18, "Employed civilians by full- and part-time status, race, and sex, 1968–1987," in the U.S. Department of Labor, Bureau of Labor Statistics (1988).

7. In this analysis, only the two race groups of white and black are examined because separate data on Hispanics, Asians, and Native Americans were not collected in 1967.

8. However, all self-employed are excluded from the analysis in 1967 and all nonincorporated self-employed are excluded from the 1987 universe because separate data on their wages and salaries could not be obtained. The addition of their numbers could change the proportional relationship between part- and full-time earners.

9. Total compensation referred to here is wages and salaries plus pension and health benefits. Legally required benefits (Social Security, Unemployment Insurance, and workers' compensation) are excluded from this estimate as are public retirement plans and group life insurance.

Chapter 3: The Middle Standard of Living

1. Of course, just as there is controversy over the parameters that define the poverty index, there would be controversy over a middle standard of living index. However, besides its use to determine transfer payment eligibility, the poverty index is an important gauge of our economy's health. For an advanced economy such as that in the United States, the middle standard of living index would be an even more important gauge.

2. Note that the household budgets from which this standard is derived are weighted to reflect the different costs of the budget in urban and rural areas.

Chapter 4: Industrial Restructuring's Influence on the Distribution of Earnings

1. The Office of Technology Assessment's (OTA) allocation of service functions in its production sector classification is a modification of the categories employed by Singlemann (1978).

2. This author has substituted the label "social infrastructure" for OTA's original label of "social services" because the production sector is much broader than that which is commonly associated with social services. A tenth production sector category—defense—has been eliminated because of limitations with the U.S. Census Bureau's Current Population Survey's (CPS) industry categories.

3. Data on the number of weeks worked in the year from the CPS is an alternative indicator that has been looked at by other researchers. However, because paid vacations and sick leave are included in the data on the number of weeks worked, this indicator is problematic. We cannot tell whether the number of weeks worked is actually increasing or whether the number of weeks of paid vacation and sick leave is increasing.

4. These data are from the U.S. Department of Labor, Bureau of Labor Statistics (1988), Table A-23. The hours worked relate to the actual number during the survey week. They include, for earners with more than one job, the number of hours worked in all jobs, with all hours then being credited to the major job.

5. See Allison (1978) as well as Theil (1967). The Theil measure is $T = 1/n$ $(Yi/uY)\log(Yi/uY)$, where uY refers to the mean of Y—wages and salaries. The Theil index differs from the better-known Gini index of inequality in two basic ways. First, although they both have a lower bound of zero, the Gini index has an upper bound of one while the Theil's upper bound is the log of n, where n is the number of earners or households in the distribution. The upper bound is reached when one worker has all earnings and everyone else has none. Theil considered the dependence of his index on n desirable "since a two-person society in which one person has everything is, intuitively, less unequal than a million person society in which one person has everything" (Allison 1978). The second difference between the Theil and Gini indexes lies in the fact that the Theil allows for decomposing the inequality of a population into that between and within groups (that is, demographic, regional, or industrial) while the Gini only summarizes the overall inequality of a given population.

6. The computation of the Theil index involves determining the mean of the income distribution. This creates a problem when CPS as well as census data are used because of the top-coding of income and earnings (that is, any individual earning more than $75,000 in a given year has his or her earnings recorded simply as $75,000). The standard procedure to correct for this problem is to fit the upper tail of the distribution to a Pareto curve, determining a mean for the upper tail. This cumbersome correcting procedure was not performed in Theil index computations here because those workers with top-coded earnings turned out to be a very small percentage of the full-time distribution, around 1%. Not performing the correcting procedure should lead to a small underestimation of inequality; only 1% of full-time workers have their earnings underestimated.

7. Not all CPS industry codes could be successfully cross-referenced for each of the four years, 1967, 1973, 1979, and 1987. The subtotal row

in Table 4.8B indicates what percent of full-time earners were placed into the trade advantage classification for each of the four years.

8. Calculated from CPS microdata files.

9. Calculated from Table B-18, "Employed civilians by full- and part-time status, race, and sex, 1968–1987," in U.S. Department of Labor, Bureau of Labor Statistics (1988).

10. See, for example, Reich (1991).

Chapter 5: The Rural and Urban Distinction in Industrial Restructuring

1. Bloomquist's (1987) analysis finds that rural areas experienced employment growth in top-of-the-cycle, bottom-of-the-cycle, and resource-based manufacturing industries over the 1969 to 1984 period while urban areas only experienced employment growth in top-of-the-cycle industries. However, in the analysis discussed in this paper, it was found that the share of urban employment in the traditional/low-wage manufacturing sector—which can be considered largely synonymous with bottom-of-the-cycle industries—grew substantially between 1979 and 1987.

2. Why the rural part-time labor force, as well as both the urban part- and full-time groups, was growing when the rural full-time group was not should be a question of some interest to rural analysts and policymakers. Was it due to the greater growth of consumer services, as compared to producer services, in rural areas? Was the rate of involuntary part-time employment increasing in the rural areas as the percentage of the overall employment that was part-time also grew, especially since 1973?

3. In this research, the decision was made to use the middle range defined at the national level for all earners as the reference point for comparing regional change among part- and full-time earners. Thus, instead of determining the median earnings figure for urban and rural part- and full-time earners, creating a middle range around each of those medians and then comparing shifts in four uniquely defined middle groups, the size of each region's middle is determined by what proportion of the region's full-time workers has earnings that fall within the national middle-earning range. This approach gives a common reference point for comparing regional change and allows us, for instance, to determine which region contains the greatest proportion of the nation's middle earners. It does not, though, directly address the issue that may not qualify as such in the urban economy (for example, what are middle-level earnings in the rural economy?). However, this issue is addressed when variations in the two economies' cost of home ownership are discussed.

4. The reader is reminded that the part-time earnings distribution is expected to have larger low and middle segments and smaller upper segments than the full-time distribution.

5. Another way to view the distribution of these sectors between the urban and rural economies is that rural high-tech employment was 15% of all high-tech employment and rural defense employment was 8% of all full-time defense employment. (From Table 5.13: rural and urban high-tech earners combined were 5,883,731 in 1987, with rural 877,755, or 14.9%; rural and urban defense earners combined were 2,601,499, with rural 202,134, or 7.8%.)

6. Conversations with Michael Teitz, John Landis, Michael Smith-Heimer, and Amy Glasmeier have helped me to formulate my ideas on the differences in the ability of rural and urban earners to purchase a home. The median sales price of new, single-family homes inside Standard Metropolitan Statistical Areas (SMSAs) was $23,800 and outside SMSAs was $19,800 in 1967. By 1987, the inside SMSA sales price had risen to $106,200 while the outside SMSA sales price had risen to $85,600; see U.S. Department of Commerce and U.S. Department of Housing and Urban Development (1967, 1987), Tables 15 and 22, respectively.

Chapter 6: The Regional Implications of Industrial Restructuring

1. That is, earnings or income per head determined by dividing a region's gross earnings or income by its total population; see Carlino (1992).

2. U.S. Department of Commerce, Bureau of the Census (1987), Table 21.

3. These rates are for unionization in the manufacturing sector. Specifically, the rates were New York, 50.3%; Illinois, 34.2%; California, 23.8%; and Texas, 15.0%; see U.S. Department of Commerce, Bureau of the Census (1991), Table 696.

4. Profit-cycle theory, it may be recalled, builds upon Schumpeterian and Marxist work on innovation and capitalist dynamics, upon the product-cycle theories of business economists, and upon theories of oligopolistic behavior (Markusen 1985a).

5. Because this analysis focuses on workers with earnings, those who lose their jobs in this process will not show up as a change in the earnings distribution.

6. Between 1967 and 1973, the number of all full-time earners in the Northeast actually declined by more than forty thousand; see Table 6.1.

7. The defense perimeter is "a ring around the nation that extends

from New England through Long Island, Florida, the southwestern states, California, Washington and Alaska" (Markusen and Carlson 1989).

8. See Gillette (1986), p. 170.

9. U.S. Department of Commerce, Bureau of the Census (1988), Table 21.

10. It is possible that all of this shift could have occurred before the bottom fell out of the building industry and that the construction earnings distribution stabilized in the early 1980s or even fell back some from a higher level. This, of course, could be determined from an analysis of the data for the intervening years, but this will not be undertaken in the present research.

11. Glasmeier (1986), footnote 15.

12. See U.S. Department of Commerce, Bureau of the Census (1981–1987), Series P-25, No. 1024.

13. See Teitz and Shapira (1989).

14. Ibid.

15. Formal economy workers are those who have a legal employment status and whose earnings—whether from self-employment or paid by an employer—are officially reported. In contrast, workers in the informal economy may not have legal residency or visitor status and their illegal employment and earnings are "off the books," that is, not counted in official statistics.

16. See chapter 2, note 5.

17. Calculated from the U.S. Census Bureau's Current Population Survey (CPS) microdata files.

18. Furthermore, we should keep in mind that since the data presented are for formal economy workers, the CPS would not contain data on workers such as illegal aliens in the informal economy. Additionally, earnings figures for the self-employed who are not incorporated cannot be determined from CPS data. Both groups, the informal economy and the nonincorporated self-employed workers, are, in all likelihood, growing in California as a result of the influx of legal and illegal Asian and Latino immigrants. If these two groups could be included in the analysis, the trend toward a growing upper-earner group would probably remain unchanged, but some of the decline in the size of the low-earner group for full-time workers might be expected.

19. See Monthly Labor Review, "A look at occupational employment trends to the year 2000" (September 1987): 46. The service worker cluster is an important exception. It will account for more of the total growth in employment than any major group, and its educational attainment requirements are not in the high group.

20. Ibid., p. 62.

21. In 1982, union membership in Illinois was 27.5% while it was 35.8% in New York State; see U.S. Department of Commerce, Bureau of the Census (1987), Table 666.

22. See "Housing Affordability Index Drops" (1989).

23. See the Bay Area Economic Forum (1989).

Chapter 7: Changing Earnings Distributions and Opportunities for Middle-Class Living: What Should Be Done?

1. Marion Clawson and Peter Hall (1973) recognized the beginnings of this trend twenty years ago in their comparison of the urban growth processes of the United States and the United Kingdom.

2. The label of "Corporatist Planning" has been given to the tripartite arrangement found in nations such as Germany; see Lehmbruch and Schmitter (1982).

3. This practice of zoning has been labeled "technocratic racism" (Feagin 1989).

4. In addition to zoning, environmental controls and environmental impact statements developed for the purposes of preserving physical attributes and unique features of communities have contributed to the rising cost of home ownership. They have done so by reducing the supply of land available for development and by lengthening the time and requirements for review of development proposals (Dowall 1984).

5. Not-in-my-backyard attitudes.

References

Abeles, P. L. 1989. Planning and zoning. In Haar, C. M. and Kayden, J. S., eds. *Zoning and the American dream*. Chicago: Planners Press.

Allison, P. D. 1978. Measures of inequality. *American Sociological Review* 43 (December): 865–880.

Apgar, W. C., Jr., and Brown, H. J. 1988. *The state of the nation's housing*. Cambridge, MA: Joint Center for Housing Studies of Harvard.

• Applebaum, E. 1981. "High tech" and the structural unemployment of the eighties. Paper presented at the American Economic Association Meetings, Washington, D.C., December 28. Philadelphia: Temple University, Department of Economics.

Arnold, A. L. and Kusnet, J. 1985. *The Arnold encyclopedia of real estate*. Boston: Warren, Gorham and Lamont.

• Ball, N. and Leitenberg, M., eds. 1983. *The structure of the defense industry*. London: Croom Helm.

Bay Area Economic Forum. 1989. *The Bay Area economy: a region at risk*. San Francisco. February.

• Bell, D. 1976. *The coming of post-industrial society*. New York: Basic Books.

• Bell, L. A. and Freeman, R. B. 1986. Increasing inequality in the U.S.? Alternative views. Paper presented at the Industrial Relations Research Association 39th Annual Proceedings, New Orleans.

• Bell, W. G. 1989. Introduction to special issue on mobility and transportation of single parents. *Specialized Transportation Planning and Practice* (November): i–vi.

• Berger, M. C. 1985. The effect of cohort size on earnings growth: a re-examination of the evidence. *Journal of Political Economy* 93, no. 3, 561–573.

• Berger, S. and Piore, J. M. 1980. *Dualism and discontinuity in industrial societies*. Cambridge, England: Cambridge University Press.

• Betson, D. and Van Der Gaag, J. 1984. Working married women and the

---

• Additional important references not cited in the text.

distribution of income. *Journal of Human Resources* 19, no. 4, 532–543.

• Bianchi, S. M. 1984. Wives who earn more than their husbands. *American Demographics* (July): 19–23.

• Bils, M. J. 1985. Real wages over the business cycle: evidence from panel data. *Journal of Political Economy* 93, no. 4, 666–689.

Blackburn, M. L. and Bloom, D. E. 1985. What is happening to the middle class? *American Demographics* (January): 18–25.

———. 1987. The effects of technological change on earnings and income inequality in the United States. Discussion Paper No. 1339. Cambridge, MA: Harvard Institute of Economic Research, September.

Blackburn, M. L., Bloom, D. E., and Freeman, R. B. 1990/1991. An era of falling earnings and rising inequality? *Brookings Review* (Winter): 38–43.

• Blair, J. P. and Premus, R. 1987. Major factors in industrial location: a review. *Economic Development Quarterly* 1, no. 1, 72–85.

• Blau, F. D. and Beller, A. H. 1986. Trends in earnings differentials by sex: 1971–1981. Presented at the Population Association of America Meetings, San Francisco, April 3.

• Bloom, D. E. and Korenman, S. D. 1986. The spending habits of American consumers. *American Demographics* (March): 22–54.

Bloomquist, L. E. 1987. Performance of the rural manufacturing sector. In Brown, D. L. and Deavers, K., eds., *Rural economic development in the 1980s*. Washington, D.C., U.S. Department of Agriculture, Economic Research Service, July.

• Beyond unions. 1985. *Business Week* (July 8): 72–77.

Bluestone, B. and Harrison, B. 1982. *The deindustrialization of America*. New York: Basic Books.

———. 1987. The grim truth about the job miracle. *New York Times* (February 1).

Bluestone, B., Harrison, B., and Gorham, L. 1984. *Storm clouds on the horizon: labor market crisis and industrial policy*. Boston: Social Welfare Research Institute, Boston College, May.

Bluestone, B., Harrison, B., and Mathews, A. 1986. Structure vs. cycle in the development of American manufacturing employment since the late 1960s. *Industrial Relations* 25, no. 2 (Spring).

• Borts, G. H. and Stein, J. L. 1964. *Economic growth in a free market*. New York: Columbia University Press.

Bradbury, K. L. 1986. The Shrinking Middle Class. *New England Economic Review* (September/October): 41–55.

• Bregger, J. E. 1984. The current population survey: a historical perspective and BLS' Role. *Monthly Labor Review* (June): 8–14.

- Brookes, W. T. 1987. Behind the big lie of low-paying jobs. *San Francisco Chronicle* (February 11).
- Brown, C. 1985. *Consumption norms, work roles, and economic growth.* Berkeley: University of California at Berkeley, Department of Economics, March.

Brown, D. L. and Deavers, K. 1987. Rural change and the rural economic policy agenda for the 1980s. In Brown, D. L. and Deavers, K., eds. *Rural economic development in the 1980s.* Washington, D.C.: U.S. Department of Agriculture, Economic Research Service, July.

- Browne, L. E. 1980. Narrowing regional income differentials: II. *New England Economic Review* (November–December): 40–59.

————. 1988. Defense spending and high technology development: national and state issues. *New England Economic Review* (September–October): 3–22.

Carlino, G. A. 1992. Are regional per capita earnings diverging? *Business Review* (March–April): 3–12.

- Caught in the middle. 1988. *Business Week* (September 12): 80–88.
- Cebula, R. J. 1983. *Geographic living cost differentials.* Lexington, MA: D.C. Heath.

Cervero, R. 1989. Jobs housing balancing and regional mobility. *Journal of the American Planning Association* (Spring): 136–150.

Cibulskis, A. and Ritzdorf, M. 1989. *Zoning for childcare.* Chicago: American Planning Association, PAS Report 422.

Clawson, M. and Hall, P. 1973. *Planning and urban growth.* Baltimore: Resources for the Future and Johns Hopkins Press.

Cohen, S. and Zysman, J. 1987. *Manufacturing matters: the myth of a post-industrial economy.* New York: Basic Books.

Coleman, R. P. 1983. The continuing significance of social class to marketing. *Journal of Consumer Research* 10 (December): 265–279.

Congressional Budget Office. 1988. *Trends in family income: 1970–1986.* Washington, D.C., February.

- Council on Competitiveness. 1988. *Competitiveness index.* Washington, D.C.

Crandall, R. W. 1988. The regional shift of economic activity. In Litan, R. E., Lawrence, R. Z., and Schultze, C. L., eds. *American living standards.* Washington, D.C.: Brookings Institution.

Danes, S. M. and Winter, M. 1990. The impact of the employment of the wife on the achievement of home ownership. *Journal of Consumer Affairs* 24, no. 1 (Summer): 148–169.

- Danzinger, S. and Gottschalk, P. 1986. Families with children have fared worst. *Challenge* (March–April): 40–47.
- ————. 1987. Earnings inequality, the spatial concentration of poverty,

and the underclass. *American Economics Association Papers and Proceedings* 77, no. 2 (May): 211–215.

- Davidson, C. and Reich, M. 1987. *Income inequality and industrial structure.* Berkeley: University of California, Department of Economics.
- Dickens, W. T. and Lang, K. 1986. Where have all the good jobs gone? In Lang, K. and Leonard, J., eds. *Unemployment and the Structure of Labor Markets.* New York: Basil Blackwell.
- Dickens, W. T. and Leonard, J. S. 1984. *Accounting for the decline in union membership.* Working Paper No. 1275. Cambridge, MA: National Bureau of Economic Research, February.
- Dickens, W. T. and Shapira, P., with Tyson, L. and Zysman, J. 1985. *The employment effects of international trade: a review of the literature.* Berkeley: Berkeley Roundtable on the International Economy, April 29.
- Dooley, M. and Gottschalk, P. 1982. Does a younger labor force mean greater earnings inequality? *Monthly Labor Review* (November): 42–45.

Dowall, D. 1984. *The suburban squeeze.* Berkeley: University of California Press.

- Drucker, P. F. 1986. The changed world economy. *Foreign Affairs* 64, no. 4, 768–791.
- Dugger, W. M. 1987. Three modes of income distribution: market, hierarchy, and industry. *Journal of Economic Issues* 21, no. 2 (June): 723–731.

Edsall, T. B. 1984. *The new politics of inequality.* New York: W. W. Norton.

Edwards, R. 1979. *Congested terrain.* New York: Basic Books.

Ehrenreich, B. 1986. Is the middle class doomed? *New York Times Magazine* (September 7): 44–64.

Employee Benefit Research Institute. 1988a. *EBRI Issue Brief,* no. 78, May.

———. 1988b. *Employee Benefit Notes* 9, January.

- Farhi, P. 1987. Middle class holds its own. *San Francisco Chronicle* (June 28).

Feagin, J. R. 1989. Areas of conflict: zoning and land use reform in critical political-economic perspective. In Haar, C. M. and Kayden, J. S., eds. *Zoning and the American dream.* Chicago: Planners Press.

- Fields, G. S. 1980. *Poverty, inequality, and development.* Cambridge, England: Cambridge University Press.
- Fisch, O. 1984. Regional income inequality and economic development. *Regional Science and Urban Economics* 14, 89–111.
- Freeman, C. 1984. Prometheus unbound. *Futures* (October): 494–507.

- Friesan, P. H. 1985. Distortion of the trend of inequality by the life-cycle profile of incomes. *Review of Economics and Statistics:* 170–174.
- Friesan, P. H. and Miller, D. 1983. Annual inequality and lifetime inequality. *Quarterly Journal of Economics* 98 (February): 139–155.

Gillette, M. L., ed. 1986. *Texas in transition.* Austin: University of Texas, Lyndon B. Johnson School of Public Affairs, Lyndon Baines Johnson Library.

Glasmeier, A. K. 1986. High-tech industries and the regional division of labor. *Industrial Relations* 25, no. 2 (Spring): 197–211.

- The good jobs riddle. 1988. *Newsweek* (September 19): 22–24.
- Gorham, L. S. 1984. U.S. industry employment trends from 1969 to 1983 and the implications for economic inequality. Master's thesis. Massachusetts Institute of Technology, June.
- Greenhouse, S. 1986. The average guy takes it on the chin. *New York Times* (July 13).

Grubb, W. N. and Wilson, R. H. 1987. The distribution of wages and salaries, 1960–1980: the contributions of gender, race, sectoral shifts and regional shifts. Working Paper No. 39. Austin: University of Texas at Austin, Lyndon B. Johnson School of Public Affairs.

Gurwitz, A. S. 1983. New York State's economic turnaround: services or manufacturing? *Federal Reserve Bank of New York Quarterly Review* (Autumn): 30–34.

- Harrington, M. and Levinson, M. 1985. The perils of a dual economy. *Dissent* 32, no. 4 (Fall): 417–426.
- Harrison, B. and Bluestone, B. 1986. *The great American jobs machine: the proliferation of low-wage employment in the U.S. economy.* Washington, D.C.: U.S. Congressional Joint Economic Committee, December.
- ———. 1987a. The dark side of labor market "flexibility": falling wages and growing income inequality in America. Mimeographed, International Labor Office.
- ———. 1987b. Who are the low wage workers? Mimeographed, March.
- ———. 1988. *The great U-turn.* New York: Basic Books.
- Hartmann, H. 1976. Capitalism, patriarchy, and job segregation by sex: the historical roots of occupational capitalism. *Signs* 1, no. 3, 137–169.

Hayghe, H. V. 1990. Family members in the work force. *Monthly Labor Review* (March): 14–19.

- Henle, P. 1972. Exploring the distribution of earned income. *Monthly Labor Review* (December): 16–72.
- Henle, P. and Ryscavage, P. 1980. The distribution of earned income among men and women, 1958–77. *Monthly Labor Review* (April): 3–10.

Hochschild, A. 1989. *The second shift.* New York: Viking Penguin.
• Holland, S. 1977. *Capital versus the regions.* London: MacMillan Press.
Housing affordability index drops. 1989. *San Francisco Chronicle* (January 31).
• Howard, M. C. 1979. *Modern theories of income distribution.* New York: St. Martin's Press.
• Huntington, E. H. and Luck, M. G. 1937. *Living on a moderate income.* Berkeley: University of California Press.
Joint Center for Housing Studies of Harvard. 1988. *The state of the nation's housing: 1988.* Cambridge, MA: Joint Center.
• Kahle, L. R. 1986. The nine nations of North America and the value basis of geographic segmentation. *Journal of Marketing* 50 (April): 34–47.
• Kahn, L. M. 1979. Unionism and relative wages: direct and indirect effects. *Industrial and Labor Relations Review* 32, no. 4 (July): 520–532.
• Kaneer, K. 1986. Distribution of consumption examined using aggregate expenditure shares. *Monthly Labor Review* 109, no. 4 (April): 50–53.
Kaufman, B. E. and Martinez-Vasquez, J. 1987. The Ross-Dunlop debate and union wage concessions: a median voter analysis. *Journal of Labor Research* 8 (Summer): 291–305.
• Kelley, A. C., Williamson, J. G., and Cheetham, R. J. 1972. *Dualistic economic development.* Chicago: University of Chicago Press.
• Kerr, C. 1954. The balkanization of labor markets. In Bakke, E. W., et al., eds. *Labor mobility and economic opportunity.* Cambridge, MA: Technology Press of MIT.
• Kim, M. 1989. Gender bias in compensation structures: a case study of its historical basis and persistence. *Journal of Social Issues* 45, no. 4, 39–50.
Kindleberger, C. P. and Herrick, B. 1977. *Economic development.* New York: McGraw-Hill.
• Kirkland, R. I. 1985. Are service jobs good jobs? *Fortune* (June 10): 38–43.
• Kosters, M. H. and Ross, M. N. 1987. *The distribution of earnings and employment opportunities: a re-examination of the evidence.* Washington, D.C.: American Enterprise Institute, September.
• Kuttner, R. 1983. The declining middle. *Atlantic Monthly* (July): 60–72.
• ———. 1991. *The end of laissez-faire: national purpose and the global economy after the cold war.* New York: Alfred A. Knopf.
• Lawrence, R. Z. 1984a. *Can America compete?* Washington, D.C.: Brookings Institution.

————. 1984b. Sectoral shifts and the size of the middle class. *Brookings Review* 3 (Fall): 3–11.

Lehmbruch, G. and Schmitter, P. C. 1982. *Patterns of corporatist policy-making*. Sage Modern Politics Series, vol. 7. London: Sage Publications.

• Leigh, N. G. 1989. National and regional change in the earnings distribution: what is happening to the middle? Dissertation, Department of City and Regional Planning, University of California at Berkeley, September.

Leitenberg, M. and Ball, N., eds. 1983. *The structure of the defense industry*. London: Croom Helm, p. 8.

• Leon, C. B. 1982. Occupational winners and losers: who they were during 1972–1980. *Monthly Labor Review* (June): 18–38.

• Leontieff, W. 1983. Technological advance, economic growth, and the distribution of income. *Population and Development Review* 9, no. 3 (September): 403–410.

• Levitan, S. A. and Carlson, P. E. 1984. Middle-class shrinkage? *Across the Board* (October): 55–59.

Levy, F. 1987. *Dollars and dreams*. New York: W. W. Norton.

• Levy, F. and Michel, R. C. 1983. The way we'll be in 1984: recent changes in the level and distribution of disposable income. *Changing Domestic Priorities Discussion Paper*. Washington, D.C.: Urban Institute, November.

————. 1986. An economic bust for the baby boom. *Challenge* (March–April): 33–39.

• ————. 1990. *The future of American families*. Washington, D.C.: Urban Institute, November.

————. 1991. *The economic future of American families*. New York: Basic Books.

Linden, F. 1984. Myth of the disappearing middle class. *Wall Street Journal* (January 23).

Linneman, P. and Wachter, M. 1988. Rising union wage premiums and the declining boundaries among noncompeting groups. *American Economic Review* 76 (May): 103–108.

• Lipsey, R. E. and Kravis, I. 1986. The competitiveness and comparative advantage of U.W. multinationals, 1957–1983. Working Paper No. 2051. Cambridge, MA: National Bureau of Economic Research, October.

• Litan, R. E., Lawrence, R. Z., and Schultze, C. L., eds. 1988. *American living standards*. Washington, D.C.: Brookings Institution.

Magaziner, I. C. and Reich, R. B. 1982. *Minding America's business*. New York: Vintage.

- McKee, D. L. and Bennett, R. E. 1987. *Structural change in an urban industrial location.* New York: Praeger.
- McMahon, P. J. and Tschetter, J. H. 1986. The declining middle class: a further analysis. *Monthly Labor Review* (September): 22–27.
- Marcoot, J. L. 1985. Revision of consumer price index is now under way. *Monthly Labor Review* 108, no. 4 (April): 27–38.

Markusen, A. R. 1985a. *Profit cycles, oligopoly, and regional development.* Cambridge, MA: MIT Press.

————. 1985b. The economic and regional consequences of military innovation. Working Paper No. 442. Berkeley: University of California, Institute of Urban and Regional Development, May.

Markusen, A. R. and Carlson, V. 1989. Deindustrialization in the American Midwest: causes and responses. Forthcoming in Roddwin, L. and Sazanami, H., eds. *Deindustrialization and regional economic transformation: the experience of the United States.* Boston: Unwin Hyman.

- Massey, D. 1984. *Spatial divisions of labour.* London: MacMillan Education.
- Mensch, G. O. 1979. *Stalemate in technology.* Boston: Ballinger.

Miller, J. and Bluestone, B. 1987. Prospects for service sector employment growth in nonmetro America. In Brown, D. and Deavers, K., eds. *Rural economic development in the 1980s.* Washington, D.C.: U.S. Department of Agriculture, Economic Research Service.

- Mills, C. W. 1953. *White collar.* New York: Oxford University Press.

Mishel, L. 1988. Better jobs or working longer for less? Working Paper No. 101. Washington, D.C.: Economic Policy Institute, July.

Mishel, L. and Simon, J. 1988. *The state of working America.* Washington, D.C.: Economic Policy Institute.

- Nasar, S. 1987. Do we live as well as we used to? *Fortune* (September 14): 32–46.
- Nilsen, D. M. 1984. Employment in durable goods anything but durable in 1979–82. *Monthly Labor Review* (February): 15–24.
- Novak, M. and Green, G. 1986. Poverty down, inequality up? *Public Interest* no. 83 (Spring): 49–56.
- Oakey, R. 1984. *High technology small firms.* London: Frances Pinter.
- Onuf, N. G. 1984. Prometheus prostrate. *Futures* (February): 47–59.
- Parker, R. 1972. *The myth of the middle class.* New York: Harper and Row.
- Pearce, D. W., ed. 1983. *The dictionary of modern economics.* Cambridge, MA: MIT Press.
- Perez, C. 1983. Structural change and assimilation of new technologies in the economic and social systems. *Futures* (October): 357–375.

- Perloff, H. S., Dunn, E. S., Jr., Lampard, E. E., and Muth, R. F. 1960. *Regions, resources, and economic growth.* Washington, D.C.: Resources for the Future.
- Pettengill, J. S. 1980. *Labor unions and the inequality of earned income.* Amsterdam: North-Holland Publishing.

Projections 2000: industry output and employment through the end of the century. 1987. *Monthly Labor Review* (September).

Reich, R. B. 1991. *The work of nations.* New York: Alfred A. Knopf.

Reiff, B. 1986. Industry and occupation employment structure and income distribution. Unpublished paper, Massachusetts Institute of Technology, May.

- Riche, R. W. 1982. Impact of new technology. *Monthly Labor Review* (March): 37–39.
- Rose, S. and Fasenfest, D. 1988. Family incomes in the 1980s. Working Paper No. 103. Washington, D.C.: Economic Policy Institute, November.
- Rosenthal, N. H. 1985. The shrinking middle class: myth or reality? *Monthly Labor Review* (March): 3–10.

Russell, L. B. 1982. *The baby boom generation and the economy.* Washington, D.C.: Brookings Institution.

- Rytina, N. F. 1982a. Earnings of men and women: a look at specific occupations. *Monthly Labor Review* (April): 25–31.
- ———. 1982b. Tenure as a factor in the male-female earnings gap. *Monthly Labor Review* (April): 32–34.
- Sahota, G. S. 1978. Theories of personal income distribution: a survey. *Journal of Economic Literature* (March): 1–55.
- Samuelson, R. J. 1984. Middle-class media myth. *National Journal* (December 31): 2673–2678.

Sassen, S. 1988. *The mobility of labor and capital: a study in international investment and labor flow.* Cambridge, England: Cambridge University Press.

- Saxenian, A. 1988. The Cheshire cat's grin. *Technology Review* 91, no. 2 (February–March): 67–75.
- Schreiber, C. T. 1979. *Changing places.* Cambridge, MA: MIT Press.
- Schumpeter, J. 1939. *Business cycles.* New York: McGraw-Hill.
- Sen, A. 1973. *On economic inequality.* Oxford: Clarendon Press.
- Shack-Marquez, J. 1984. Earnings, differences between men and women: an introductory note. *Monthly Labor Review* (June): 15–16.
- Siegel, J. 1978. Inflation: robbing consumers of their discretionary income. *Consumer Business Review* (Spring): 3–13.
- Sieling, M. S. 1984. Staffing patterns prominent in female-male earnings gap. *Monthly Labor Review* (April): 29–33.

Singlemann, J. 1978. The sectoral transformation of the labor force in seven industrialized countries, 1920–1970. *American Journal of Sociology* 83, no. 3, 1224–1234.

• Smith, J. P. and Ward, M. P. 1984. *Women's work and wages in the twentieth century.* Rand Report 3119-NICHD. Santa Monica, CA: Rand Corporation. October.

• Smith, M. P. 1985. Global capital restructuring and local political crisis in U.S. cities. Paper presented in session on "The Role of the State and Planning in the New International Division of Labor," Center of Urban Studies and Urban Planning Conference, University of Hong Kong, August.

• Solo, R. A. and Anderson, C. W. 1981. *Value judgement and income distribution.* New York: Praeger.

• Stapleton, D. C. and Young, D. J. 1984. The effects of demographic change on the distribution of wages, 1967–1990. *Journal of Human Resources* 19, no. 2, 175–201.

• Steinberg, B. 1983. The mass market is splitting apart. *Fortune* (November 28): 76–82.

• Sternlieb, G. and Hughes, J. W. 1983. *Income and jobs: USA.* New Brunswick, NJ: Rutgers—The State University of New Jersey, Center for Urban Policy Research.

Storper, M. 1982. The spatial division of labor: technology, the labor process, and the location of industries. Thesis, University of California, Berkeley.

• Sylas-Labini, P. 1984. *The forces of economic growth and decline.* Cambridge, MA: MIT Press.

Teitz, M. B. and Shapira, P. 1989. Growth and turbulence in the California economy. Forthcoming in Roddwin, L. and Sazanami, H., eds. *Deindustrialization and regional economic transformation: the experience of the United States.* Boston: Unwin Hyman.

• Terry, S. L. 1983. Work experience, earnings, and family income in 1981. *Monthly Labor Review* (April): 13–20.

Theil, H. 1967. *Economics and information theory.* Chicago: Rand McNally.

Thurow, L. C. 1984. The disappearance of the middle class. *New York Times* (February 5).

• ———. 1985. A general tendency towards inequality. Paper prepared for the American Economics Association Meetings, New York, December.

U.S. Congress, Office of Technology Assessment. 1988. *Technology and the American economic transition: choices for the future.* OTO-TET-283. Washington, D.C.: U.S. Government Printing Office, May, 148.

• U.S. Department of Commerce, Bureau of the Census. 1969a. *Current population reports*. Series P-60, No. 60. Income in 1967 of persons in the United States. Washington, D.C.: U.S. Government Printing Office.

• ————. 1969b. *Current population reports*. Series P-60, No. 64. Supplementary report on income in 1967 of families and persons in the United States. Washington, D.C.: U.S. Government Printing Office.

• ————. 1970. Census of population 1970. *Subject report: final report PC (2-6A)*. Employment status and work experience. Washington, D.C.: U.S. Government Printing Office, Table 11, p. 127.

• ————. 1978. *The current population survey: design and methodology*. Technical Paper 40. Washington, D.C.: U.S. Government Printing Office, January.

• ————. 1988. *Current population reports: population estimates and projections*. Series P-25, No. 1024. State population and household estimates with age, sex, and components of change: 1981–1987. Washington, D.C.: U.S. Government Printing Office.

• ————. 1986. *Current population reports*. Series P-20, No. 411. Household and family characteristics: March 1985. Washington, D.C.: U.S. Government Printing Office.

————. 1986, 1988, and 1991 editions. *Statistical abstract of the United States*. Washington, D.C.: U.S. Government Printing Office.

U.S. Department of Commerce, International Trade Administration. 1988. *United States trade performance in 1987*. Washington, D.C.: U.S. Government Printing Office, June.

U.S. Department of Commerce and U.S. Department of Housing and Urban Development. Annual. *Construction reports*. C25-67-13 and C25-87-13. Washington, D.C.: U.S. Government Printing Office.

U.S. Department of Labor, Bureau of Labor Statistics. 1967. *Three standards of living, for an urban family of four persons*. Bulletin No. 1570-5. Washington, D.C.: U.S. Government Printing Office, Spring.

• ————. 1986. *Linking employment problems to economic status*. Bulletin 2270. Washington, D.C.: U.S. Government Printing Office, September.

————. 1988. *Labor force statistics derived from the current population survey, 1948–1987*. Bulletin 2307. Washington, D.C.: U.S. Government Printing Office, August.

• Vroman, W. 1982. Union contracts and money wage changes in U.S. manufacturing industries. *Quarterly Journal of Economics* 97, no. 4 (November): 571–594.

• Walker, R. 1985. Is there a service economy? *Science and Society* 49, no. 1 (Spring): 42–83.

- Walker, R. and Storper, M. 1979. Systems and Marxist theories of industrial location: a review. Berkeley: University of California, Institute of Urban and Regional Development.

Watts, H. W. 1980. Special panel suggests changes in BLS family budget program. Reprinted from *Monthly Labor Review* (December).

- Wessel, D. 1986. U.S. rich and poor increase in numbers; middle loses ground. *Wall Street Journal* (September 22).

Williamson, J. G. and Lindert, P. H. 1980. *American inequality.* New York: Academic Press.

- Wilson, J. O. 1980. *After affluence.* San Francisco: Harper and Row.
- Women at work. 1985. *Business Week* (January 28): 80–85.